Tectonic Shifts

Tectonic Shifts
Haiti Since the Earthquake

Edited by Mark Schuller and Pablo Morales

Kumarian Press
An Imprint of Stylus Publishing

Published by Stylus Publishing, LLC
22883 Quicksilver Drive
Sterling, Virginia 20166-2102

Copyright © 2012 by Kumarian Press, an imprint of Stylus Publishing, LLC.

Design by Pro Production Graphic Services
Copyedit by Bob Land
Proofread by Beth Richards
Index by Robert Swanson
The text of this book is set in 11/13 Adobe Garamond

Printed in the United States of America

 All first editions printed on acid free paper that meets the American National Standards Institute Z39-48 Standard.

Library of Congress Cataloging-in-Publication Data
Tectonic shifts : Haiti since the earthquake / edited by Mark Schuller and
 Pablo Morales. — 1st ed.
  p. cm.
 Includes bibliographical references and index.
 ISBN 978-1-56549-511-1 (cloth : alk. paper) — ISBN 978-1-56549-512-8
 (pbk. : alk. paper) — ISBN 978-1-56549-513-5 (library networkable e-edition) —
 ISBN 978-1-56549-514-2 (consumer e-edition)
 1. Haiti Earthquake, Haiti, 2010. 2. Earthquake relief—Haiti. 3. Haiti—
Social conditions—21st century. 4. Haiti—Economic conditions—21st century.
I. Schuller, Mark, 1973–   II. Morales, Pablo, 1976–
 HV600 2010. H2 T43 2011
 972.9407'3—dc23

                                                        2011033765

13-digit ISBN: 978-1-56549-511-1 (cloth)
13-digit ISBN: 978-1-56549-512-8 (paper)
13-digit ISBN: 978-1-56549-513-5 (library networkable e-edition)
13-digit ISBN: 978-1-56549-514-2 (consumer e-edition)

Bulk Purchases

Quantity discounts are available for use in workshops and for staff development.

Call 1-800-232-0223

First Edition, 2012

    10 9 8 7 6 5 4 3 2 1

Contents

Part 2 On-the-Ground Realities:
Displacement and Its Discontents

Part 3 Emerging Movements:
Political Restructuring in Haiti

Illustrations

Figures

Tables

Abbreviations

BAI	Bureau des Avocats Internationaux
CARE	Cooperative for Assistance and Relief Everywhere
CARICOM	Caribbean Community and Common Market
CCCM	Camp Coordination and Camp Management (Cluster)
CDC	Centers for Disease Control and Prevention
CEP	Provisional Electoral Council
CEPR	Center for Economic and Policy Research
CESCR	International Covenant on Economic, Social, and Cultural Rights
CONAP	National Coordination for Advocacy on Women's Rights
CRC	Christian Reformed Church
DAP	Disaster Accountability Project
DTM	Displacement Tracking Matrix
FAO	Food and Agriculture Organization
FAVILEK	Famn Viktim, Leve Kanpe (Women Victims, Stand Up)
FEMA	Federal Emergency Management Agency
FRAKKA	Fòs Refleksyon ak Aksyon sou Koze Kay (Force for Reflection and Action on Housing)
FRAPH	Front for the Advancement and Progress of Haiti
GBV	Gender-based violence
GPPi	Global Public Policy Institute
HAWG	Haiti Advocacy Working Group
HDI	Human Development Index

HNP	Haitian National Police
HRC	Haiti Response Coalition
HRF	Haiti Reconstruction Fund
IACHR	Inter-American Commission on Human Rights
ICCPR	International Covenant on Civil and Political Rights
ICF	Interim Cooperation Framework
ICRC	International Committee of the Red Cross
ICVA	International Council of Voluntary Agencies
IDB	Inter-American Development Bank
IDP	Internally displaced person
IFI	International financial institution
IFRC	International Federation of Red Cross and Red Crescent Societies
IHRC	Interim Haiti Recovery Commission
IICA	Inter-American Institute for Cooperation on Agriculture
IJDH	Institute for Justice and Democracy in Haiti
IMF	International Monetary Fund
IOM	International Organization for Migration
KOFAVIV	Komisyou Fanm Viktim Por Viktim (Commission of Women Victims for Victims)
LAMP	The LAMP for Haiti Foundation
LDC	Least developed country
LERN	Lawyers Earthquake Response Network
MINUSTAH	UN Stabilization Mission in Haiti
MSPP	Haitian Ministry of Public Health and Population
NGO	Nongovernmental organization
OAS	Organization of American States
OCHA	Office for the Coordination of Humanitarian Affairs
OHCHR	Office of the United Nations High Commissioner for Human Rights
PARDN	Action Plan for National Recovery and Development
PDNA	Post-Disaster Needs Assessment
PPD	Public policy documents
PRGF	Poverty Reduction and Growth Facility
PRSP	Poverty Reduction Strategy Papers
SME	Small and medium enterprises
SMS	Sphere Minimum Standards
SOFA	Solidarité des Femmes Haïtiennes (Haitian Women's Solidarity)

SOUTHCOM	United States Southern Command
TPS	Temporary Protected Status
UDHR	Universal Declaration of Human Rights
UN	United Nations
UNDP	United Nations Development Programme
UNFPA	United Nations Population Fund
UNHCR	United Nations High Commissioner for Refugees
UNICEF	United Nations Children's Fund
UNPOL	United Nations Police Division
URD	Urgence Réhabilitation Développement
USAID	United States Agency for International Development
WASH	Water, sanitation, and hygiene
WHO	World Health Organization

Introduction

Mark Schuller and Pablo Morales

THE EARTHQUAKE THAT STRUCK HAITI on January 12, 2010, will forever be re-
membered as one of the world's deadliest disasters. For 35 seconds the
earth shook and reduced a nation—already struggling with the historical
weight of slavery, underdevelopment, imperialism, and intense internal
divisions—to rubble. One in seven people were suddenly rendered homeless, while as many as 316,000 people lost their lives, according to official
estimates. Haiti dominated the airwaves and cyberspace for weeks, bom-
barding world citizens with words and images at once contradictory, con-
troversial, consuming, and ultimately confusing; the earthquake seemed to
have as many meanings as people with access to a blog. In this volume we
aim to sort out critical perspectives on the disaster. As each of the chapters
herein shows, understanding the disaster means understanding not only the
tectonic fault lines running beneath Haiti but also the deep economic, political, social, and historical cleavages within and surrounding the country.

Haiti will never be the same. The changes wrought by the disaster—
social, political, economic—do indeed amount to shifts of a tectonic scale.
It is no exaggeration to say that the earthquake permanently changed
Haiti. Of course, it was a tragedy that gripped the nation and the world.
But as a disaster it was also the platform for a series of other changes. For
some, like former president Bill Clinton, it was an opportunity to "build
back better," to undo the damage wrought by policies he championed as
president. Seen from another point of view, however, Haiti's earthquake was
a manifestation of the social ills that beset the island nation in the United
States' diplomatic and geopolitical shadow. Particularly, the quake exposed

1

centuries of underdevelopment and recent economic policies, and their impact on social inequality and exclusion within Haiti.

The events of January 12, 2010, also demonstrated Haiti's longstanding tradition of *youn ede lòt,* Haitian Creole for one helping the other. Throughout the earthquake-affected region, not only Port-au-Prince but the area to the south, including Léogâne, Jacmel, Petit-Goâve, and Grand-Goâve, the first emergency response came from people themselves: Complete strangers pulling out children or the elderly half-buried under slabs of concrete. Neighbors pooling together what scraps of food, utensils, charcoal, and water they could find, sleeping next to one another on the ground, in the street. Community brigades pulling out material goods and living and dead bodies from the remains of houses. Makeshift clinics set up under borrowed tarps or bedsheets. Store owners giving out stocks of candles, water, batteries, and medicines to passersby. Huddled meetings assessing the damage, the loss of life, needs, and community assets. Homeowners opening their *lakou*—the family compound—to family members, fellow churchgoers, neighbors, coworkers, and friends. Teams of able-bodied young men and women clearing debris from roads and corridors. Stories like these were not the exception: this was the story of how the Haitian people put away their economic and political differences and worked together, in dignity and solidarity, to collectively survive.

Unfortunately this wasn't the story that was broadcast into people's living rooms across the world. News from within Haiti first trickled out through Twitter, because the earthquake damaged other satellite-based Internet and cell phone towers. Soon thereafter, CNN reported the earthquake nonstop for more than a week, capturing the most horrific scenes and broadcasting them throughout the world. The images—edited for maximum impact—could not have been more graphic. It was presented as hell on earth. World citizens responded to the collective hailing. In the first week, private US citizens contributed $275 million, mostly to large NGOs like the Red Cross. By contrast, the donations in the first week after Japan's March 2011 earthquake, which triggered a nuclear crisis and killed at least 18,000, totaled $87 million.

The contribution to Haiti was sustained, reaching $1 billion until March 1, the deadline for claiming donations on citizens' 2009 taxes and peaking at $1.4 billion for the year. Sixty percent of US households and more than 80% of African American families contributed to the Haiti earthquake response, despite feeling the pinch from the recession. Begun by international hip-hop star and disqualified presidential candidate Wyclef Jean for his Yéle Haïti charity, donating to the relief effort via text messaging was aimed particularly at younger people. Even the Red Cross adopted this strategy, which continued in the Japan earthquake effort. In addition to private citizens, who collectively donated $2 billion, foreign governments, IFIs, and the UN offered support. At a March 31, 2010, UN conference, 58 donor agencies pledged $5.3 billion over the next year and a half.

Lending their international star power, Hollywood celebrities embraced the cause and helped raise its profile. George Clooney won an Emmy award for his *Hope for Haiti* telethon, which raised more than $57 million. Wyclef re-recorded Michael Jackson's "We Are the World" using stars of this generation. And the day before Sean Penn was set to present the Best Actor award at the Oscars, he unveiled his plan to help Haiti: the J/P Haitian Relief Organization, which adopted one of the largest IDP camps at the Pétion-Ville club, home to some 50,000 people.

What people see and how they understand the earthquake and its aftermath are largely determined by where they stand, their point of view. The story of Haiti's earthquake has been told and retold in tens of thousands of blog entries, news stories, YouTube videos, and at least 10 English-language books. Given the inequalities that marginalize Haiti, particularly the poor majority, the points of view presented to date are dominated by white, foreign do-gooders, either volunteer missions or professional humanitarians. Their stories necessarily celebrate their good intentions and minimize and even denigrate the contribution of Haitians, while also often failing to fully and accurately report the many difficulties that too many Haitians still face.

This book aims to fill this gap. Bringing together 46 individually and collectively authored pieces, *Tectonic Shifts* addresses the various levels of the emerging disaster that tend to get overlooked, ignored, or suppressed. Half of the contributors herein are Haitians—scholars, journalists, and activists—who were living in Haiti before, during, and after the earthquake. The three sections that make up the book focus, respectively, on the geopolitical structures that Haiti is a part of, the on-the-ground realities following the earthquake, and the social movements that have emerged since the disaster.

We call the book *Tectonic Shifts* because these three areas of focus roughly correspond to three interrelated geological aspects of earthquakes. First, the structural aspects: earthquakes take place when tectonic plates, or large land masses that generally stay put, move along fault lines, causing the earth to shake violently. Like the motion of tectonic plates, Haiti's disaster needs to be examined as a larger process involving geopolitical structures and transnational tensions. Second, Haiti's earthquake caused considerable damage to Haiti's social landscape. Assessing the "social rubble" on the ground requires direct on-the-ground reporting, which we have taken care to include. Finally, earthquakes create movement, moving the earth and sending out shock waves. From a political point of view, the earthquake created shock waves through a round of questionable elections, while social movements, facing an enormous task, have attempted to move the earth under their feet.

Geopolitical Structures

Tectonic Shifts offers an account of the forces that led to the disaster that killed some 316,000 and leveled a capital city. Disaster researchers have long argued against those who argue that disasters are an act of God, usually in punishment for a nation's sins (like, for example, Pat Robertson and many other religious fundamentalists). True, the tectonic plates that shifted along the faults underneath Haiti were by no means products of human action. But to be a *disaster* requires vulnerability. As many political ecologists argue, disasters are the material consequences—expressed in dramatic form—of the pent-up contradictions and inequalities in capitalist exploitation of the world's limited resources over time.[1]

Yet Haiti *was* punished—not by God but by France, for its Revolution of 1791–1804, one of the most important events in the history of human freedom. For this sin, France extorted the fledging Black Republic for an indemnity in 1825, plunging Haiti into a 120-year debt. The United States, repeatedly invading Haitian waters and formally taking control in 1915, set into motion the centralization of power, resources, and people in Port-au-Prince. Many people in Haiti understand this, reserving the word *disaster* for the national and global system of inequality that led to the excessively high death toll and the indignities that followed, not the earthquake itself.

An earthquake of this magnitude and this close to a big city is bound to cause major damage, as did recent quakes in Iran, Turkey, and New Zealand. Much of Haiti's death toll can be linked to the extreme density of Port-au-Prince, whose population exploded as a direct consequence of neoliberal push and pull factors. As contributor Alex Dupuy notes (Chapter 1), 732,000 people lived in Port-au-Prince in the 1980s, growing to 3 million by 2008. Unplanned, uncoordinated *bidonvil* (shantytowns) sprung up to accommodate the 2 million people who were pushed off their land and pulled into low-wage factory jobs. Where were these 2 million new residents going to live?

Even for the lucky few who made a steadily declining minimum wage, what kind of house could they afford? Many lived in square, seven-by-seven-foot cinderblock dwellings with patchwork tin roofs that barely kept out the pouring rain or scorching Caribbean sun. These structures offered no privacy and were not connected to any water-supply system, thus no toilet or shower. With state services privatized under neoliberalism, families (especially mothers) have to pay for their children's education (40% of a minimum wage salary for one child) and health care, on top of high housing costs and increasing food costs. Most tenants had to build their own houses on land they rented; predictably, given the other expenses, many dwellings were built as cheaply as possible. These were the structures that, in combination with the earthquake, killed so many people. Reduced to rubble, they crushed those underneath. Of the homes built since 1990, 86% were destroyed on January 12, according to contributor Yolette Etienne (Chapter 1).

For all these reasons, Haiti's earthquake was a *human* disaster, the result of human action, social structure, and policy, together with the individual families making their way through the labyrinth of neoliberal restructuring. As a product of human action, it could have been avoided. The pictures of the wreckage circulating on the Internet, each more horrible than the next, are the clearest symbol yet of the failure of neoliberal capitalism and the centuries of plunder that preceded it.

These same agencies that forced Haiti to privatize its essential services and social safety net took even greater control of the situation following the earthquake. While the world community responded with a generous pledge of solidarity for Haiti's reconstruction at a March 31, 2010, conference—$10 billion with more than half to be given in the first year and a half—foreign agencies kept control of the decisions and the purse strings. Following a rushed planning document dominated by foreign experts, the government of Haiti dissolved itself, ceding power to a foreign-led reconstruction commission.

Again solidifying the tectonic shifts in Washington, Ottawa, and Brussels about how aid is to be delivered and the trend of NGO-ization, post-quake Haiti is today often called a Republic of NGOs. With an already hollowed-out state structure leveled by the earthquake, a patchwork of thousands of NGOs coordinated by UN "clusters" implemented the immediate and medium-term relief effort. With billions of dollars at stake in the provision of daily necessities of water, and the long-term rebuilding and reconstruction contracts, the earthquake presented an opportunity for disaster capitalism, a veritable "gold rush," in the words of the US ambassador in Haiti.

On-the-Ground Realities

Tectonic Shifts includes documents of lived experiences of the quake and its aftermath. As the glare of the media fades over time, with ever dwindling resources being deployed to assist the victims of the catastrophe, Haiti's on-going humanitarian crisis risks becoming forgotten. What impact have the billions of dollars had in this privatized, NGO-ized, militarized response? While some individuals have been pulled out of poverty, and thousands have benefited from emergency surgery and prosthetic limbs, the realities for too many people remain grim.

A growing defensive response to these failures is to blame Haitian culture, Haitian people's mentality, or the persistent poverty before the earthquake. Indeed, on one level, the seismic event just exposed the social ills besetting Haiti before January 12: without access to adequate health care, education, sanitation, water, jobs, and housing, Haiti's poor majority has long faced a precarious life. Haiti was already suffering a humanitarian disaster, though one that was ignored. A close look at exclusion and inequality highlights a shocking degree of continuity before and after the temblor. However, an honest assessment also reveals that the event—and the aid response—only increased these inequalities and marginalization of peasants, tenants, women, and the poor majority excluded from education.

Despite the efforts and some individual successes, seen collectively and from the ground—especially by the 1.7 million people who lost their homes in the earthquake—the aid response was far from adequate. Up to a sixth of Haiti's population has become internally displaced. While the IDP camps have dwindled, they are not going away any time soon. We offer several perspectives of this reality, with many voices from the camps.

IDPs' right to exist and Haitians' right to housing are supposedly guaranteed by international human rights law and the Haitian constitution, yet many of Haiti's remaining half a million IDPs must face the ongoing threat of forced eviction. Then there is the threat of fatal disease. A cholera outbreak triggered by UN troops stationed in Haiti's Central Plateau in October 2010 claimed almost 5,000 lives within its first six months. The outbreak underscores the need for an understanding of health and human rights in disaster-relief efforts.

Finally, as heads of household, women IDPs are the most at risk. The deplorable conditions in the camps—with inadequate lighting or security, overcrowding, and a lack of privacy—also constituted a breeding ground for an alarming rise in GBV. Women's organizations and their supporters abroad have rallied to pressure the various authorities in Haiti to protect women's rights and provide adequate services for rape victims. But as with the fight to secure every other kind of basic service in the camps, the battle has been uphill.

Emerging Movements

In the face of the devastation, Haiti's people were not silent, passive victims waiting for a handout. If the earthquake knocked down concrete walls protecting private property, it also helped dissolve some prejudices dividing classes or sectors of the popular movement. In the immediate aftermath, there was a glimmer of a new society based on solidarity and unity. Unfortunately, this moment did not last, particularly when the militarized, privatized, NGO-ized foreign aid apparatus reproduced and augmented the longstanding ills of exclusion, inequality, and division in Haiti. When it was clear that only some people would get tarps, tents, and then T-shelters; that only some people would receive clean water and medical care; that only some people would return to school; that only some people would have relatively lucrative jobs and service contracts; and that only some people would be allowed inside the UN logistics base to make decisions about this aid, a range of social movements organized in resistance.

As scholars have noted, disasters are primarily political events.[2] Haiti's earthquake and aftermath are no exception. In the midst of the fears of cholera, Haiti held national elections for president and both houses of Parliament. The Haitian government even warned that it was too soon. Despite ample early-warning signs, the international community pressed ahead with the elections that excluded viable candidates and Haiti's largest political party, and looked the other way when signs of corruption and logistical difficulties were impossible to ignore. That said, the international community funded the elections when they held tight to their purse strings regarding promised aid.

One ray of hope is the emergence of new social movements, whose interventions challenge us to think about politics from outside the usual top-down perspective. These movements are coming together across political divisions to demand greater popular participation in the new Haiti. We end the book on this theme to suggest new ways of thinking about, framing, and acting in solidarity with the Haitian people.

Aims of the Book

Taken together, these three elements—the geopolitical structures, changing on-the-ground realities, and emerging movements—offer tools for engaged, principled reflection and action. Moreover, *Tectonic Shifts* offers a range of critical analyses from a range of perspectives: from Haiti and the Haitian Diaspora, as well as from non-Haitians in solidarity with the country's struggle for social justice: activists, journalists, and scholars. Together, these voices highlight the many struggles that Haitian people are facing with dignity, offering lessons not only for those directly affected and involved in relief but also for people engaged in other struggles for justice and transformation, as well as members of the general public who were moved by the earthquake and wish to know more.

This project grew out of the July/August 2010 special issue of *NACLA Report on the Americas,* titled "Fault Lines: Perspectives on Haiti's Earthquake." We were urged by several people to consider publishing an expanded version of the issue as a book that could serve as an important source for students, scholars, development practitioners, journalists, policymakers, and activists. We believe this was not only because of the timeliness of the issue but also because it, like *Tectonic Shifts,* brought together many different voices from different perspectives. Half of the contributors are individuals or groups based in Haiti. The Diaspora has made many important contributions; we include a few here, as well as contributions from foreigners who have committed to be on the ground, accompanying Haiti's people. This book also brings together an equal mix of activist, journalist, legal, and scholarly approaches. Ultimately, we are uniting our efforts to help inspire, empower, educate, and challenge readers to help accompany the Haitian people in their quest for justice and dignity.

Notes

1. This is the "pressure and release" model elaborated by Ben Wisner et al., *At Risk: Natural Hazards, People's Vulnerability and Disasters,* 2nd ed. (New York: Routledge, 2004).

2. Neil Middleton and Phil O'Keefe, *Disaster and Development* (London: Pluto Press, 1998), Adolph Reed, "Class Inequality, Liberal Bad Faith, and Neoliberalism: The True Disaster of Katrina" in N. Gunewardena and M. Schuller, eds., *Capitalizing on Catastrophe: Neoliberal Strategies in Disaster Reconstruction* (Lanham, MD: Alta Mira Press, 2008), 147–54.

Part I

Geopolitical Structures
The Earthquake, Underdevelopment, and International Political Economy

1

Haiti's Vulnerability to Disasters

In May 2011 Agence France-Presse triggered a prolonged and heated debate about the official death count of the Haitian earthquake by publishing a leaked report to the United States Agency for International Development (USAID) authored by US anthropologist Timothy Schwartz. While contracted to study the impact of the housing evaluation system (red for demolish, yellow for repair, and green for habitable), Schwartz insisted on challenging the death toll by Haitian prime minister Jean-Max Bellerive of 316,000. Based on an ultimately suspect methodology not similarly leaked to the press, Schwartz estimated that the events of January 12, 2010, claimed 66,000 lives. While USAID distanced itself from the report, the mainstream international press took this uncritically and seized the opportunity to wag its fingers at the Haitian authorities—followed by some NGOs—accusing them of having inflated the goudougoudou's[1] death toll for self-interested reasons. For one, editor Mark Schuller finds the higher estimate plausible, given that of the 84 people on his street in Port-au-Prince, 14 people perished. Small Arms Survey's Athena Kolbe and Robert Muggah also came up with an estimate based on their research that directly focused on the death toll, much higher than Schwartz's.

With all due respect to our colleagues, this debate is a red herring. The people who died in the temblor had families, friends, community ties, aspirations, experiences, talents, skills, and hopes. Out of respect for the dead, and their living relatives struggling to survive, the majority of people in Haiti do not engage in this post hoc estimation. The lack of precision on the question of the death toll owes largely to numerical and societal uncertainties that predate the

11

*earthquake (the dearth of official birth records and national ID cards, for ex-
ample). Many records that did exist, along with family heirlooms, baby photos,
and other personal effects, are now buried beneath the rubble; cadavers, tens
of thousands of them, are now buried in a series of unmarked mass graves in
Titanyen, an area north of Port-au-Prince that has long been the dumping
ground for cadavers. Haiti's dead—like the living—do not count, a feature of
what Cameroonian intellectual Achille Mbembe termed "necropolitics."[2]*

*Whether it was 66,000 or more than 300,000 who perished, Haiti's
earthquake was one of the world's deadliest "natural" disasters ever recorded.
Comparing the January 12 earthquake to the tremors 500 times more powerful that shook Chile a mere five weeks later is instructive. While a significant
tragedy, especially to the affected Chileans' loved ones, Chile's temblor claimed
723 lives. True, Chile's earthquake was farther away from a major city. An
earthquake of the same magnitude as Haiti's struck just outside the major city
of Canterbury, New Zealand, in September 2010. No deaths were recorded.*

*Explaining the differences requires attention to what disaster researchers
call "vulnerability," which results from human action: social policies, political
decisions, conflicts, land-use decisions, exclusion, economic forces, and so on.[3]
For this reason, many scholars and Haitian survivors (some being both, including many contributors to this volume[4]) define the disaster not as an earthquake
but as the* kriz konjonkti—*a conjunctural crisis—meaning the intersection of
neoliberalism and foreign control, together with the complicity of Haiti's elite
and government.*

*We begin this chapter with a report by Haitian anthropologist Rachel
Beauvoir-Dominique, describing similarly exaggerated fallout following Tropical Storm Jeanne in 2004. Beauvoir-Dominique's report highlights the continuities in Haiti's vulnerabilities to disaster: change "Gonaïves" to "Port-au-Prince,"
"tropical storm" to "earthquake," and history eerily repeats itself—from vulnerability to land use, from the bottom-up solidarity, cash-for-work programs, and
extended deplorable conditions in tent camps to the role of the UN troops. One
of the founders of disaster studies, anthropologist Anthony Oliver-Smith, offers
here a historical overview of the many factors contributing to Haiti's heightened
vulnerability. Oliver-Smith discusses the indemnity France imposed in 1825 to
recognize Haiti's independence, keeping Haiti chained by debt until after the
Second World War.*

*Respected Haitian American social scientist Alex Dupuy sharpens the focus
on the particular damage wrought by neoliberalism, the gospel of the free market
imposed by the World Bank and other foreign agencies in the so-called Washington
Consensus. Dupuy focuses on the negative consequences of the low-wage assembly*

industry that exploded Port-au-Prince's population. Finally, Haitian civil society leader and development expert Yolette Etienne pulls together many of these strands, while focusing in particular on the uncontrolled urbanization and centralization stemming from the 1915 US occupation of Haiti. Etienne discusses the mismatch between aid and need, challenging us to examine the lessons not learned from previous disasters. All four contributors sharpen our attention to the ultimately changeable human causes of the disaster.

* * *

Humanitarian Assistance in Gonaïves after Hurricane Jeanne

Rachel Beauvoir-Dominique

Vulnerability

IN 2004 HAITI SUFFERED TWO major disasters in less than a year: torrential rains on May 23–24 caused massive flooding in the southeast, especially the municipalities of Fonds Verrette and Mapou, killing more than 2,000 people; then, on September 18, Hurricane Jeanne struck, killing more than 3,000 and affecting 300,000, especially in the northern city of Gonaïves.[5] These disasters were all associated with natural phenomena (hurricanes, floods) but revealed the profound vulnerability of Haitian society and, therefore, the disasters' principally human causes.

In Gonaïves we were directly confronted with the problems of a city that had to rebuild everything, especially its municipal functions, even as Haiti was in the throes of a difficult political transition (President Jean-Bertrand Aristide had been ousted in a coup the previous February). Even before Hurricane Jeanne, most of the city's infrastructure was already deteriorated, if not destroyed, including the police office, the jail, the Court of Appeal, and city hall.

The city's evolution was typical for those in less industrialized countries: stagnant during the nineteenth and early twentieth centuries, its population exploded during the transition to capitalism, which destroyed rural areas and caused massive waves of migration to urban areas. Indeed, Gonaïves grew from a tiny population of about 600 during the colonial period to a city of 35,000 inhabitants in 1982. By 1997 it reached 130,000, increasing to 170,000 in 2000. The developed area had increased from 290 hectares in 1987 to 665 hectares in 1997.

The extreme poverty of services in Gonaïves makes the situation almost unbearable and explains the vulnerability of such a dense population (only one of eight areas in the city identified by the firm Beta has drainage).

The Emergency Relief

Humanitarian assistance after the hurricane primarily came from the affected population themselves. As the Sphere International Humanitarian Charter and Minimum Standards, drafted in the 1990s and adopted by hundreds of humanitarian agencies, recognizes, "It is firstly through their own efforts that the basic needs of people affected by calamity or armed conflict are met."[6] The survivors of the massive floods that Hurricane Jeanne caused in Gonaïves went first to more sturdy, neighboring houses, where the owners welcomed them in solidarity, sometimes even on the roofs (in one case, a house owner sheltered more than 80 people). The neighborhoods of Gatereau and Bienac, which were spared total destruction, were remarkable in this sense; in Gatereau, a relatively elevated area, drinking water from wells was distributed. Similarly, given the absence of food, utensils, or fuel, the first shipment of aid arrived from outside the city in the Artibonite Valley; this included pots, clothes, and food.

The international response to requests from supporters of the Gonaïves victims was exceptional. Indeed, more than the total requested funds were obtained: an estimated $31,983,515 was collected by various organizations for the UN Flash Appeal of September 30, 2004.[7] This was similar to the aid collections following the South Asian tsunami the following December. Yet the shock of the human misery was followed by one of the pitiful offers of support from so-called friends. US President George W. Bush shocked the world by announcing, in the aftermath of the disaster, a disbursement of $60,000 for the victims—less than 25 cents per person. The very same week he announced $7 billion in aid for the damage the hurricane wreaked in Florida (five deaths versus 3,000). Similarly, France, in its "compassion" under President Jacques Chirac, immediately offered 260,000 euros (less than one per person). While these two nations did catch up a little later, the shame remains.

What Are the Results?

Cleanup
The cleanup of Gonaïves did not take place until December (probably in response to many complaints and government visits on January 1, Independence Day), through the mobilization of national actors like the Public and Community Works and private companies. This initiative emerged from the central government.

Another problem was the Cash for Work (CFW) program. Normally designed to allow disaster victims to earn a little money, the operation provided the minimum daily wage (70 gourdes at the time, or $1.75) to a large segment of deprived Gonaïviens in exchange for "intensive labor" in the houses filled with mud as in the urban canals and ravines. Of course, in the destroyed city, where almost everyone ended up losing their savings and their source of revenue, candidates were abundant.

However, in terms of its substance as well as its form (jobs with a rapid rotation, lasting just a few days and with long delays for payment), opposition arose from all sides and fed lively debates during the coordination meetings among the NGOs. People called the CFW program "slavery" or *corvée* (meaning "chore," a term used to refer to the abuses of the first US occupation of Haiti in 1915). This insulting practice was even more offensive to local workers after CARE, the largest NGO in the city, pressured other NGOs like Oxfam, which paid workers 100 gourdes a day, to reduce their salary!

Shelter and Housing
Beyond direct humanitarian assistance with food or drinking water, NGOs' contributions in terms of shelter were the most appreciated. As such, getting "out of the street," restoring one's family, and getting a place were experienced as part of the fundamental rights relating to human dignity. People were happy and saw it as a sign of respect when they obtained a tent or even simple tarps to cover the structural elements of damaged houses.

The negative aspects of this appeared only later. In January 2005 the World Health Organization (WHO) reported that about half of the 56 shelters meant for overnight stays continued to house many thousands of souls in Gonaïves, not to mention countless reconverted family homes. Within these camps of tents and makeshift shelters, living conditions deteriorated rapidly: excessive heat, overcrowding, problems with trash disposal, water problems, torn tents, proximity, and so on, visibly tarnishing the image of humanitarian assistance in Gonaïves. It then became a priority to get out of providing services. Yet international experience reveals the great delicacy of such operations. Creating new shantytowns, self-construction, land issues—there were many things to manage, and each case told much more about the medium- to long-term reality than about the emergency phase, especially in places where social organization was already destroyed.

This may explain the very slow and painful progress at this point. The continued existence of the tent camps, each with deplorable living conditions, remains a sore spot in the management of the crisis, revealing without any doubt the difficulties that would show up later when the aid ended.

Safety vs. Security

The security situation seriously deteriorated in Gonaïves the first week after Hurricane Jeanne. In this city where the social climate was already extremely tense, the sound of gunshots broke the silence every night, a sign of violence carried out on popular sectors to extract the little they had left. This situation persisted in and particularly around the city, where residents said many months later that they were under a curfew, barring them from the streets starting at 6 p.m.

The National Police were manifestly absent. The police station and jail were flooded during the disaster, and after prisoners escaped from one section of the jail, the police chose to release prisoners from a second section. Without weapons, uniforms, or buildings the police suffered important personal losses, leading to their absence.

This explains, but does not justify, the deployment of the UN Stabilization Mission in Haiti (MINUSTAH) forces in the city. The almost 750 blue helmets were unable to ensure citizens' safety and were accused by the population of "strolling around." The relative futility of its nightly patrols could possibly be explained by the insufficiency of the troops' cultural familiarity with Haiti, according to the humanitarian coordinator of the region.

The Disaster and Human Rights

The Code of Conduct of the Red Cross clearly states the following:

• *"Aid is given regardless of the race, creed, or nationality of the recipients and without adverse distinction of any kind. Aid priorities are calculated on the basis of need alone."* Despite this, some social sectors, particularly practitioners of Vodou (especially in sacred sites such as Souvenance, Desronvilles, and Badjo) were deliberately excluded from distributions by certain institutions in favor of surrounding Protestant communities, sharpening a destructive division of the people in this region. There were also numerous allegations of insufficient attention to vulnerable populations (the elderly, women—especially pregnant women—and children).

• *"Relief aid must strive to reduce future vulnerabilities to disaster as well as meeting basic needs."* Operations to restore civil protection in Gonaïves seem to have started only in the successive phase of rehabilitation, in the spring of 2005, which meant that as the next rainy season (May) approached, the population found itself in the same situation of insecurity and anxiety.

• *"We hold ourselves accountable to both those we seek to assist and those from whom we accept resources."* The population was basically not informed of expenses incurred during all these operations, nor of the origin of the money or how much it totaled. Although commitments of $43,331,920 made as of June 2005 are ridiculous compared with the $7 billion from President Bush for the damage in Florida, the population, from Gonaïves in particular, had the right to explanations of how these funds were used.

When Will the "Second" Phase Begin?

The rapid intervention and involvement of the multinational apparatus during the emergency phase of humanitarian aid only reluctantly authorized desirable levels of local or even national participation. The shocking thing, however, is the almost total withdrawal of national institutions like the National Police in the early days of the disaster. Similarly, five months after the launch of the second phase of recovery, called "reconstruction," the following problems arose:

• Little or no transition was anticipated to prepare the population for the sudden, total stop of food assistance.
• No debate was initiated, locally or nationally, on the orientations and options of this vital phase of operations.
• Essential criticisms of affected residents were ignored, rejected, and even maligned.
• National control over many NGOs' interventions was very minimal, relegated instead to the United Nations Development Programme (UNDP).
• Certain redevelopment contracts, in the housing sector in particular, did not include any national company, and even originated in the United States.
• Despite the established coordination structures, a cliquishness among the intervening actors was clearly noticed.
• Humanitarian coordination work performed by MINUSTAH, a mainly military organization, led to a confusion of roles.

* * *

Haiti's 500-Year Earthquake

Anthony Oliver-Smith

DISASTERS ARE NOT ACCIDENTS OR acts of God.[8] They are deeply rooted in the social, economic, and environmental history of the societies where they occur. Moreover, disasters are far more than catastrophic events; they are *processes* that unfold through time, and their causes are deeply embedded in societal history. As such, disasters have historical roots, unfolding presents, and potential futures according to the forms of reconstruction. In effect, a disaster is made inevitable by the historically produced pattern of vulnerability, evidenced in the location, infrastructure, sociopolitical structure, production patterns, and ideology that characterize a society. Nowhere is this perspective more validated than in Haiti, which on January 12 in some respects experienced the culmination of its own more than 500-year earthquake.

Like the written histories of many Latin American and Caribbean nations, Haiti's begins in tragedy and devastation. The Taino, the original population of the island later named Hispaniola, were decimated by European diseases contracted from the earliest Spanish settlers in 1493. After fitful attention from the Spaniards and other European powers for more than 125 years, the French West India Company established control over the colony, by then called Saint-Domingue, which constituted about a third of the island. By the end of the seventeenth century, African slavery, a foundational element in the long-term construction of Haiti's vulnerability, was instituted to obtain labor to work on plantation crops of sugar and coffee for export. By the end of the eighteenth century, the colony's African slaves were producing 40% of all the sugar and 60% of all the coffee consumed in Europe, for the benefit of European planters and their offspring with slave concubines, offspring whom the French colonial system often defined as free and able to inherit property and own slaves; many of these *mulâtres* would emerge as Haiti's first national elites.[9]

The revolutionary zeal of 1789 in France spread to these early elite free people of color in Saint-Domingue, initiating a series of reform and resistance movements in 1790 that progressed into full-scale slave revolts and ultimately culminated in the colony's independence in 1804. Haiti, its name chosen from the original Taino name for the island, became the world's first black republic. Despite the Haitian victory, however, France refused to recognize the new republic until reparations were paid for lost "property," primarily in the form of slaves and land, in the amount of 90 million gold francs (reduced from 150 million). Haiti was subjected to new threats of invasion by France and a crippling embargo maintained by France, Britain, and the United States until it agreed in 1825 to that payment. The entire debt was paid off only in 1947, after Haiti had taken out high-interest loans to do so. Haiti thus began its existence under the weight of crippling debt and embargo. Bearing that burden, the country went from being the richest Caribbean colony, "the pearl of the Antilles," to the most impoverished nation in the Western Hemisphere.[10]

To punish the upstart black republic, European and US leaders early in the nineteenth century began a campaign to isolate Haiti politically and economically, essentially channeling through debt obligations the nation's extracted resources—income largely from sugar, coffee, and indigo—toward metropolitan nations, first France and later the United States, following the 1915 US invasion.[11] The Haitian government and elites brokered the extraction process with foreign powers, principally the United States, and began accumulating power and wealth while draining the nation's resources. While impoverishing the population with brutality, militarism, mismanagement, and corruption, Haitian elites did little to construct a viable infrastructure or a functional institutional framework in the country.[12]

The historical construction of Haiti's impoverishment and vulnerability has been exponentially compounded by more recent developments during the last quarter of the twentieth century. Following the brutal dictatorship of "Papa Doc" Duvalier, the ruinous reign of his son "Baby Doc" left the nation in even greater debt to foreign lenders because of either misappropriation or outright theft by the dictator. The second Duvalier regime, a virtual kleptocracy, coincided with the catastrophic USAID-ordered slaughter of all of Haiti's pigs to limit the spread of African swine flu virus. The loss of the pig population—the source of peasant savings, emergency capital, and nutrition—left rural people, the majority of the population, even more impoverished and vulnerable.[13]

Ever more bereft of resources, rural Haitians were forced to cut down more and more trees to produce charcoal, eventually deforesting almost all of Haiti's territory. USAID programs, working with large landowners, encouraged the construction of agro-processing facilities, while International Monetary Fund (IMF)–imposed tariff reductions opened Haitian markets to subsidized US rice surpluses, undercutting local production of the nation's staple crop and dismantling the rural economy. The goal of these measures was to develop Haiti's cities into centers of export production for

US companies. The destruction of the rural economy and investment in urban export production stimulated a massive migration to the nation's cities, where impoverished migrants took up residence in festering slums and hillside shantytowns with few services of any sort. The demand for jobs by displaced rural people quickly outstripped the supply, deepening the impoverishment of ever denser populations in vulnerable locations in cities. Political instability during the last 20 years has also led to a reduction of companies available to offer jobs.[14]

Thus, as 2010 began, Haiti found itself extraordinarily vulnerable to the natural hazards of its environment. In the previous quarter-century, few development efforts, misguided and mismanaged as they were, had privileged the issue of environmental security or hazard mitigation. A lack of building codes, together with informal settlements, widespread under-nourishment and hunger, disease, poor access to clean water or electricity, inadequate educational and health facilities and services at the national and municipal levels, and crime and corruption led to the presence of extreme vulnerability. In addition, Haitians were largely unaware of the seismic risk on the island, although seismologists had been warning of the possibility of a strong earthquake.

Because of this social construction of extreme vulnerability, more than 300,000 Haitians died, according to Haitian government estimates. The unregulated and informal housing stock of the city of Port-au-Prince has been flattened, its basic service lifelines, inadequate as they were, destroyed. A million people now without shelter awaited the summer's torrential rains and the oncoming hurricane season in conditions of extreme exposure and deprivation.

A scant five weeks after the Haitian earthquake, Chile was hit by an earthquake that was more than 500 times more powerful. Nonetheless, because of the epicenter's depth and location farther from densely pop-ulated areas, the number of Chileans killed in the quake was limited to hundreds rather than hundreds of thousands, as in Haiti. But the differ-ence in mortality can be traced not only to the location and depth of the earthquakes but also to the levels of vulnerability that characterized the two societies. Because of the frequency and severity of earthquakes in the re-gion, Chile's government and population are sensitized to the need for precautionary measures. For example, Chile has an excellent building code, first instituted in the 1930s and later modernized under the Salvador Allende administration and strengthened again in 1985.[15]

In contrast, Haiti has no building code, and the vast majority of the population of its capital, Port-au-Prince, lived in poorly constructed houses in densely packed slums. Moreover, rampant corruption in Haiti virtually assured that even buildings constructed in the formal sector had little engineering input and substandard construction. The high rates of damage and collapse of formal building stock were clearly a function of corruption among high-level officials, who turned a blind eye to these irresponsible practices that resulted in the total destruction of 13 of 15 federal ministry buildings. Transparency International ranks Haiti at 168 and Chile at 25 in their least-to-most-corrupt index.[16]

In terms of development levels, Chile, despite having its share of poverty and inequality, has a much better Human Development Index (HDI) than Haiti. The HDI is a composite index measuring the average achievements of 182 nations in three basic aspects of human development: health (life expectancy at birth), knowledge (adult literacy rate and the combined primary, secondary, and tertiary gross enrollment ratio), and standard of living (GDP per capita). In the 2009 Human Development Report, Chile ranked 44th, well into the high-development category, while Haiti ranked 149th, toward the bottom of the medium-development category and quite close to the low-development category, occupied primarily by African states (23 of 24 listed).[17] These levels of poverty and underdevelopment, while not identical with vulnerability, coincide very frequently with high vulnerability. Such indicators also demonstrate that Chile has a functioning state apparatus that delivers a certain level of service to its citizens, which was evident in the earthquake emergency and aftermath, whereas Haiti's government was virtually invisible, if not nonexistent, for several days after the disaster.

Yet the relationships between citizen and state as evidenced in behavior during the two disasters in Haiti and Chile displayed some significant differences. In the context of the almost total absence of the state in Haiti, the response of the population—apart from some relatively few cases of looting—was characterized by social solidarity and self-organization resulting in collective efforts at rescue and assistance to those in need. Looters in Haiti, meanwhile, were subjected to the rough justice of the community. In contrast, in Chile, with its powerful centralist state apparatus, the population depended largely on government responses. When these did not prove adequate to the situation, individualist impulses took over, unleashing more social violence and looting than in Haiti.

Raúl Sohr, a Chilean journalist, suggests that the lack of social solidarity and organizational capacity in the general population was a result of the corrosive effect of a neoliberal political and ideological model that prompts individualist gain-seeking rather than collective responses to crisis.[18] The contrast between the social responses in Chile and Haiti resonates with findings that resource constraints under neoliberal regimes in Latin

America have eroded previously dense social networks of the poor, reducing community solidarity and interhousehold cooperation.[19] Thus, there may in fact be more to reconstruct in Chile than infrastructure and housing stock. On the other hand, in Haiti, potential social resources on which to base reconstruction may be more abundant than expected.

The fundamental question that needs to be asked is how reconstruction can address the complex of environmental, economic, political, and social variables that produced the Haitian disaster in such a way that will be sustainable, reduce vulnerability, and enable people at the household and community level to survive. In other words, Haiti has to reconstruct and recover economically without reinstituting the same system that generated the extreme vulnerability in the first place. However, predisaster systems, regardless of levels of incompetence and corruption, have shown themselves to be remarkably resilient, very often achieving quite rapid reinstitution in aftermaths. In effect, reconstruction becomes a test of the system's capacity to respond to a clear demonstration that the catastrophic death and destruction that took place in Haiti were deeply rooted in the changes enacted in the country's social and political-economic history, particularly in the twentieth century.

Reconstruction, to be truly transformative, has to address that complex of factors that made the earthquake into the horror that it became. In other words, reconstruction will have to recognize the responsibility of international forces and local interests in the high vulnerability of Haiti, which then must be reflected in policies and practices that address not only the symptoms manifested in the destruction, but also the causes, both proximate and distant, of the disaster. If we view the death and destruction of the Haitian earthquake as due in part to economically and socially inscribed practices and the capital and commodity flows that created and sustained them nationally and internationally, the challenge of reconstruction lies not just in rebuilding Haiti but in changing its marginal place within the world system.

In contemporary disasters, perhaps our most important task is to discover and implement those aspects of reconstruction that within the limits of action permitted by existing structures can feasibly reduce environmental degradation and vulnerability to hazards. Post-earthquake Haiti provides an important opportunity for economic forms and practices to be altered toward more sustainable forms of use. By the same token, the earthquake has created a space in which political power balances can be reassessed and shifted to better reflect local realities and the needs of society.

Furthermore, reconstruction can help to establish the range of possibilities for sustainability as an achievable goal of specific directed policies within the limitations established by current economic practice. However, whether the political and economic structures of the nation can, even with the necessity and the incentive of reconstruction, truly ever come to grips with a set of endemic conditions that are so deeply embedded by both national and international forces in their own forms and practices remains in doubt.

In the final analysis, much of the devastation and misery caused in Haiti by the earthquake of January 12 was a product of historical processes set in motion since the time of independence, and even earlier. These processes, emerging from the international response to the abolition of slavery and the struggle for independence, cumulatively over time, produced the conditions of profound vulnerability in which most of Haiti's population lived. Thus, the accentuated vulnerability that the island nation exhibited before the earthquake, and still exhibits, is a socially created phenomenon—a historical product brought into being and maintained by identifiable forces.

* * *

The Neoliberal Legacy in Haiti

Alex Dupuy

HAITI HAS HAD A LONG history of foreign interference in its domestic affairs since it gained its independence in 1804, culminating in the US invasion and occupation of the country from 1915 to 1934.[20] Thenceforth, the United States displaced other powers, notably France, Great Britain, and Germany in the nineteenth century, and placed Haiti firmly under its sphere of influence. For our purposes, however, we can consider the 1970s as having marked a major turning point in creating the conditions that existed on the eve of the earthquake and contributed to its devastating impact.

In return for military and economic aid from the United States and other core countries (notably Canada and France), the regime of Jean-Claude "Baby Doc" Duvalier (1971–1986), which succeeded that of his father, François "Papa Doc" Duvalier (1957–1971), turned over the formulation of economic policy for Haiti to the international financial institutions

(IFIs). These institutions pursued a twofold strategy that succeeded, on the one hand, in turning Haiti into a supplier of the cheapest labor in the Western Hemisphere for the export-assembly industries established by foreign and domestic investors, and, on the other hand, one of the largest importers of US food in the Caribbean Basin. These outcomes were achieved through a series of "structural adjustment" policies that kept wages low, dismantled all obstacles to free trade, removed tariffs and quantitative restrictions on imports, offered tax incentives to the manufacturing industries on their profits and exports, privatized public enterprises, reduced public-sector employment, and curbed social spending to reduce fiscal deficits.

Foreign investors were attracted to Haiti for a number of reasons: its abundant supply of unskilled, low-wage workers kept in check with violent repression; its proximity to the US market; its lack of foreign-exchange controls and other kinds of government interference; its policies allowing the free circulation of the US dollar; its tax incentives with exemptions on income and profits; and its tariff exemptions on imported raw materials, machinery, or other inputs used in the assembly industries, as well as on the export of the assembled products.[21] Even though the gap between the wages of Haitian workers and those in other countries in the region was high enough to offset transportation, tariff, and other costs, the World Bank argued that they still might not offset the bureaucratic and political risks in Haiti. The country's wages should therefore not be raised, as workers were demanding, to prevent investors from going elsewhere, the Bank argued.

The other side of the US and IFIs' urban industrial strategy was to dismantle Haiti's trade barriers and open its economy to food imports, principally from the United States. Although the Duvalier dictatorship embraced the assembly industry, it resisted demands to remove the 50% tariffs on imports of food, especially rice, and thereby enabled Haitian farmers to continue producing all the rice consumed in Haiti while limiting other food imports to about 19%. All that changed after Jean-Claude Duvalier was overthrown in February 1986. The US government successfully pressured the government of General Henri Namphy to "liberalize" the Haitian economy by, among other things, slashing import tariffs and reducing subsidies to domestic agriculture.

When Jean-Bertrand Aristide was elected by a landslide in November 1990 and assumed the presidency in February 1991, he sought to change these policies to protect domestic food production, especially rice, against cheaper imports, and raise the minimum wage of workers in the assembly industries. These efforts failed because of stiff resistance from the Haitian

Chamber of Commerce, the IMF, and USAID. The Haitian army soon toppled Aristide in September 1991. In October 1994 President Clinton returned Aristide to office on the back of 20,000 US marines to finish out his first five-year term. Despite opposition from the Haitian business class, Aristide raised the daily minimum wage to 70 gourdes (about $1.75) in 1995. But he also agreed to lower tariffs on rice and other food imports to 3%.[22] They have remained at that level since, including during Aristide's truncated second term (2001–2004).

By the end of the 1980s and early 1990s, however, the Bank came to realize that despite all the advantages of the export-assembly strategy it advocated, the strategy did not create the conditions for a more sustainable development of the Haitian economy. Even at the height of its operation in the mid-1980s, the assembly industry never employed more than 7% of Haitian workers and did not contribute significantly to reducing the underestimated 38% unemployment rate of the active urban labor force. The industry had at best a neutral effect on income distribution, but a negative effect on the balance of goods and services, since it encouraged more imports of consumer goods.

The industry also contributed little to government revenues because of the tax exemptions on profits and other fiscal incentives, which, along with the subsidized costs of public services and utilities, represented a transfer of wealth to the foreign investors and their entrepreneurial Haitian subcontractors who operated the assembly industries. Other than construction and services (like transportation and catering), the assembly industry did not contribute to the expansion of other industrial sectors, not only because it imported its raw materials and other industrial inputs rather than relying on domestic supplies, but also because the poverty wages of its workers did not stimulate the economy. Moreover, the products of the assembly industry were not used as inputs by other Haitian industries but exported to the United States. The processing industry is entirely dependent on the United States or other developed markets for its products because it relies on contracts from companies in those countries. Thus, when the limits on import quotas are met, or if demand decreases, the industry cannot expand its production.

In sum, the assembly industry drained more foreign exchange than it brought in, which the industry accomplished in two ways. First, most of foreign investors' profits were not reinvested in that sector but expatriated, and the absence of expanded investment opportunities led even Haitian entrepreneurs to invest their savings outside of Haiti, most often in the

United States. Second, the importation of consumer and producers' goods (intermediate and capital goods) surpassed the total exports of the modern industrial sector, thereby draining foreign exchange from the economy. In light of its own analysis, then, the World Bank could not but conclude that the assembly industry's impact on developing the Haitian economy as a whole had "remained limited." "Even [in the years when the industry] was particularly marked," the Bank noted, "little of this dynamism trickled down to other sectors."[23]

Meanwhile, Haiti's neoliberal agricultural policies had drastic consequences for the country's farmers. Whereas in the 1970s Haiti imported about 19% of its food needs, it now imports 51%. It went from being self-sufficient in the production of rice, sugar, poultry, and pork to becoming the fourth-largest importer of subsidized US rice in the world and the largest importer of foodstuffs from the United States in the Caribbean. Eighty percent of all the rice consumed in Haiti is now imported. Trade liberalization, then, essentially meant transferring wealth from Haitian to US farmers, especially rice farmers in Arkansas and the US agribusiness companies that export to Haiti and those Haitian companies that resell it on the domestic market. Not surprisingly, rice imports were more profitable than other food imports.[24]

Trade liberalization not only exacerbated the decline of agriculture and the dispossession of farmers, but when combined with an industrial strategy that located assembly industries primarily in Port-au-Prince, it also propelled migrants from the rural areas to the capital city and its spreading squalor. Port-au-Prince grew from a city of 150,000 inhabitants in 1950 to 732,000 in the early 1980s, and to about 3 million in 2008, or almost one-third of Haiti's population of 9.8 million. Those who could not find employment in the assembly industries swelled the ranks of the unemployed or the informal sector, which became the largest source of employment for the urban population. Since the 1970s migration to the neighboring Dominican Republic, the Caribbean, and North America increased dramatically to the point that Haiti is now heavily dependent on emigrants' remittances, which in 2008 represented 19% of Haiti's GDP.[25]

But if the dual-development strategy devised by the IFIs exacerbated Haiti's underdevelopment and poverty, it also aggravated the disparities between the wealthy elites and the subordinate classes. Along with Bolivia, Haiti has the largest income inequality in the hemisphere. In 1976, three-quarters of the population lived in absolute poverty, while about 5% appropriated more than half of the national income. By 2007 the richest

10% appropriated 47% of national income, and 2% controlled 26% of the nation's wealth. By contrast, the poorest 20% received 1.1% of national income; 76% of the population lived on less than $2 a day, and more than half lived on less than $1 a day.[26]

Yet despite these lamentable outcomes, the economic development strategy now under way in Haiti is nearly identical to that of the past.

* * *

Haiti and Catastrophes
Lessons Not Learned

Yolette Etienne

EIGHTEEN MONTHS AFTER THE disaster of January 12, 2010, the situation of the affected population remains precarious.[27] More importantly, hope seems to have faded away. We seem to plunge into a trivialization of the situation and the repetition of practices that do not offer a change in the living conditions of the most vulnerable. The direction of the response has been assumed largely by international agencies. The response has mobilized the full range of humanitarians, ranging from the most specialized organizations to amateur groups and even criminals on the lookout to exploit all forms of human misery. We must also recognize that almost all actors have groped around in their interventions because of the scale and urban nature of the disaster. The consequences of this approach are heavily felt by a population whose initiatives have been neither strengthened nor valued.

What have we learned? How have we managed this trauma, this nightmare? Has the disaster of January 12 opened a new period? Can we still hope for a redefinition of the relationship between the population and decision makers, or even the relationship between Haiti and the world system? The country, though disenchanted, still hopes for a leadership capable of bringing about a reconstruction that breaks with discrimination and exclusion and mobilizes energies to create capacities and opportunities to escape from the fatalism of a failed state and to build a new collective space. To achieve this, we must continue to deepen the assessment of the post-earthquake era's results, learn the lessons, and identify the challenges we are facing today.

Let Us Remember the Numbers of the Apocalypse, Against All Odds

Official figures confirm a situation of apocalyptic dimensions: more than 200,000 dead, more than 300,000 injured, thousands of amputees, 1 million orphans, 2 million displaced, and more than half a million homeless citizens still spread about in makeshift camps. We have seen a mass exodus of more than 30,000 professionals. Two hundred and eighty-five thousand houses and buildings destroyed, with productive and social sectors annihilated. Forty-nine university buildings collapsed; 3,978 schools were destroyed (representing more than 23% of the schools nationwide), including more than 90% of schools in the Port-au-Prince metropolitan area; and more than 1,500 teachers died. The health sector was also severely affected with the collapse of 30 out of 49 hospitals and health centers in the metropolitan area. Food insecurity and health risks have increased significantly.

A Crisis of Confluence or a Structural Crisis?

We cannot repeat enough that the extent of earthquake damage can be explained only by general context: a long and deep structural crisis. A city built for 250,000 people had 3 million on January 12, with population densities close to those of Calcutta or Mumbai. To cite just one example, a shantytown called Jalousie in the hills of Pétionville houses 43,475 people per square kilometer. Eighty percent of the capital city's population lived on 20% of the territory. The territorial layout inherited from the 1915 model and the hyperconcentration around Port-au-Prince—both resulting from the 19-year US occupation—is to a large extent responsible for the casualties Haiti suffered during the earthquake. Add to this the lack of a social housing policy faced by a flood of some 12,000 to 15,000 migrants coming to live in Port-au-Prince every month. The lack of urban planning and of any control mechanism over housing construction (large estates of the middle class and the rich have proliferated in areas formally forbidden for buildings, such as the neighborhood of Juvenat), materials, standards of resistance, and construction techniques all played a crucial role. According to available statistics, 86% of houses destroyed were built between 1990 and 2010. With anguish and indignation we witness an irresponsible re-occupation of the space with new buildings that continue to elude any norms, together with the restoration of buildings that somehow escaped the Earth's fury on January 12.

The events that day violently destroyed a ramshackle system that showed its limits in a permanent, structural, and multidimensional crisis. The answer to this conjunctural crisis requires the promotion of new models that will challenge the centralization, exclusion, polarization, financial speculation, and the extreme dependence that characterized Haiti during the last 50 years.

International Aid and Its Contradictions

Since the first anniversary of the disaster, and even before, numerous evaluations and analyses have emerged. What is the overall impact of various actors' responses? We must continue to reflect on the virtues and contradictions of the international aid channeled through different mechanisms that played a role in this conjuncture. These reflections are not only useful to pull Haiti out of its quagmire but also to change the patterns of humanitarian interventions called upon to rescue any population in the world: Haiti is not the exception but a perfect example of the intersection of threats that can affect men and women in a given place.

We must first recognize and continue to welcome the extraordinary spirit of solidarity and generosity toward the victims of the earthquake that emerged spontaneously with an unprecedented mobilization of citizens around the world. Half the US population contributed in various ways, and we received donations from more than 17 African countries and many Asian countries. The contributions from governments and civil societies of Europe and the Americas reached impressive levels. Significant contributions came from our Caribbean neighbors: Cuba, the Dominican Republic, Puerto Rico, Trinidad and Tobago, and Venezuela.

Despite this great solidarity, TV cameras insisted on zeroing in on looting or youth fighting over a small bag of water (see Ulysse essay later in this volume). They have systematically overshadowed the positive aspects: the extraordinary and wonderful spirit of inter-Haitian solidarity dominated by generosity, sharing, personal sacrifices, and the mobilization of an economy based on solidarity. Little was shown of the Port-au-Prince neighbor-hoods' extraordinary capacity for self-organization—neighborhoods that were able, in brotherhood and without violence, to reorganize rapidly to protect life in an exceptional context of destruction. Not much was shown of the enthusiastic involvement of farmer organizations that came to help city dwellers in all the affected urban areas (Petit-Goâve, Léogâne, Jacmel, Port-au-Prince) to deliver food and that could accommodate without flinching an extraordinary influx of people, estimated at 690,000, by pro-viding them shelter, a plate of food, and effective support (see Jean-Baptiste essay in Chapter 5 of this volume).

The international humanitarian aid saved tens of thousands of lives and humanized conditions in some of the makeshift camps in the metro-politan area, Léogâne, and Petit-Goâve. Despite this, many observers re-ported serious imbalances and inequality in the distribution of aid, which focused primarily on the central regions that enjoyed a higher visibility. Massive food aid has played a crucial role in the survival of the displaced populations, but it has had pernicious effects on domestic production by reducing retail prices of grain products. Direct support to domestic pro-duction has been grossly inadequate, according to an Oxfam report.[28]

But despite undeniable positive results, the way aid was configured and structured triggered numerous criticisms and anger against the state—its absence and chronic irresponsibility—and against NGOs with consid-erable resources but with limited results in the end.

The aid architecture and organizational structures generally proposed by international organizations are for the most part not grafted onto Haiti's traditional structures and have therefore weakened the socioeconomic or-ganizations and structures that should have been tasked in this new phase. The injection of funds through Cash for Work (CFW) programs failed to support activities and did not bring about new leadership or new social commitment (see the Haiti Grassroots Watch essay in Chapter 4 of this volume). Most of the CFW activities, easy and badly selected, strengthened the syndrome of "assistantship" and its corollaries of apathy, dependency, and fatalism, reinforcing the loss of an entire generation's self-esteem.

Voices from all over question the tendencies that lock Haiti in a hu-manitarian framework while neglecting investments that could strengthen productive capacity. However, the trend persists, and we still wait for a reconstruction plan and above all a financing plan for the reconstruction on par with the Marshall Plan for Europe after the Second World War. Figure 1.1 illustrates well the priorities of aid that is disengaging from pro-ductive investment to focus on humanitarian dependency.

Figure 1.1 Food Aid and Aid to Agriculture in Haiti (2008 $m)

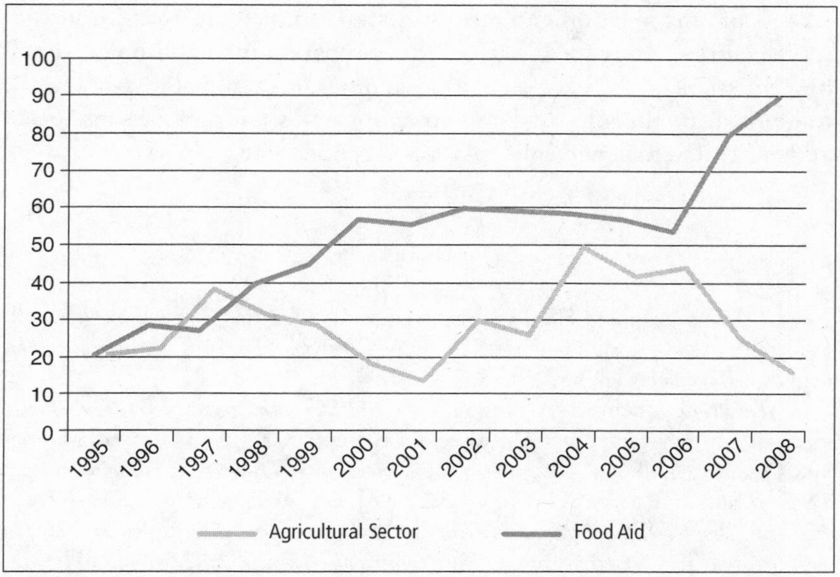

Source: Organisation for Economic Co-operation and Development

Conclusion

The announced re-foundation remains quite hypothetical in the present context. What we need is a powerful national revival and a powerful, continued citizen mobilization to create the conditions for a real end to the crisis. After 15 years of UN missions, the international community shows no sign of changing course. Despite the presence of MINUSTAH, the country has not really restored a climate of stability and security (see Chapter 2, this volume). The foundations to ensure progress on democratic elections do not exist. The culture of impunity prevents a sustainable structuring of the justice system. The country does not control its borders with the Dominican Republic and has not drastically reduced the transit of drugs. MINUSTAH has already cost nearly $3.7 billion between June 2004 and October 2010. We should question the validity of these strategies and results in terms of structuring the productive sectors and state institutions to meet the challenges of socio-natural disasters and the challenges of underdevelopment that the country will continue to face.

International assistance in its humanitarian form, just as in its development form, will still have an important role to play in supporting the process of rehabilitation and reconstruction. To play this role, it must respect Haiti's sovereignty and its self-determination in establishing a development strategy (see Chapter 2, this volume). It should also abandon the traditional, dominant paradigms to adopt paths and innovations for an authentic, fraternal, and solidarity-based cooperation.

Notes

1. Many people in Haiti are suspicious of naming the phrase, *tranblemanntè a,* for fear of its return. They use the phrase *bagay la,* "the thing," mimicking the sound of the earth shaking.

2. Achille Mbembe, "Necropolitics," *Public Culture* 15, no. 1 (2003): 11–40.

3. For more on vulnerability, see, for example, Greg Bankoff, Georg Frerks, and Dorothea Hilhorst, eds., *Mapping Vulnerability: Disasters, Development, and People* (London: Earthscan Publications, 2004); Ben Wisner et al., *At Risk: Natural Hazards, People's Vulnerability and Disasters,* 2nd ed. (New York: Routledge, 2004).

4. See also Myrtha Gilbert, *La Catastrophe N'était Pas Naturelle* (Port-au-Prince: Imprimeur II, 2010).

5. This is an excerpt from Rachel Beauvoir-Dominique, *Impact de l'assistance humanitaire aux Gonaïves suite au Cyclone Jeanne au regard des droits humains fondamentaux,* Centre de Recherches Urbaines–Travaux (C.R.U.–T.), Plateforme des Organisations Haïtiennes de Défense des Droits Humains (POHDH), July 2005. Translated from the French by Joris Willems.

6. Project Sphere, *The Humanitarian Charter and Minimum Standards* (Geneva: Project Sphere, 2004), 18.

7. UN Flash Appeals are solicitations of emergency humanitarian assistance following disasters.

8. This article originally appeared in *NACLA Report on the Americas* 43, no. 4 (July–August 2010): 32–36, 42.

9. Alex Dupuy, *Haiti in the World Economy: Race, Class and Underdevelopment since 1700* (Boulder, CO: Westview Press, 1989).

10. Ibid.

11. Seumas Milne, "Haiti's Suffering Is a Result of Calculated Impoverishment," *The Guardian* (UK), January 20, 2010.

12. Mark Schuller, "An Anthropology of Disaster Capitalism," unpublished manuscript (n.d.); "Haiti's 200-Year Ménage-à-Trois: Globalization, the State, and 'Civil Society'": *Caribbean Studies* 35, no. 1 (2007): 141–79.

13. Bernard Diederich, "Swine Fever Ironies: The Slaughter of the Haitian Black Pig," *Caribbean Review* 14, no. 1 (winter 1985): 16–17.

14. Leah Chavla, "Has the US Rice Export Policy Condemned Haiti to Poverty?" *Hunger Notes,* April 23, 2010.

15. Naomi Klein, "How Socialism Protected Chileans From Earthquake Fall-Out," *The Nation,* March 4, 2010.

16. "Corruption Perceptions Index 2009," Transparency International, available at transparency.org.

17. "Human Development Report 2009—HDI Rankings," United Nations Development Programme, hdr.undp.org/en/statistics.

18. Raúl Sohr, "Historia de dos terremotos," *La Nación* (Santiago, Chile), March 5, 2010.

19. Mercedes González de la Rocha, "Economic Crisis, Domestic Reorganization and Women's Work in Guadalajara, Mexico," *Bulletin of Latin American Research* 7, no. 2 (1988): 207–23; Agustín Escobar Latapi and Mercedes González de la Rocha, "Crisis, Restructuring and Urban Poverty in Mexico," *Environment and Urbanization* 7, no. 1 (1995): 57–76.

20. This article is excerpted and adapted from Alex Dupuy, "Disaster Capitalism to the Rescue: The International Community and Haiti After the Earthquake," *NACLA Report on the Americas* 43, no. 4 (July–August 2010): 14–19, 42.

21. For a fuller analysis, see Alex Dupuy, "Globalization, the World Bank, and the Haitian Economy," in *Contemporary Caribbean Cultures and Societies in a Global Context,* ed. Franklin W. Knight and Teresita Martinez-Vergne (Chapel Hill: University of North Carolina Press, 2005), 43–70.

22. See Leah Chavla, "Haiti Research File: Bill Clinton's Heavy Hand on Haiti's Vulnerable Agricultural Economy: The American Rice Scandal," Council on Hemispheric Affairs, April 13, 2010; Jonathan M. Katz, "With Cheap Food Imports, Haiti Can't Feed Itself," Associated Press, March 20, 2010.

23. Cited in Dupuy, "Globalization, the World Bank, and the Haitian Economy," 53.

24. Katz, "With Cheap Food Imports, Haiti Can't Feed Itself"; Claire McGuigan, *Agricultural Liberalisation in Haiti* (London: Christian Aid, 2006).

25. Dilip Ratha, Sanket Mohapatra, and Ani Silwal, "Migration and Development Brief 11," Migration and Remittances Team, Development Prospects Group, World Bank, November 3, 2009; International Monetary Fund, "Haiti: Poverty Reduction Strategy Paper Progress Report," *IMF Country Report,* no. 09/290, February 2009; and "Haiti: Sixth Review Under the Extended Credit Facility," *IMF Country Report,* no. 10/35, January 22, 2010.

26. IMF, "Haiti Poverty Reduction Strategy"; IADB, *IDB: Country Strategy with Haiti, 2007–2011* (2007).

27. Translated from the original French by Joris Willems.

28. Oxfam, *Planting Now: Agricultural Challenges and Opportunities for Haiti's Reconstruction,* Oxfam Briefing Paper 140, October 2010.

2

Rat Mode, Soufle
Foreign Domination

*As argued in Chapter 1, Haiti's vulnerability and its oft-referred-to "weak state"
are direct consequences of foreign-imposed neoliberalism. On January 12, 2010
the earthquake leveled Port-au-Prince, the country's nerve center—centralized
in large part because of foreign policies since the 1915 US invasion—devastating the already weak capacity of Haiti's government. In this vacuum, in which
as many as 18% of Haiti's public workforce died, foreign actors assumed control
of the immediate response.*

A Haitian proverb explains, Rat mode, soufle *(First the rat bites, then
it blows on the wound). As Yolette Etienne explains, people all over the world
contributed to the effort following Haiti's earthquake. But unfortunately this
global solidarity came at the price of foreign control. Most visible was the rapid
deployment of 20,000 US troops. Several commentators, including Deputy UN
Special Envoy Paul Farmer, praised their willingness to "get their boots dirty,"
to accomplish logistical tasks that they were uniquely suited to accomplish, and
to work alongside medical teams to provide needed emergency services.[1]*

*Even granting its best intentions, however, the US military inherited a legacy
of imperialism, mistrust, and racism. Haiti's sovereignty had already recently suffered numerous indignities at the hands of a UN occupation force, MINUSTAH,
inaugurated following the forced removal of former president Jean-Bertrand Aristide in 2004, Haiti's bicentennial year. Many see MINUSTAH's presence as an
insult to Haiti's sovereignty, keeping the country firmly under control while international financial and development institutions maintain a grip on the country's
finances, suppressing the movement for higher wages in 2009 and blocking the
implementation of Petro Caribé, a deal with Venezuela that would provide*

lower-priced fuel, to cite two examples. Haiti's macroeconomic plan remains under foreign supervision, as Dupuy demonstrates. To many, MINUSTAH's primary role is to keep Haiti as a leta restavèk, *a child domestic worker serving foreign interests.*

Many commentators see the earthquake as a pretext, a justification, for even deeper foreign control. Writing a day after the devastating earthquake, the conservative think tank the Heritage Foundation called upon the US government to seize the moment to solidify US influence in the region. Although US soldiers left Haiti after several months, MINUSTAH—with increased troop strength—remains. Haitian economist Roland Bélizaire details the pre- and post-earthquake continuities in foreign domination over the official development or reconstruction plans. Haiti's Post-Disaster Needs Assessment (PDNA) was dominated by foreign experts promoting foreign capital interests such as privatization. Haiti Support Group's Joris Willems writes about the Interim Haiti Recovery Commission (IHRC), cochaired by Bill Clinton in his role as UN special envoy. Willems documents IHRC's failures on its own terms, including a lack of transparency and the "preferencing" of funds.

While the IHRC makes decisions about reconstruction, the humanitarian response is coordinated by UN "clusters." Melinda Miles of the Haiti Response Coalition details the many ways that these clusters exclude Haitian people and their perspectives from the aid and reconstruction process. As Miles argues, UN agencies insulate themselves from Haitian people. A white paper by solidarity group UnityAyiti outlines MINUSTAH's myriad human rights abuses. The text selected here focuses on these abuses and questions the justification for MINUSTAH's continued presence given regional crime statistics. This chapter offers tools to pull apart and critique the many ways that the earthquake gave way to ramped-up foreign control and ultimately the impact of outsiders on the country's governance.

* * *

Foreign Domination in Haiti
When Will We See a Rupture?

Roland Bélizaire

DURING THE PERIOD OF RECONSTRUCTING or re-founding Haiti after January 12, 2010, the country's social movement should focus on channeling the aspirations of the population in matters of public policy.[2] This should be achieved by exercising pressure on the state to redefine its interventions and take into account its aspirations regarding various economic, social, cultural, and environmental issues—which itself should take place within a coherent and strategic framework of cooperation and planning.

In a chronic and cyclical way, Haiti's rural and urban working classes have been excluded from participating in drawing up public policy. If public policy exists, it has been defined by "experts" from IFIs, representatives of diplomatic missions and international organizations, and Haitian bureaucrats or technocrats, politicians, and members of so-called civil society, especially during the first decade of the 2000s.

The main orientations in public policy come from the IFIs and Western powers, because they hold the financial resources and allegedly the expertise necessary to implement policies. As such, the support from this so-called international community is always conditioned by a set of measures aimed primarily at keeping the so-called third-world countries dependent and under domination. From the IMF's structural adjustment programs to the Washington Consensus, domination today is exercised through programs of "sound economic governance" and the fight against poverty.

Thus, past economic-development plans drafted by the IFIs and the Haitian government, such as the Emergency and Economic Rehabilitation Program (PURE I and II, 1994–2004), the Interim Cooperation Framework (ICF, 2004–2006), the Interim Strategy Document for Poverty Reduction (PRSP-I, 2006–2008), the Document of National Strategy for Growth and Poverty Reduction (PRSP, 2008–2010), and the final documents of Public Policy (DPP), are followed by today's Post-Disaster Needs Assessment (PDNA) and the Action Plan for National Recovery and Development (PARDN). These last two documents and the associated IHRC show, once again, Haiti's dependence and the weight of the international community as a consequence of the weakening of the state. These documents and their catastrophic consequences for most Haitians highlight the need to think in a totally alternative way about public policy in Haiti.

PDNA and PARDN: Cooperation or Domination?

The PDNA arose in a very different context than the one that gave birth to the old public policy documents like the PURE, ICF, the PRSP-I, and the PRSP. The earthquake of January 12 and its social and infrastructural consequences have caused strong emotions among Haitians and members of the international community. An extraordinary spirit of solidarity with the Haitian people was observed throughout the world. However, if some countries want to instantly develop ties of cooperation and solidarity with the Haitian people, others see the opportunity to advance their macabre plans, disguised as humanitarian assistance, by strengthening their domination over the country. Experience shows that the deployment of 20,000 US troops and the strengthening of MINUSTAH were not worth the effort and have not solved the problems the population faces.

The PDNA and PARDN offer nothing different, neither in terms of the proposed steps, methodology, approach, nor content, compared to previous public policy documents (PPD). It all comes down to the straight line of ultraliberal policies defined and imposed by the IFIs. Thus, like other PPD, Haiti's development is conditioned on the sources of international funding while the emphasis is put on economic governance and reducing poverty.

On the one hand, PARDN proposes a few territorial, economic, social, and institutional re-foundations, and makes great statements on an ideal society—"a fair, just, united and friendly society living in harmony with its environment and culture"—and on the alleged ownership of the plan by "all sectors of Haitian society." On the other hand, PARDN establishes the IHRC, an exclusive body with little Haitian representation that will "eventually become the Agency for the Development of Haiti, and a Multiple Donor Fiduciary Fund that will enable the preparation of files, the formulation of programmes and projects as well as their financing and execution, all with a coordinated and coherent approach."[3] PARDN aims first to fulfill the wishes of international and bilateral donors, not those of most Haitians.

As for the PDNA, it reflects a strategic action framework in different sectors: social, economic, political, and environmental. But given the level of simplification and superficiality of its hypotheses and ideas, speaking of the PDNA as a "reconstruction plan" for the country, much less as a Haitian public policy, is incorrect. The PDNA presents some scraps of ideas and sets out some general guidelines, which usually only respond to the logic of selling the program rather than reflecting a desire to really solve a problem. This is the case, for example, for the free access to higher education, to which the Constitution of 1987 was already dedicated but for which the Haitian government has never taken the necessary steps.

Let's look closer at the PDNA strategies in the following areas: education, environment, agriculture, health, and telecommunications. Apart from telecommunications, these sectors are treated only in relation to poverty. Is this the reason that higher education, research, and management training are totally ignored? Other sectors are no better off. Tourism and culture, for example, are treated only marginally. Even worse, the government's general political orientation, that of dependence and neoliberalism, is embedded in the document, and the ministries will be simply reproduced without bothering to consult concerned sectors in creating a genuine public policy, as we have mentioned above.

However we evaluate the PDNA, its proposals and assessment of the sectors it will address are often complete strangers to the social and political context. Its analysis relates only to the functioning of the institutions outside of the population's actual demands, the Haitian conjuncture, and the new social dynamics that had evolved before January 12, 2010. Telecommunications is one example. The government was set to privatize the state company, Teleco, just a few days before January 12, and one of the first steps of the "reconstruction," in its interpretation by President René Préval and the IFIs, is to continue the process of liquidating it (see Chapter 4, this volume). According to data from three reports of the IMF, the same institution that required the company's privatization, Teleco generated a gross profit of 5 billion gourdes from 1994 to 2004. After taxes and transfers, the net profit was almost 4 billion gourdes.

"Reconstruction," in this famous document, offers no alternative-development paradigm whatsoever and no vision of the national reality. The PDNA and PARDN are drinking from a draft of ideas and proposals, a traditional patching-together of IFI remedies that represent only the continuation of policies from before January 12, remote-controlled from abroad. The only truth contained in this process—interestingly *not* in the PDNA itself—comes from the Haitian government:

> The earthquake has exposed the structural weaknesses of the country's development process, but at the same time it has promoted, among many citizens and some elite groups, the hope for a new era of change. However, before we begin, we must formulate a new vision for the country's economic future, hence laying out new fundamental options concerning, first of all, the international positioning of the country and the type of democratic society and state that we should promote in Haiti. Only after we lay these foundations can we propose the model of market economy that would support these profound changes.

In the light of this assertion, we can better understand why the PDNA could not ask the Haitian state to break with neoliberal policies, to stop the violation of the country's sovereignty, and to end its dependence on international and bilateral donors. The PDNA's strategic objective is to reinforce the country's financial and political dependence by reestablishing or strengthening the market economy. The ideology of the PDNA is very clear: "The first strategic element to underline is the process of economic reformulation, based on a differentiated approach that combines a demand-driven approach funded essentially through international aid linked with a fiscal and monetary policy in compliance with a stable macroeconomic environment with a stimulation of sectors presenting high short-term flexibility such as agriculture."

The process of stimulating growth will be based on two levers: (1) a dynamic process of revaluating the productive sectors supported by structural reforms, public investment, and proactive macroeconomic policy, and (2) a very dynamic role of the least-developed countries. We must remember that in the jargon of IFIs and so-called development institutions, structural reforms underpin the pursuit of policies applied in the country before January 12, 2010, under the Structural Adjustment Program, renamed the Poverty Reduction and Growth Facility (PRGF). These policies include the following:

- Reducing the fiscal deficit by increasing the tax burden to the detriment of the population and the decrease in social expenditures like subsidies to agriculture
- Increasing the interest rate under the pretext of controlling inflation
- Devaluing and dollarizing the currency
- Removing state controls on prices, leaving consumers and the bulk of the population vulnerable to the greed of the mercantile bourgeoisie
- Liberalizing the economy in favor of international capital in the form of foreign direct investment
- Deregulating and the eliminating all forms of state subsidy to the rural and urban masses
- Privatizing public enterprises and squandering all cultural, historical, and natural heritage

In sum, the PDNA and the IHRC are only attempts by the IFIs and Western capitalist countries, particularly the United States, to counter any real alternative reconstruction. The United States does not want Haiti to join the axis of Cuba, Venezuela, Bolivia, and Ecuador, afraid that it will achieve self-determination, which does not serve US interests. The earthquake of January 12 made it possible to implement "the shock strategy."

In this context, proposals coming from progressive sectors and local populations had to be dismissed from the elaboration process of the PDNA and PARDN, and the team of Préval and Prime Minister Jean-Max Bellerive, who seem to be good servants of the international system, had to be maintained in power. To do this, the support of international finance is essential.

* * *

Deconstructing the Reconstruction
The IHRC

Joris Willems

THE INTERIM HAITI RECONSTRUCTION COMMISSION (IHRC) was proposed by the Haitian government at the International Donors' Conference Towards a New Future for Haiti, held in New York on March 31, 2010, "to provide effective co-ordination and deployment of resources and to respond to concerns about accountability and transparency."[4] Half of its members are Haitian, and the other half are international donors and institutions. The commission is cochaired by Haitian Prime Minister Jean-Max Bellerive and UN Special Envoy Bill Clinton.

Functioning of the IHRC

The IHRC approves or rejects proposed projects on the basis of criteria that are supposedly publicly available. Despite multiple requests, no such criteria were ever published. While a public list of approved projects gives some basic project details, there is no information on rejected projects. More than a third of the needed funds for approved projects were still unavailable until June 2011. On March 17, 2011, eight months after the IHRC's first meeting, the minutes of the four first meetings were finally published after weeks of pressure from multiple researchers, but no more minutes were published until at least the end of June 2011. The IHRC Secretariat received substantial critiques from researchers and board members for the total lack of transparency, supposedly one of its guiding principles.

According to the IHRC bylaws, any person or entity should submit to the IHRC its development or reconstruction projects that involve any pledge, donation, or grant of debt relief. The same process applies for any activity by any person or entity that involves private funding exceeding $500,000 and relates to a matter of national significance. While this means that practically all reconstruction and development projects should pass through IHRC, projects like the multimillion-dollar project from the

Prince Charles Foundation for the reconstruction of downtown Port-au-Prince bypass the IHRC completely.[5]

Projects submitted to the IHRC are reviewed by the projects department, sector leaders at the IHRC Secretariat, and relevant ministries. Once the green light is given, the IHRC executive director or the cochairs can approve the project for up to $10 million. For projects above that amount, the board members decide.

At least until the February 28, 2011, IHRC meeting, some board members remained confused about the project approval procedure.[6] They complained that they were to vote on projects based on the very limited information available in the single-page summaries of the originally submitted Project Concept Notes. These summaries consisted of a short project description and checked boxes indicating whether the project had fulfilled specific criteria. In an interview, a board member trying to clarify the procedural matters stated bluntly that "the more we advance [with IHRC], the less we understand."[7]

There is no financial requirement whatsoever to submit a project. A donor can submit a proposal without having funds available for the project, so many have been approved that lack substantial portions of necessary funding. Of the 87 approved projects worth $3.2 billion, there remained a funding gap of $1.2 billion, or 37% of the necessary funds. The approval of unfunded projects was a conscious choice made during the first meetings of the IHRC, as Bill Clinton noted at the April 8, 2011, IHRC board meeting: "We made a decision that we would try to always approve more projects than we had money for. Because we wanted to show the world we were up and going."

At the December 14, 2010, board meeting, members fiercely criticized the Secretariat. The first came from Caribbean Community and Common Market (CARICOM) representative P.J. Patterson. At the same meeting the Haitian board members presented a letter stating that they felt completely disconnected from the activities of the IHRC. They also complained about the last-minute delivery of documents:

> Projects are often forwarded as summary tables to the Board, only on the eve of meetings. Procedural changes related to the formalities around submission of online projects vary without notice. Staffing and consultant selection are undertaken unbeknownst to the Haitian members of the board. . . . In reality, Haitian members of the board have one role: to endorse the decisions made by the Director and Executive Committee.[8]

The Haitian members also recalled the special board session of September 20, 2010, in New York:

As far as protocol goes, the way Haitians who are not members of the Executive Committee [the co-chairs] are being treated is very revealing of the desire to minimize their part in the council. This was made evident in the unacceptable reception they were given at the September 20, 2010 meeting in New York, where several Haitian members of this committee were not even granted a place at the table.[9]

This special session also addressed at least two important issues far beyond the mandate of the IHRC: the OAS-CARICOM Election Observation Mission and the extension of MINUSTAH's mandate. No minutes of this meeting have been published.

The Anti-Corruption Office (PAO), responsible for transparency, accountability, impact assessment, and complaint investigation, only became operational in March 2011, when PricewaterhouseCoopers (PWC) won the bid. The bid was written by PWC while it was working in the IHRC in 2010.

The Financial Picture

The New York donors' conference resulted in a pledge of $9.9 billion for the Haitian Reconstruction Plan in the five to 10 years following the earthquake. For the IHRC's 18-month mandate, $5.54 billion was pledged, of which little more than $1 billion was debt relief, leaving some $4.5 billion of "programmable cash." An unspecified amount of these funds were to be delivered to the Haiti Reconstruction Fund (HRF), a multidonor trust fund managed by the World Bank, that was proposed in PARDN. The HRF's *raison d'être* was described as facilitating "harmonization between programs and projects needing funding and funds available," making it possible "to assemble funds for programs whose scale exceeds the capacities of a single donor."[10]

All the HRF participants signed an agreement that no earmarking would be allowed. Yet donors clearly want to manage their own funds. As a solution, it appears the term "preferenced" is now used by multiple donors to earmark their contribution without calling it "earmarking." Of the $313 million in "programmable cash" that had actually been delivered to the HRF as of March 31, 2011 (out of the $577 million pledged from the $4.5 billion total), there remains only $75 million in "unpreferenced" money, which represents 24% of the total. Former IHRC executive director Gabriël Verret strongly criticized these practices of preferencing: "The U.S. largely contributed to that because it put 120 million USD in the HRF

and preferenced every single penny of it. In other words, there is no difference between that and the US simply deciding we want to do these projects
bilaterally. . . . Had the World Bank been honest, it would have said we
don't accept this, this is the limitation that we put on. But it didn't."[11]

Brazil, which initially said it wanted to serve as an example by making
an unpreferenced contribution, later retroactively preferenced $40 million
of its $55 million for a hydroelectric power plant on the Artibonite River,
a project that was initiated in 2008. While there have been incitements for
donors not to preference their money for the HRF, Japan preferenced all of
its contributed money in a letter dated February 28, 2011. In other words,
while the IHRC and the HRF are supposed to be models of multilateral cooperation and coordination, in reality it is bilateral aid often tied to return
to the country of origin or specific individuals who wield political influence. (See the Doucet and Macdonald essay in this volume for an example.)

While such practices somewhat limit the operational capacity and indeed the initial objectives of the HRF, donors' failure to fulfill their original
pledges is even far more limiting. Of the 55 public donors that pledged
money for 2010 and 2011, 22 had not disbursed anything as of June 24,
2011, and only seven have fulfilled their original pledge.[12] As of the end of
June 2011, less than 38% of the money had been disbursed and some 35%
had been committed, whereas 27% was still pending.

Conclusion

Although there is little doubt that the Haitian government needed help to
accomplish the immense task of rebuilding, the IHRC's functioning has
raised important concerns. As far as transparency goes—one of the IHRC's
guiding principles—the IHRC has failed. Its reluctance to share supposedly public information with journalists, researchers, and even its own board
members is obvious: board meeting minutes were slowly and incompletely
published, selection criteria were not shared despite multiple requests, and
the list of rejected projects was not made public. Concerning projects and
their financing, donors still prefer to finance their own projects instead of
supporting existing ones already approved by the board. The HRF completely bypasses its very own objectives—financing projects of strategic importance—by earmarking most of the available funds.

The promising amount of money pledged after the donor conference,
$5.4 billion, is extremely misleading. One might mistakenly think that
the Haitian government could decide how to use those funds. The truth

is far from that. Of course, the Haitian government is represented in the IHRC. But major donors have an equal vote in the project bidding. The institutional strength of the international members gives them a substantial advantage over the Haitian members, who often lack offices and staff to review and comment on proposed projects. The Haitian state doesn't have the best corruption record, and neither does it always respect its own Constitution, communities, or human rights treaties. But one thing should be clear from this experience: you only learn to walk again by standing on your own feet, not by being pushed forward in a wheelchair.

* * *

Assumptions and Exclusion
Coordination Failures
During the Emergency Phase

Melinda Miles

————

IN THE FIRST WEEKS AND months after Haiti's earthquake, the humanitarian response was colored above all by a series of assumptions about the Haitians whom the disaster most affected. Pervasive stereotypes of Haiti—"poorest country in the Western Hemisphere," chaotic, and wracked with political violence—created a fear not based on reality but rather on mainstream-media depictions that frequently generalize, demonize, and sensationalize the Haitian people (see Ulysse essay, this volume). Haitians used whatever tools they could find to try to dig loved ones and neighbors out of the rubble, but as with African Americans following Hurricane Katrina in New Orleans, foreigners saw not survivors but looters and gang members roaming the streets with machetes.

Stereotypes went hand in hand with the exclusion of Haitians from the recovery process. A perfect example of exclusion was quickly solidified after the earthquake in the form of the Office for the Coordination of Humanitarian Affairs (OCHA) cluster system. Begun in 2005 by the UN Inter-Agency Standing Committee, the system identified a series of "clusters" of UN agencies, NGOs, and other international organizations around a particular sector or service provided during a humanitarian crisis (for example, Camp Coordination and Management, Water Sanitation and Hygiene, Health, and so on).

With OCHA operations taking place behind the heavily guarded walls of the UN Logistical Base (Log Base) in Port-au-Prince, the message that Haitians were "others" of the most dangerous kind was reinforced. Aid workers believed they had to be protected from the victims of the earthquake by UN or US soldiers during distributions of lifesaving food and water, and were restricted from walking in the streets or through the spontaneous camps they were serving.

Despite the fact that most Haitians self-organized to provide protection in the parks, empty lots, streets, and other places where people sought safety after the quake, the humanitarian community quickly declared that there was no local capacity to assist with the emergency relief phase. The UN system focused on camps rather than communities, and only camps that met criteria centered on the number of families were included in distribution plans, which created a false dichotomy: dividing families living in public spaces and those still surviving in the yards of their homes or in the streets in front of their property. IDPs quickly became referred to as "camp dwellers" and even "squatters." One internal e-mail circulated to the Protection cluster list in June 2010 went so far as to accuse homeless earthquake victims of "trespassing."

Between assumptions that Haitians couldn't help themselves and were dangerous, and the derogatory terms used to describe homeless earthquake survivors, pervasive, overt racism characterized the initial emergency response. It also quickly became apparent that Haitians would not be allowed to participate in their own relief process. In February 2010 the Haitian Response Coalition (HRC) held a conference that included Haitian civil society organizations, grassroots groups, and activists to counteract their exclusion. The HRC, a broad group of small- and medium-size NGOs with a long history of working in Haiti and a shared focus on local leadership, sustainability, and self-determination, formed within days of the quake as a collaborative effort to get assistance to the communities that were being systematically neglected. The conference, called "Initiative for a New Haiti," included more than 40 organizations and community leaders and included a basic training on the OCHA cluster system and on how aid money was being distributed. Nigel Fisher, who would go on to become the UN humanitarian and resident coordinator in Haiti, participated and gave a detailed explanation of the PDNA process, which was open to Haitian participation. The Haitian attendees created working groups by sector and assigned representatives to attend cluster meetings.

It didn't take long, however, for HRC's effort to fail. Most of the representatives were refused entry to the Log Base, even though their names appeared on the official security list. As a white American, I was never challenged by security guards and often brought others onto the base without showing any kind of identification. One Haitian American member of HRC was repeatedly turned away by the guards until I started picking her up on the road so she could enter in my vehicle.

When Haitians made it through this first obstacle to participation, they found themselves transported to a foreign place. The Log Base was filled with soldiers from several countries, and the cluster meetings were filled beyond capacity with foreigners, mainly young people with very little field experience or language skills. Despite the fact that English is not one of Haiti's official languages, for months the cluster meetings were held almost exclusively in English, effectively preventing Haitian participation.

A report from the International Council of Voluntary Agencies (ICVA) stated, "If local NGOs (and other local stakeholders) are to participate in coordination—it's basic—language and location. Providing a neutral forum for open discussion enables [local NGOs] to make their own decisions regarding participation and if necessary representation."[13] After the Urgence Réhabilitation Développement (URD) and Global Public Policy Institute (GPPi) made their three-month evaluation, most clusters started using French, even though most Haitians do not speak French. Translation to Haitian Creole was seldom provided.

By June 2010 French was used exclusively within the Protection Cluster and acted as a tool to silence NGO advocates condemning the lack of response to forced evictions. Members of the HRC spoke Creole fluently, but not French. During one tense meeting, a representative respectfully requested a brief translated summary in order to participate. The cluster coordinator's response was so harsh that other NGO representatives intervened to defend the request and provided the translation. Language was not the only way the HRC was excluded; in another incident, HRC members were told a Protection Cluster meeting had been canceled when it had in fact been moved to a different room on the Log Base.

By holding nearly all of its meetings within the confines of the Log Base and refusing to offer Creole translation, Haitians and the hybrid international-Haitian HRC were effectively kept out of the process. The URD/GPPi described the overall earthquake response as "highly exclusive," adding,

> The affected population was not consulted, informed or included in the design, planning and implementation of the humanitarian response. As a

consequence, the affected people and NGOs interviewed for this evaluation underlined that they had often felt they were not respected by international aid organizations.[14]

In addition to coordination, the OCHA system had an impact on
aid distribution. Most of the largest aid agencies allowed through the US
military–controlled airport refused to distribute desperately needed supplies without military escorts. For Haitians, this enhanced the notion that
instead of receiving relief they had unwittingly become victim to yet another occupation of their country. Furthermore, it made large-scale distributions nearly impossible to carry out. Nonfood items, shelter, and food were
unavailable to smaller NGOs, even those with competent local staff and
long-term, preexisting relationships with the most affected communities.

The HRC, for its part, was a unique partnership of experienced Haitian community organizers and foreigners, and was focused on identifying
self-organized camp committees to carry out collaborative assessments of
community needs. However, it could not access the aid it was so well posi-
tioned to deliver. As Reed Lindsay reported in *The Nation,*

> In the first days after the earthquake, the coalition's member organizations
> had difficulty sending aid, blocked from landing planes in Port-au-Prince
> by the US government, which controlled the airport and initially gave
> priority to troop deployments and the delivery of military equipment.
> But even when the transportation lines were loosened, the aid has come
> slowly, and Ruth [a Haitian community organizer with the HRC] has
> helped organize more camps than she has aid to deliver. Meanwhile, the
> well-heeled major relief aid agencies have often ignored camp commit-
> tees, and conditioned handouts on the presence of US or U.N. troops.[15]

Additionally, weak leadership within the international community's efforts resulted in lack of coordination within the OCHA clusters. UN Emergency Relief Coordinator Sir John Holmes criticized his team in an internal
e-mail leaked on February 17, 2010, more than a month into the relief efforts:

> Regarding coordination, I was disappointed to find that despite my calls
> for the Global Cluster Lead Agencies to strengthen their cluster coordi-
> nation capacity on the ground, very little progress has been made in this
> critical area. . . . I would therefore like to repeat my request to Global
> Cluster Lead Agencies to boost their cluster coordination teams imme-
> diately, and to provide sustained coordination capacity on the ground.[16]

The capacity to coordinate was challenged by the large number of NGOs that flooded into the country in the first weeks after the earthquake. The URD/GPPi report noted that "a major challenge for cluster coordination was the massive influx of international NGOs with varying capacity, levels of professionalism and resources."[17] Cluster coordinators thus needed to be both creative and flexible, yet "only some cluster lead agencies (first WHO and IFRC, later FAO) reacted creatively to this situation and adapted cluster coordination accordingly."[18]

UN coordination staff effectively insulated themselves from their Haitian counterparts and the affected population behind the walls of the Log Base. They traveled the city in SUVs, afraid of the people around them in the streets that led to their organizations' camps. Even after moving into apartments in the upscale neighborhoods of Pétionville, curfews forced them to stay indoors after 6 p.m., and most could not stray more than a block from their residence. Most had short-term assignments in Haiti, and because of the misperception concerning security and Haitians, they were unaware of urgent problems all around them.

The URD/GPPi report asked and answered fundamental questions about the performance of the OCHA clusters and the disaster response: "Did the aid system save lives? Yes, but not that many. . . . Did the aid system alleviate suffering? Yes, but too superficially." An opportunity to set a good example for the rest of the world instead established a model of how best to act against the interests of a devastated people and render them invisible.

* * *

Mission Accomplished?
MINUSTAH in Haiti, 2010–2011

Kevin Edmonds, Deepa Panchang, Marshall Fleurant,
Brennan Bollman, Lindsay Schubiner, and Rishi Rattan

———

ACCORDING TO THE STANDARD OF insecurity that is used to justify MINUSTAH's continued presence in Haiti, the much higher levels of violence in several neighboring Caribbean states—Jamaica, Trinidad and Tobago, and the US

Virgin Islands—could warrant international stabilization efforts (see table 2.1). Yet, for political reasons, this is not the case. Even the US Department of State remarked in March 2011 that "despite grinding poverty, inadequate policing, and lax gun laws, some studies have shown Haiti to have a lower homicide rate than many of its neighbors in the Caribbean and Latin America."[19] It is ironic that in Brazil, the national leader of MINUSTAH, levels of civilian violence exceed those in Haiti by more than 300%.

It is thus becoming increasingly difficult to justify MINUSTAH's presence. A detailed analysis of MINUSTAH's actions documented in the available reports after the earthquake reveal that the force is doing little more than policing activities related to crimes against persons and property—work that falls under the responsibility of the Haitian National Police (HNP), which could better carry out these tasks with more resources and training. Furthermore, the UN security mission has itself been the perpetrator of human rights violations.

MINUSTAH's Pre-Earthquake Human Rights Record

From 2004 to 2010 several independent legal and human rights organizations published reports supporting Haitians' charges that MINUSTAH not

Table 2.1 2010 Homicide Rates in Brazil, Haiti, Jamaica, Trinidad and Tobago, and the US Virgin Islands

Country	Population	Murders	Rate per 100,000
Haiti	9,600,000	795[a]	8.2
Brazil*	189,953,000	50,113[b]	26.38
Jamaica	2,600,000	1,428[c]	54.9
Trinidad and Tobago	1,300,000	472[d]	36.3
US Virgin Islands	100,000	66[e]	60

Notes: *Data published on Brazil's murder rate by the Brazilian Ministry of Justice from 2008

a. United States Department of State, Bureau of Diplomatic Security, Haiti 2011 Crime and Safety Report, https://www.osac.gov/Pages/ContentReportDetails.aspx?cid=10560.

b. Julio Jacobo Waiselfisz, Mapa Da Violência 2011, Sao Paulo, Instituto Sangari, Ministry of Justice, 2011, http://www.sangari.com/mapadaviolencia/pdf2011/MapaViolencia2011.pdf.

c. Mark Wignall, "Why Has Jamaica's Crime Rate Fallen?" *Jamaica Observer*, February 3, 2011, http://www.jamaicaobserver.com/columns/Why-has-Jamaica-s-crime-rate-fallen_8329778.

d. "In the Shadow of the Gallows: Trinidad Debates the Death Penalty," *The Economist*, February 10, 2011, http://www.economist.com/node/18114940.

e. Daniel Shea, "Homicides in V.I.," *Virgin Islands Daily News*, January 13, 2011, http://virgin islandsdailynews.com/news/homicides-in-v-i-1.1089794#axzz1RC9AESqx.

only failed to protect rights as required by its mandate but also directly violated Haitian citizens' human rights. In 2005 the research organization Center for Global Justice, in collaboration with the Human Rights Program
at Harvard Law School, found that MINUSTAH had neither initiated a
disarmament program nor protected civilians from murderous paramilitary
attacks and extrajudicial killings—particularly supporters of Fanmi Lavalas,
the political party of ousted former president Jean-Bertrand Aristide. Furthermore, they protected HNP officers who were carrying out extrajudicial
killings, either directly with personnel or indirectly by failing to investigate.[20]

By mid-2005 MINUSTAH itself was attacking civilian communities
without the HNP. In a July 2005 assault on Cité Soleil, a Port-au-Prince
shantytown, MINUSTAH targeted a single alleged gang leader and five of
his associates, but ended up firing 22,000 rounds of ammunition, killing
some 70 people. The final death toll is unknown because MINUSTAH
deemed the mission a success and did not seek to enumerate the civilian deaths.[21] Two years later, human rights lawyers were still documenting
similar violent military strikes. They concluded that MINUSTAH's actions violated its own charter, as well as international law. However, the
MINUSTAH mandate included a clause that essentially gave perpetrators
of crimes immunity from the Haitian justice system.[22]

In addition to physical violence, sexual violence committed by members of MINUSTAH has run rampant and gone unpunished.[23] Most
notably, in 2007, 114 Sri Lankan soldiers were repatriated for having commercial sex with underage Haitian girls.[24] Because the soldiers enjoyed de
facto immunity in Haiti, the United Nations recommended they be pros-
ecuted in Sri Lanka. To date, no prosecution has occurred, and despite
UN threats to the contrary, Sri Lanka remains part of the MINUSTAH
mission.[25] This tarnished history led to the growing perception in Haiti of
MINUSTAH as an occupying force.

MINUSTAH's Post-Earthquake Human Rights Record

Protection Failures and Direct Violations

Since the earthquake, Haitians have faced heightened threats to security,
life, and health in makeshift displacement camps. Gender-based violence,
which has affected women in hundreds of camps, has gone virtually ignored
by MINUSTAH. The force has taken only a few measures to address it,
in name only, and even in instances when patrols are sent to camps, most
troops can barely communicate with camp residents enough to react ap-
propriately (see Chapter 7, this volume). Forced evictions from camps have

also affected hundreds of thousands of IDPs, with nearly no protective action by MINUSTAH, despite domestic and international laws that classify
these evictions as illegal (see Chapter 8, this volume). Compounding these
protection failures was the introduction of cholera into the country by MI-
NUSTAH troops, the subsequent failure to investigate, and lack of proper
response to the growing epidemic (see Piarroux et al. essay in Chapter 9,
this volume). Counter to its mandate to assist in free and fair elections,
MINUSTAH also played a role in propping up a US-supported but illegitimate presidential election that excluded a majority political party and a
large part of the population (see Chapter 10, this volume).

In addition to these main areas of concentration are a number of other
issues related to MINUSTAH's involvement in Haiti—for example, its
complicity in the Les Cayes prison massacre of January 19, 2010, when
the HNP stormed the facility to put down a riot triggered by deteriorating conditions. Although 19 unarmed inmates were killed and 40 others
injured, MINUSTAH effectively helped the HNP orchestrate a cover-up.[26]
Another telling incident is the death of Jean Gérald Gilles, a 16-year-old
boy who was found hanging inside a MINUSTAH base in Cap Haïtien on
August 17, 2010.[27] Despite suspicions that he was murdered on the base,
MINUSTAH has refused to investigate.[28]

MINUSTAH has also developed a record of violently responding to
peaceful popular demonstrations, gassing students and IDP camps,[29] as-
saulting journalists, shooting at children,[30] and killing peaceful protesters.[31]
Given that these protests were often targeting the presence of MINUSTAH
itself, the mission's unprovoked, violent responses only provide further examples of its failure to build a positive relationship with the Haitian people
and its suppression of the democratic process.

Lack of Security Coordination

MINUSTAH's failure to coordinate its activities with other governmental,
domestic, and international organizations has either duplicated or under-
staffed critical positions, siphoned money from groups documenting abuses
and protecting citizens, and created fatal mistakes in military operations.
Despite being made aware of this issue since its inception, MINUSTAH
fails to devote personnel and money toward more efficient coordination.

Despite designating to Haiti a nonmilitary security force, the United
Nations Police Division (UNPOL), MINUSTAH's failure to coordinate
with community leaders in post-earthquake Haiti has left IDPs "at the
mercy of landowners and gangs."[32] The lack of sufficient translators to
accompany missions exacerbates MINUSTAH's inability to effectively

document abuses and communicate with the very people it is charged to protect. Such a lack of commitment to understanding the on-the-ground reality of Haitian civilians is unconscionable given that the UN has been present in Haiti in one form or another for almost 20 years.

Conclusion

MINUSTAH's failure to uphold its mandate and the force's consistent violation of human rights have made it a significant threat to the Haitian people. Especially given the relatively low levels of violence in Haiti, the justification for the mission's continued presence, well beyond its initial mandate, is on unstable ground. In light of the collected evidence, and in support of the growing demand from Haitians, the humane solution is for MINUSTAH to develop a timetable for withdrawal. Concurrently, international resources should be rerouted to support humanitarian relief and capacity building for those still suffering the effects of the earthquake, the cholera outbreak, and decades of pernicious foreign policy. MINUSTAH's yearly budget of $865 million would be better spent on cholera treatment and water infrastructure than on soldiers and bullets.

Notes

1. Paul Farmer, *Haiti After the Earthquake* (New York: Polity Press, 2011).

2. This is an excerpt from a report published under the same title by the Haitian Platform to Advocate for Development Alternatives (PAPDA) in July 2010. Translated from the French by Joris Willems.

3. PARDN (Action Plan for National Recovery and Development of Haiti, English version), March 2010, 5, www.haiticonference.org/Haiti_Action_Plan_ENG .pdf.

4. PARDN, "HICR Mission and Mandate," 7.1.1, p. 54.

5. For more information, see Ayiti Kale Je, Haiti Grassroots Watch, Haïti Veedor, "Impasse? What's Blocking the Capital's Path to Reconstruction?" June 9, 2011, http://www.ayitikaleje.org/7pap1eng.

6. Speeches of IHRC board members Lut Fabert-Goossens (European Union), Rebecca Grynspan (United Nations), Pierre Duquesne (France), and Jean-Claude Lebrun (Haiti), "Minutes of the Board Meeting of the Interim Haiti Recovery Commission (IHRC)," February 28, 2011, www.cirh.ht/files/pdf/cirh_procesverbal _20110228.pdf.

7. Author interview with Philippe Bécoulet, representative for international NGOs, Port-au-Prince, March 2011.

8. "Protest Letter from Haitian IHRC Members to Commission Co-Chairs," *Le Matin,* December 14, 2010, trans. Isabeau Doucet.

9. Ibid.

10. PARDN, 55.

11. Author interview with Gabriël Verret, Port-au-Prince, March 31, 2011.

12. Office of the Special Envoy for Haiti, Assistance Tracker, http://www.haitispecialenvoy.org/assistance-tracker.

13. Kerren Hedlund, *Strength in Numbers: A Review of Humanitarian Coordination in the Field, Case Study: Haiti 2010,* International Council of Voluntary Agencies, February 11, 2011, www.icva.ch/doc00004599.pdf.

14. François Grunewald and Andrea Binder, *Inter-Agency Real-Time Evaluation in Haiti: 3 Months after the Earthquake,* Groupe Urgence Rehabilitation Developpement and Global Public Policy Institute, August 21, 2010, ochanet.unocha.org/p/Documents/Haiti_IA_RTE_1_final_report_en.pdf.

15. Reed Lindsey, "Haiti's Excluded," *The Nation,* March 29, 2010.

16. Colum Lynch, "Top U.N. Aid Official Critiques Haiti Aid Efforts in Confidential Email," *Foreign Policy,* Turtle Bay blog, February 17, 2010, http://turtlebay.foreignpolicy.com.

17. Grunewald and Binder, *Inter-Agency Real-Time Evaluation in Haiti,* 33.

18. Ibid.

19. US Department of State, Bureau of Diplomatic Security, *Haiti 2011 Crime and Safety Report,* https://www.osac.gov.

20. Harvard Law Student Advocates for Human Rights and Centro para la Justicia Global, *Keeping the Peace in Haiti? An Assessment of the United Nations Stabilization Mission in Haiti Using Compliance with Its Prescribed Mandate as a Barometer for Success,* March 25, 2005, http://www.ijdh.org/Haiti(English)(Final).pdf.

21. International Tribunal on Haiti, *Preliminary Report of the Commission of Inquiry, First Inquiry October 6–11, 2005,* 5, www.ijdh.org/pdf/COIReport.pdf.

22. Bri Kouri Nouvèl Gaye (BKNG), Mennonite Central Committee Haiti, Let Haiti Live, Unity Ayiti, *Haiti's Renewal of the MINUSTAH Mandate in Violation of the Human Rights of the Haitian People,* March 2011, submission to the UN Universal Periodic Review, http://ijdh.org/archives/17957.

23. Information of MINUSTAH rape and sexual assault taken from the following: BBC News, "UN Troops Face Child Abuse Claims," November 30, 2006; Stephanie Busari, "Charity: Aid Workers Raping, Abusing Children," CNN, May 27, 2008; Colum Lynch, "U.N. Faces More Accusations of Sexual Misconduct," *Washington Post,* March 13, 2005; Ansel Herz, "Haiti: Looking More Like a War Zone," Inter Press Service, March 30, 2010; Athena R. Kolbe and Royce A. Hutson, "Human Rights Abuses and Other Criminal Violations in Port-Au-Prince, Haiti: A Random Survey of Households," *The Lancet* 368, no. 9538 (September 2, 2006): 864–73; Save the Children, "No One to Turn To: The Underreporting of Child Sexual Exploitation and Abuse by Aid Workers and Peacekeepers," (2008), http://www.savethechildren.org.uk/en/docs/No_One_To_Turn_To.pdf.

24. Carol J. Williams, "U.N. Confronts Another Sex Scandal," *Los Angeles Times,* December 15, 2007.

25. BKNG et al., *Haiti's Renewal of the MINUSTAH Mandate.*

26. Deborah Sontag and Walt Bogdanich, "Escape Attempt Led to Killings of Unarmed Inmates," *New York Times,* May 22, 2010.

27. Thalles Gomes, "Morte de jovem haitiano gera novos protestos contra a Minustah," *Brasil de Fato,* September 13, 2010, trans. David Holmes Morris, http://lo-de-alla.org/2010/09/death-of-youth-sparks-protests-against-minustah.

28. Center for Economic and Policy Research (CEPR), "What Happened to Gerard Jean Gilles?" September 24, 2010, http://www.cepr.net.

29. Kim Ives, "As MINUSTAH Gasses Students, CEP Sets New Elections for November 28th," *Haiti Liberté,* May 26, 2010.

30. CEPR, "MINUSTAH: Securing Stability and Democracy from Journalists, Children and Other Threats," October 18, 2010.

31. Al Jazeera English, "Haiti Cholera Protest Turns Violent," November 16, 2010.

32. International Action Ties, *Vanishing Camps at Gunpoint: Failing to Protect Haiti's Internally Displaced,* July 14, 2010, http://ijdh.org/archives/13424.

3

The Republic of NGOs

Haiti's earthquake triggered a massive and unprecedented mobilization of NGOs. Because of the neoliberal policies discussed in Chapters 1 and 2, the Haitian government's capacity was severely weakened even before the earthquake. Donors began preferring to fund NGOs instead of governments in the 1980s and increasingly so in the 1990s, following US Vice President Al Gore's National Partnership for Reinventing Government initiative, which spearheaded neoliberal reforms in the US government. Haiti, often referred to as a "laboratory" for foreign policy, was ahead of the curve. In 1995 the Republican-controlled US Congress forbade USAID funds to go directly to the elected government of Haiti, where President Jean-Bertrand Aristide had recently returned because of Bill Clinton's intervention.[1] Other donors followed suit. After the 2010 earthquake the Haitian government only received 1% of emergency aid.

In 2009 Clinton, in his role as UN special envoy, declared there to be 10,000 NGOs working in the country, the highest per capita anywhere in the world. This statistic confirmed what many Haitian people have been calling an "invasion" of NGOs.[2] NGOs are playing ever more central roles in Haiti as elsewhere. There were 3,800 NGOs working in multiple countries in 1996, twice the number from ten years prior.[3] Currently, there are so many NGOs that we can't even guess at their number.[4] This rise in the number of NGOs is matched by an increase in funding flowing through them. Globally, in 2005, it is estimated that NGOs channeled anywhere from $3.7 billion to $7.8 billion of humanitarian assistance,[5] and $24 billion in overall development funding.[6]

Because of the sheer number of NGOs, coordination immediately became a challenge acknowledged by all levels of the effort. Bill Clinton himself, as well as US Secretary of State Hillary Clinton, publicly questioned the overdependence on these private structures that willingly or not tend to undermine public capacity and coordination. People began to use the phrase "Republic of NGOs" to describe how thoroughly privatized Haiti's services have become, such as 80% of schools and 90% of clinics, with accountability structures oriented toward their foreign donors and not the Haitian people, the supposed beneficiaries. People also disparagingly referred to an insular "NGO class" characterized by its higher salaries, bigger and newer cars, offices, and so on. The public sector was even more undermined, as qualified staff fled to NGOs that paid much higher wages. Reports of $1,000-per-day contracts circulated soon after the earthquake, even as the majority of the displaced still had not received a proper tent.

Because of their central role and the greater visibility accorded to Haiti, NGOs as a structure came under the spotlight in the global media and among policy makers. But much of the analysis—success stories as well as criticism—remained superficial, focusing on the individual level. Without a doubt, many individual NGOs have performed lifesaving humanitarian work. The media is replete with heartwarming tales of good Samaritans pulling individuals out of their misery. However, the overall progress on a range of indicators—camp conditions, cholera, rubble removal, rehousing, and education—remained minimal even a year and a half after the earthquake and billions spent.

Explaining this seeming contradiction requires a structural analysis. Building where the discussion left off with MINUSTAH, Haitian professor and humanitarian specialist Charles Vorbe interrogates the militarism and instrumentalization within the humanitarian response to Haiti's earthquake. While offering many specific details of the earthquake response, Vorbe grounds the Haitian case in an analysis of the global humanitarian enterprise. In an early critique of the trends of privatization and the militarization of aid, solidarity activist and NACLA researcher Kevin Edmonds poses a series of questions about the impact, sustainability, and accountability of the NGO-ized response.

Accountability and transparency—the reasons donors gave for their preference of funding NGOs in the first place—are the key themes in the Disaster Accountability Project's One-Year Report. Arising from a survey of 196 US-based nonprofits seeking private aid, the report finds that the vast majority have a long way to go. The late Janil Lwijis, activist professor at the State University of Haiti who perished on January 12, grounds the experience of NGOs in Haiti's history. Lwijis argues that NGOs are in fact "government" bodies implanting the logic, ideology, and structures of global capitalism. Collectively this chapter shifts the focus to NGOs as a structure, the one empowered to respond to the disaster and hence responsible for its overall impact.

* * *

Earthquake, Humanitarianism, and Intervention in Haiti

Charles Vorbe

HAITI'S JANUARY 12 EARTHQUAKE KILLED about 300,000 people, more than the human cost of the 13 years of Haiti's War of Independence 200 years earlier. For the UN, it was one of the greatest humanitarian catastrophes the planet has ever known. It gave rise to an unprecedented mobilization of humanitarian aid, with countries, multilateral institutions, NGOs (there are more than 10,000 in Haiti), charitable institutions, evangelical missions, associations of every kind, celebrities, and every kind of organization from what could be called "the charity business sector" all bustling about and rushing to the aid of the disaster victims. For the whole world, one thing was certain: this was the hour for humanitarianism, and nothing but.[7]

The usage of the word "humanitarian" itself is precisely the problem that beckons us. To get to the essence of humanitarianism in today's Haiti, whatever its form, one must avoid the pitfall of evidentiary truths, of sentiments that reassure, of received, convenient, acritical, and nonsubversive ideas in order to question, in all objectivity, certain current mystified and mystifying representations of reality. To do so, all the semantic enchantment of words like "solidarity," "charity," "rescue," "pity," and "aid," and the noble sentiments that they evoke, must also be left behind so that the concrete representations of humanitarianism in today's Haiti can be examined in the harsh light of day.

Since the end of the Cold War, humanitarian action has become an important, and even essential, component of certain states' foreign policy playbook. Vulnerability has grown in the Global South, and emergency situations have multiplied across the globe. Thus, with increasing frequency, we witness deployments of not only civil but also military aid in order to respond "effectively" to the complexities of the "emergency" situations. Following the fiasco of the US intervention in Somalia in 1993 and also the absence of a coordinated action among the different humanitarian aid protagonists (civil governmental, nongovernmental, and military) in Haiti in 1994 when Aristide was returned, successive US administrations have attempted to better coordinate their multidimensional responses to these emergency situations. More often than not, NGOs have been at the heart of these strategies. As vice president, Al Gore advocated the insertion of NGOs "into the global humanitarian aid system where they are associated with small and medium-sized business in order to promote democracy and the development of a free market system."[8]

The events of September 11, 2001, accelerated this process of integrating humanitarian responses with other components of governmental response—including diplomacy and military action. Former US secretary of state Colin Powell, with a notable hint of sincerity sufficiently rare at this level of responsibility, has acknowledged that the US government has "excellent relations with the NGOs which can be a 'force multiplier'" and "an important part of our combat team . . . because we are all working toward the same single goal, humanitarian aid."[9] The NGOs, that is, contribute to what has come to be called "soft power." According to Makki, "They constitute an essential pillar of an overall strategy on the part of the US which depends upon establishing a *noopolitics*"—from the Greek root *noo* for "spirit," meaning mental or ideological politics—"which is founded on the development of networks and on the mastery of informational processes."[10]

Since the 1990s there has been a general evolution of the practice of NGOs in the "age of humanitarianism." They have moved away from the traditional and classical approach of volunteer humanitarianism based on the principles of neutrality, impartiality, and independence as proclaimed and defended, for example, by the International Committee of the Red Cross (ICRC). But this is a dangerous situation. The association of humanitarianism with militarism and politics can lead to the disappearance of authentic humanitarianism. Nonetheless, we need to be honest: the principle of neutrality of the organization founded by Henri Dunant is becoming increasingly uncertain, to the same extent that the concept of humanitarianism increases its monopoly on people's minds.

The confusion of genres is in itself perverse and in fact can lead to the violation of international humanitarian law and to its crisis, a situation that largely facilitates the establishment of a modus vivendi around a "third type of colonialism," what might be called "humanitarian neocolonialism," wherein the NGOs gradually find themselves assigned by governments to a compensatory function, secondary tasks, or subcontracting. However honest many NGO activists might be, and whatever the sincerity of their humanitarian commitment, the implicit role of the overwhelming majority of the "nongovernmental" organizations is to reinforce existing systems of domination and exploitation.[11] According to French legal scholar Robert Charvin, "More than 50% of the resources of the entire NGO apparatus have public origins."[12]

The humanitarian apparatus in Haiti constitutes a hegemonic US military presence. Early in the earthquake relief efforts, an image made the rounds of the national and international media: US soldiers perched in an army helicopter in full flight, tossing sacks of food overboard to earthquake victims, who, on the ground, come running from everywhere and fight among themselves to collect whatever they can. This image is highly symbolic. The degrading nature of the procedure—which shocked those of good conscience and sparked a veritable global outcry—makes clear the absolute incompatibility between, on the one hand, the security preoccupations of any army and, on the other hand, the respect for the dignity and the humanity of the beneficiaries of the aid rightfully called humanitarian.

The other forces on the Haitian scene are the ubiquitous "blue helmets"— the MINUSTAH units of the French, Canadian, even Israeli armies. They number in the tens of thousands but are nothing in comparison to the impressive deployment (in personnel and equipment) of Uncle Sam during the first days after the catastrophe. Washington mobilized 22,000 people for initial emergency intervention. The United States had exclusive control of the strategic points (the airport and the seaport at Port-au-Prince, among others) and designated the United States Southern Command (SOUTHCOM) as the "principal agency" in Haiti. SOUTHCOM's explicit role in Latin America and the Caribbean is to "lead military operations and promote a cooperation of security forces to attain US strategic objectives." SOUTHCOM's presence in Haiti spoke volumes about the intentions of US imperialism and how it addresses Haiti's humanitarian crisis. General Douglas Frazer, commander of SOUTHCOM, was clear about the mission given to the forces under his command: "We are concentrating on the organization of command, control, and communications over there [in Haiti], in order to better understand what is happening."[13]

Other players, both official and private, complained about the complications of emergency action stemming directly from the centralization of the decisions by the US authorities beyond any control of the Haitian administration. Cuba, Venezuela, Ecuador, Nicaragua, and other countries denounced what seemed to them to be a military occupation. Nobel Peace Prize laureate Argentine Adolfo Pérez Esquivel declared during a mission of investigation and solidarity: "The problem facing Haiti is not of a military nature. In consequence, it cannot be resolved by the presence of foreign troops on Haitian territory or other measures of this nature."[14] He also sharply disapproved of "the presence of international occupying forces in Haiti, because these seriously impact the sovereignty of the country." More surprising was the official position of France, albeit under the rubric of secondary contradictions between the forces allied against the United States in Haiti. French President Nicolas Sarkozy raised his voice against the notion of placing Haiti in trusteeship, "defending" the sovereignty of its people as well as its right to self-determination.[15] The very conservative French newspaper *Le Figaro* even ran a headline on January 25, 2010, that read, "Haiti in a Game of Influence Dominated by the United States."[16]

If one doubts the strategic importance of Haiti for its big neighbor to the north, the history of the relations between the two countries provides indisputable proof. Noam Chomsky notes, "Between 1849 and 1913, US warships penetrated 24 times into Haitian national waters 'to protect American lives and property.'"[17] Considering the humanitarian situation provoked by the January 12 earthquake, one of the most influential US think tanks, the neoliberal Heritage Foundation, merely a day after the earthquake didn't hide that "the earthquake has both humanitarian and US national security implications," namely that an effective response from Venezuela or Cuba could "diminish US influence in the region." Consequently, Washington "should initiate a rapid response that is not only bold but decisive, mobilizing US military, governmental, and civilian capabilities for both a short-term rescue and relief effort and a longer-term recovery and reform program in Haiti."[18]

Today's humanitarianism, beyond the soldiers' paternalistic pity and the humanist doctrine that grants it legitimacy in a world "without heart or soul," constitutes a veritable ideology in the sense that it gives a false representation—a reverse, deformed, and deforming image—of reality. This distortion of the real, which is not by chance, contributes to the global endeavor to mystify, which is necessary to implement the new humanitarian neocolonialism or, better, neocolonial humanitarianism. And the world's interventionist powers, those that maintain and fund the world's leading neocolonial humanitarian aid organizations, have figured out how to take full advantage of this doctrine.

Such is the case in Haiti, where humanitarian action, placed under the control of the military, serves objectively as an instrument to reinforce the domination of the country by the US superpower and the "international community," which Washington utilizes, in this event, to its own ends. This said, this "recolonization" is being strongly contested. Beyond provoking the discontent and irritation of numerous governments throughout the world, Haitians themselves are beginning to become aware of and mobilize against what appears to them to be an endeavor to dispossess them of their sovereignty—or what remains of it—and of their right to determine the reconstruction of their country. To the extent that humanitarian aid management, within the context of Haiti's neocolonial system, shows its serious deficiencies, it will end up fueling the already simmering anger of the population that has lived through decades of slow-cooking disaster followed by the eruption of the January 12 catastrophe.

* * *

NGOs and the Business of Poverty in Haiti

Kevin Edmonds

HAITI HAS THE MOST PRIVATIZED social-service sector in the Americas, with some 80% of the country's basic services provided by the private sector through NGOs.[19] No other country in the world has more NGOs per capita. Edmond Mulet, head of the UN mission in Haiti, conservatively estimates that there were more than 10,000 before the January 12, 2010, earthquake. Many Haitians ironically refer to their country as a "republic of NGOs."

The Haitian government, regularly accused of corruption by the US State Department, has been marginalized in post-earthquake recovery and rebuilding efforts.[20] Less than one cent of each dollar of US earthquake relief is going to the Haitian government. As reported by the Associated Press, NGOs working on disaster assistance receive 43 cents, while 33 cents of that same dollar ends up with the US military.[21] This has been the pattern of aid since deposed Haitian president Jean-Bertrand Aristide—not one of Washington's favorite politicians—was elected in 1990.

An umbrella organization of anti-Aristide activists and NGOs called the Group of 184, for example, was largely financed by USAID, the International Foundation for Electoral Systems, and the International Republican Institute. As Peter Hallward reports in his book *Damming the Flood,*

USAID and other government agencies from Northern countries provide 70% of the funding of NGOs in Haiti.[22] The other 30% comes from corporate and individual donations. Thus, the label "nongovernmental" is a bit of a misnomer.

In Haiti, the state has been circumvented, and unelected organizations that are unaccountable to the Haitian people have been carrying out a program of neoliberal transformation. The relationships between the NGOs and their donors continually undermine the Haitian people's right to self-determination, while the organizations are at the same time cultivating and profiting from the poverty they are entrusted to fight.

One of the largest NGOs, the American Red Cross, has come under fire for its handling of earthquake relief funds.[23] It collected $255 million in private donations, but allocated only $106 million to Haiti relief. This left $149 million of donations unaccounted for, 18 months after the earthquake.[24] Exposing the massive overheads of the big NGOs, Bill Quigley of the Center for Constitutional Rights noted that more than $200 million was given to the Red Cross, which had only 15 employees in Haiti before the earthquake, while Partners in Health and their 5,000 (mostly Haitian) employees received $40 million.[25]

Despite the passage of two months and the raising of billions of dollars of relief aid worldwide, the lack of transparency and accountability has negatively affected the delivery of services. [26] Haitian Prime Minister Jean-Max Bellerive stated his frustration with the disorganization: "We don't know who has given money to NGOs and how much money have they given. . . . At the moment, we can't do any coordination or have any coherent policies for giving to the population."[27]

The PDNA donor conference in Santo Domingo, the Dominican Republic, on March 16, 2010, did little to change the status quo of NGO-led development. The meeting was another example of Haitians' exclusion from the decision-making process in the rebuilding of their own country. The paternalistic nature of the meeting led Haitian President Réne Préval to angrily challenge the US State Department, calling its allegations of corruption "arrogant" and demanding that the Haitian government have veto power over any reconstruction projects.

Despite Préval's challenge, the result was more of the same. There was no discussion of working with popular Haitian organizations, which are crucial to local development. The "experts" decided that Haiti should take steps to further strengthen the private sector, transparency, and good governance. The final irony of the Donors' Conference is that the NGO prescription to the Haitian government is what the NGOs themselves desperately need: more transparency and accountability.

* * *

The Transparency of Relief Organizations in Haiti

Disaster Accountability Project

THIS REPORT SEEKS TO (1) determine whether 196 organizations that solicited donations for Haiti disaster relief produced regular, factual reports on their activities, and if so, (2) how comprehensive, frequent, factual, and publicly accessible such reports were, and (3) to determine how much money has been raised for Haiti relief, how much of that has been spent, and on what (i.e., health care, food, clean water, etc.).[28]

Through this report, the DAP aims to promote accountability and transparency by (1) highlighting relief organizations that provide the public with complete and detailed situation/activity reports and (2) identifying those relief organizations that do not release situation reports to the public or publish situation reports infrequently or include little concrete factual information.

Process and Scope

DAP's Relief Oversight Initiative is dedicated to increasing transparency in the policies and activities of relief/aid organizations. Following up on our six-month report released on July 12, 2010, the team again sought to obtain information from nearly 200 relief groups responding to the high-magnitude earthquake that shook Haiti on January 12, 2010. Data collected fell into two categories: data from self-report surveys and internal research.

Most correspondence with relief organizations regarding the survey occurred via e-mail. The majority of groups were sent e-mails directly to established contacts or general/media inquiry e-mail addresses. Most organizations were e-mailed four times, an initial request to fill out the survey and three follow-up reminders that included the survey link. Most questions were responded to within 48 hours.

One difficulty the team encountered in soliciting responses from relief groups was the way in which some organizations limit initial contact. Some groups only allow contact via online forms with predetermined inquiry topics. Any additional information can be obtained only by signing up for a newsletter or mailing list. While directly contacting an actual representative did not itself guarantee a response, "contact via online inquiry" forms further decreased the possibility of correspondence with an organization.

In our last report, about 10% of the contacted organizations responded to our survey, and of those, a number provided incomplete answers. We are pleased to announce that in this report, the percentage of responses has nearly doubled to 38 submitted surveys. However, this still means that roughly 80% did not comply with our survey request. While many of the completed surveys provide descriptive observations, many organizations also left questions blank or incomplete.

Analysis of these surveys allowed the Relief Oversight Initiative team to examine the extent to which relief organizations value transparency in their activities in Haiti. The surveys also provide a picture of the scope of relief that each organization provides. Although organizations such as Guide-Star and Charity Navigator offer much fiscal information regarding relief groups, making public the details of the actual day-to-day activities and programs of relief groups in Haiti is crucial to achieving greater transparency and effectiveness in aid.

In addition to the survey, the Relief Oversight Initiative team visited each of the surveyed organizations' websites to assess the availability/accessibility of situation and activity reports and their level of detail, frequency, and factual content. Quality of assessments relates directly to the ultimate goal of bolstering standards of transparency. Availability of information, such as the policies and day-to-day activities of relief work, is representative of the openness of relief organizations. Recognition of deficiencies in reporting, such as infrequent updating, limited information, or long gaps between entries, and correcting for them, will enable the public and donors to make more informed decisions before donating based on emotional appeals and high-end advertising, and enable more efficient coordination to improve delivery of aid.

Although the scope of this report is limited to those groups responding to the 2010 earthquake in Haiti, the need for increased transparency in other relief/aid settings is evident. While the specific circumstances of each aid operation may vary, all relief organizations should be held accountable not only for the consequences of their actions but also for maintaining a high level of transparency, and should therefore adopt policies that allow the public and international community to better monitor their activities. While it may be argued that such public scrutiny could deter some organizations from responding as quickly to a disaster by limiting their flexibility, this is a false dilemma. The responses to this survey suggest that relief organizations with a genuine interest in promoting sustainable development and providing essential needs have nothing to fear from increased transparency.

Our hope is that this methodology used to study relief groups in Haiti can be applied to relief and aid work worldwide. The scope of such work is only limited by relief/aid organizations themselves, insofar as they control the information relevant for transparency studies. We of course recognize and would exclude from such a study, as appropriate, those settings where aid workers need to maintain anonymity and work in secret for fear of reprisals; such environments may be more suitably studied in a different fashion. Furthermore, we acknowledge that aid organizations with very low budgets may not have the capacity to provide as frequent updates as organizations with larger budgets.

Highlights of Report Findings

Responses

The one-year follow-up survey was sent to 196 relief organizations working in Haiti. Of those, 38 completed the survey by the given deadline. Although the response rate to our follow-up survey was nearly double that of the six-month mark, nearly 80% of contacted organizations did not respond. This lack of response is one indicator of how severely lacking transparency is among aid groups. Of the 38 groups that responded, many completed the survey with detailed information; however, some groups left questions blank or incomplete.

Money Raised vs. Spent

Collectively, the organizations that responded to the survey reported receiving over $1.4 billion in cash donations and government and/or foundation funds and grants. To date, these groups report spending about $730 million, or 52%, on Haiti relief efforts. In comparison, at the six-month mark, survey respondents reported having raised more than $825 million and spending about 33% of that.

Interest Raised

More than $1.8 million has reportedly been raised in interest by just five of the survey respondents. Ten of the 38 groups reported that they did not know how much interest they have raised, and the rest did not respond either way, indicating that this figure is likely higher. Eleven organizations report that the interest raised will be spent directly on Haiti relief efforts, while four groups explicitly state that the interest they raise will be used for general operating fund purposes.

Transparency

A critical focus of this survey is transparency. Therefore, organizations were asked several questions about the transparency of their activities in Haiti. Only three of the surveyed groups (Haiti Maycare, Help the Children, and Compassion International) reported that they do not provide "publicly available situation/activity reports detailing their specific activities on the ground," and 35 groups indicated that they did provide such information. Most commonly, groups reported that they publish information quarterly, while several groups reported publishing activity reports more often.

The survey questions regarding transparency were detailed, asking about the specific types of information reported (that is, hard facts vs. anecdotes from the field, blog stories, or donation appeals). Four members of the DAP team conducted a search of the websites of all 196 organizations that were sent the survey for publicly available information about their activities on the ground.

In the year since the Haiti earthquake, DAP has considered an acceptable level of transparency to be frequent provision of detailed and specific information; or, otherwise stated, not information that is anecdotal, infrequent, aggregate-heavy, or lacking in factual details of activities. Of the 38 survey respondents, 35 reported that they provide factual, public information on their websites. Those and many other organizations do provide some information on their websites, but based on the DAP's standard of transparency, only one of the 196 organizations (Architecture for Humanity, also a survey respondent) provided what DAP considers to be an acceptable level of information.

On-the-Ground Work

Another critical focus of this survey is to make use of transparency to improve delivery of services. Thirty-two organizations report having staff on the ground for a total of 7,822 staff members operating in Haiti. Six groups report that they have no staff currently on the ground in Haiti, though half of these organizations are still soliciting donations for Haiti relief (Association of Baptists for World Evangelism, Episcopal Relief and Development, and World Food Program USA). Of the 38 groups that responded, 26 report raising money specifically for clean water efforts and 21 organizations report raising money for sanitation efforts.

Considering the recent cholera outbreak, it is critical that organizations focusing on water and sanitation efforts provide frequent and thorough updates of their activities. More knowledge about what is happening on the ground is necessary to better assess existing efforts and for all involved to determine what is already being done and what is needed to battle the current crisis and improve lifesaving infrastructure. More knowledge will enable organizations to better coordinate, maximize resources, and build upon their current on-the-ground efforts.

* * *

NGOs: What Government Are You?

Janil Lwijis (Jean-Anile Louis-Juste)

Everyone repeats: NGOs are organizations working on development but that are not governments.[29] The first international decree on NGOs reinforces this discourse. For our analysis, we need to not only focus on NGOs' activities that appear in front of our eyes. We need to get at the roots of NGOs as well, and take a good look at the branches to which they are connected. In this way we look at Article 71 of the UN Charter, which fleshes out the roles of NGOs within the UN system, defining NGOs' activities as based in community-development projects. So we need to say that NGOs are another category of government: a government that is mingled directly with the "international community" but acts locally.

Haiti was one of the first countries to become accustomed to community development projects. The UN established a pig project in the town of Jacmel in 1948. Despite formal recognition of NGOs within the UN Charter, the agency worked with the Haitian government. The same was true of the Alliance for Progress (1960) in its battle against the Cuban Revolution: international agencies collaborated with the public sector.

This support to public agencies changed. In the 1970s the Catholic Church made a change in the alliance it formed with the Duvalier dictatorship in 1966. A cultural movement arose from the Latin American and Caribbean conference declaring a "preferential option for the poor" in Medellín, Colombia, in 1968. The first peasants' training centers were founded: in Papaye and Bassin Bleu (1972), Jean-Rabel (1973), and the Institute for Technology and Community Organizing (ITECA, 1978). True, François "Papa Doc" Duvalier (1957–1971) closed all political spaces in the country. But in 1969 Nelson Rockefeller participated in the negotiations to replace Duvalier, who was ill. Rockefeller achieved two political successes: first negotiating the acceptance of US-based evangelists, creating an invasion of Protestant churches, and, second, the implantation of export-processing factories.

As a consequence, before 1960, a few people heard talk of CARE, the Haitian-American Community Help Organization (HACHO), Christian Service, and so on, but in the 1970s, NGOs became a symbol diffused throughout every corner of the country. This propaganda succeeded in controlling our thought, because today the majority of Haitian organizations function in the form of community development projects. That is, they take a social problem (be it political, economic, or cultural) out of its local realities and turn it into a situational problem for foreign actors to solve. Using their intellectual capacity, they create a project to execute with foreign capitalist funding.

NGOs: International Government on National Territory?

In the struggle against the government that became a crisis, NGOs fight to occupy the social field in the country that never had a social welfare state [*Leta Byennèt*].[30] Meanwhile, "democratic transition" was capital's political and ideological response to workers. NGOs came with civil society, a new social contract, citizenship, the rule of law, and so on, which represents another body for the soul of capital. Like this, development aid was reinforced as support for "envelopment."[31]

In Western European countries, social welfare policies for well-being were the most effective weapon for the international community to prevent the international Communists from gaining ground. The international community used social policy as a measure to keep former colonized countries under the domination of the colonizer countries. In this version of international development, the local dominant class associates with the colonizers' dominant class. This alliance is a consequence of financial dependence, pillaging natural resources, and sucking the labor of peasants and factory workers dry. Therefore, countries being drained only had public aid for envelopment.

While the international community privatized public aid for envelopment to respond to capital's demands against the workers that diminished because of the success of workers in wealthy imperialist countries,[32] it presented Article 71 for application, creating legal spaces for NGOs. The pillage and draining of wealth already prepared the ground for disasters they want to call "natural." These so-called natural disasters are really social disasters (see Chapter 1, this volume) that require international rescue, certainly given the lack of prevention work in colonized countries sucked dry.[33] NGOs gain legitimacy in this process to create a legal framework for capitalism.

Therefore, NGOs are not an initiative created by private citizens. The NGO system is an ideological and political tool used by capital to reproduce itself following the economic crisis of the 1980s. NGOs manage aid to develop capital in the heart and spirit of the poor masses—in other words, to disable workers. NGOs perform local development for international capital. They function to treat the population's social problems. By passing existing social realities through a mill of social engineering, existing class realities turn into a number of development projects that can receive funds from large foundations and capitalist governments. Therefore, NGOs are the social body that today most exemplifies the sham solidarity between rich and poor. The history of NGOs as a structure is full of contradictions inherent to modern colonialism: capital against labor.

Some NGOs manage international aid; others run social issues through the mill of technical solutions. The international aid managers dominate the implementing agencies when they decide how to evaluate the work of the latter. They apply all of the capitalist administration's keywords within their evaluation: "effectiveness," "cost-benefit analysis," "efficiency," and so on. These scientific tools arose from the dictatorship of capital over labor to reject people who face social problems. Therefore, at their core, NGOs mask the political struggles within a society under a guise of partnership between NGOs coming from colonizer and colonized countries, because the international division of labor remains one of the largest elements of NGOs' foundation.

On this land that is the mother of liberty, NGOs zombify the poor masses. Many of them say that they give peasants their souls, for example, because they do popular education in the style of Paolo Freire.[34] All of this is true. However, they refuse to recognize how they are already woven together with capitalist foundations and governments, or recognize that all their popular education is conducted inside a capitalist relationship, that community development projects expose and bring capital into the midst of the popular masses.

NGOs meet a few small needs. They take control over the heart and soul of the popular masses. This governance is done in the interest of capital, with the international community making all the decisions. Educated people in colonized countries are applying this governance in their own societies. Is this not enough to recognize NGOs as an international government on national territory?

Notes

1. This intervention included the Governor's Island Accord, calling for foreign control of Haiti's economic policies, as well as privatization.

2. See Sauveur Pierre Etienne, *Haïti: L'Invasion des ONG* (Port-au-Prince: Centre de Recherce Sociale et de Formation Economique pour le Développement, 1997).

3. Scholte, J. A. and A. Schnabel, *Civil Society and Global Finance* (London: Routledge, 2002), 250.

4. Roger Riddell, *Does Foreign Aid Really Work?* (Oxford: Oxford University Press, 2007), 53.

5. Development Initiatives, *Global Humanitarian Assistance 2006* (London, 2006), 46.

6. Riddell, *Does Foreign Aid Really Work?* 259.

7. Consciously or not, some imply that the humanitarian crisis stems from the January 12 earthquake. But a look at any of numerous reports from international organizations or NGOs—with their statistics concerning access to water, health care, sanitation, and housing—makes it clear that the Haitian population has been living in a "humanitarian crisis" for decades.

8. Robert Charvin, "Notes sur les dérives de l'humanitaire dans l'ordre international," *Revue belge de droit international* 2 (1995): 468–85.

9. Conférence à Washington, 26 octobre 2005 citée par Rony Brauman "Mission civilisatrice, ingérence humanitaire" *in Le Monde diplomatique* de septembre 2005.

10. Sami Makki, "Militarisation de l'humanitaire ? Le modèle américain de l'intégration civilo-militaire, ses enjeux et limites," communication au colloque GRIP-ECHO, Bruxelles, le 17 nov. 2004.

11. Charvin, "Notes sur les dérives de l'humanitaire dans l'ordre international."

12. Robert Charvin, with Brigitte Henri, *Relations internationales, droit et mondialisation. Un monde à sens unique* (Paris: L'Harmattan, 2000), 205.

13. Michel Chossudovsky, "La militarisation de l'aide d'urgence à Haïti: opération militaire ou invasion?" January 22, 2010, http://www.mondialisation.ca/index.php?context=va&aid=17168.

14. Press note, April 12, 2010, published on Alterpresse.org.

15. See the speech of President Sarkozy on his visit to Haiti, http://www.consulfrance-miami.org/spip.php?article1317.

16. Tanguy Berthemet, "Haiti in a Game of Influence Dominated by the United States," January 26, 2010.

17. Noam Chomsky, *L'an 501: la conquête continue,* Ecosociété, Montréal, Epo, Bruxelles, 1995, p. 231.

18. James M. Roberts and Ray Walzer, "American Leadership Necessary, to Assist Haiti After Devastating Earthquake," January 13, 2010, http://s3.amazonaws.com/thf_media/2010/pdf/wm_2754.pdf.

19. Adapted from an article originally published April 5, 2010, https://nacla.org/node/6501.

20. Eighty percent figure cited in Alex Dupuy, "Beyond the Earthquake: A Wake-Up Call for Haiti," Social Science Research Council, January 22, 2010, http://www.ssrc.org/features/pages/haiti-now-and-next/1338/1339.

21. Joseph Guyler Delva, "US Report on Corruption in Haiti Angers Préval," *Jamaica Observer,* March 19, 2010, http://www.jamaicaobserver.com/business/Corruption-in-Haiti_7493359.

22. Peter Hallward, *Damming the Flood* (London: Verso, 2010), 179.

23. Amadi Ajamu, "Red Cross Under Fire! Where's the Money for Haiti?" *San Francisco Bay View,* March 30, 2010, http://sfbayview.com/2010/red-cross-under-fire-wheres-the-money-for-haiti.

24. American Red Cross, Haiti Earthquake Response, July 2011 Update, http://www.redcross.org/www-files/Documents/pdf/international/Haiti/Haiti Earthquake_18MonthReport.pdf.

25. Bill Quigley, "Haiti Numbers—27 Days After Quake," *Huffington Post,* February 9, 2010, http://www.huffingtonpost.com/bill-quigley/haiti-numbers---27-days-a_b_454755.html.

26. Financial Tracking Service: Tracking Global Humanitarian Aid Flows. The United Nations Office for the Coordination of Humanitarian Affairs. http://fts.unocha.org/pageloader.aspx?page=emerg-emergencyCountryDetails&cc=hti

27. Quoted in Mathew Bigg, "Haiti Wants More Information on Foreign Aid," Reuters, March 3, 2010.

28. Adapted from Disaster Accountability Project, "Executive Summary," *One Year Follow-Up Report on the Transparency of Relief Organizations Responding to the 2010 Haiti Earthquake* (December 2010–January 2011).

29. Excerpted from *ONG: Ki gouvèman Ou Yè?,* a book originally published in 2009 by Asosyasyon Inivèsite/ Inivèsitèz Desalinyen, a group within the Faculté des Sciences Humaines at the Université d'Etat d'Haïti, founded by the late Janil Lwijis. Translated from the original Haitian Creole by Mark Schuller.

30. *Leta Byennèt* refers to revolutionary Haitian leader Jean-Jacques Dessalines' prioritization of well-being and not simply political liberty.

31. Play on the phrase "public aid for development."

32. The original phrase, *peyi sousè,* refers to countries that suck the wealth from others.

33. The original phrase, *peyi sousè,* literally means "countries sucked dry."

34. Paulo Freire, *Pedagogy of the Oppressed,* trans. Myra Bergman Ramos (New York: Continuum Publishing Corporation, 1985).

4

Disaster Capitalism

Activist journalist Naomi Klein struck a nerve with the phrase "disaster capitalism." Social movement activists and scholars instantly had new language to critique the ballooning budgets for wars and their reconstruction, the no-bid contracts, and the rapid, prefab social-engineering proposals that undermined decades of movement advances. The invasions of Afghanistan and Iraq at the turn of the twenty-first century were followed closely by another "regime change" in the Americas. On February 29, 2004—in the midst of the celebration of Haiti's bicentennial and the first time slaves forged a free nation—President Jean-Bertrand Aristide was ushered out following a several-months-long confrontation. Even before WikiLeaks' release of some 1,900 cables from the US Embassy in Haiti to Haïti Liberté, it was clear that, whatever legitimate concerns some of Aristide's opposition had, the international community was clearly engineering Aristide's withdrawal. Unlike Afghanistan or Iraq with vast oil reserves, the benefits to transnational capitalist interests were less than clear in Haiti. The regime change wrought increased repression relatively muffled by the international press and a wave of violence and kidnapping that justified MINUSTAH's continued presence. Looking at the policy decisions during the 2004–2006 interim period, neoliberal measures like privatization, tariff reduction, and export orientation were well served by the interim Boniface-Latortue regime.[1]

What is disaster capitalism? In a previous work, editor Mark Schuller defined it as "national and transnational governmental institutions' instrumental use of catastrophe (both so-called 'natural' and human-mediated disasters,

*including post-conflict situations) to promote and empower a range of private,
neoliberal capitalist interests."[2] Essentially, there are two components of disaster
capitalism. The first, what can be called "(non)profiteering," is the more widely
reported, particularly by journalists. While nonprofits and increasingly for-
profit corporations are receiving growing no-bid contracts for reconstruction—
justified by a systematic undermining of state capacity that neoliberal policies
portend—disasters are opportunities for radical policy reform. These neoliberal
social engineering reforms—"shock therapy" in the form of austerity measures,
privatization, trade liberalization, and the like—constitute the second and more
long-term element of disaster capitalism.*

*If Aristide's forced removal triggered this social experiment, the earthquake
was an automatic charge. Noted earlier, donors pledged over $10 billion for
Haiti's reconstruction, over $5.4 billion for the first 18 months. As Joris Wil-
lems reported, much of these funds were "preferenced" right back to the source,
what used to be called "tied aid" or earmarking.[3] Based on a belief in the private sector, Bill Clinton made a pitch to the World Economic Forum in Davos,
calling Haitians "creative" and "entrepreneurial." Given this, it might follow
that investment would flow to Haitian companies, but the Center for Economic
and Policy Research (CEPR) reported in April 2011 that only 2.5% of funds
went to Haitian firms. But car-rental companies, office-supply retailers, water
trucks, and landlords sought their own individual "dividend" of the billions. It
wasn't uncommon for NGO workers, with monthly housing allowances, to pay
$2,500 in monthly rent, 10 times greater than pre-quake housing costs. NGO
and international aid policies encouraged this, with specific procurement procedures that saw the bulk of aid funds return to foreign companies and allied
Haitian elite families.*

*It was, as US Ambassador Kenneth Merten noted in a WikiLeaked cable,
a "gold rush." Solidarity activists and journalists Ansel Herz and Kim Ives
follow the case of Lewis Lucke, who, leveraging political connections, sued a
contractor for half a million dollars for his "finder's fee." Following a Nation
Institute investigation, journalists and graduate students Isabeau Doucet and
Isabel Macdonald examine the political connections of Clinton campaign contributor Warren Buffett in a project trumpeted up by the Clinton Foundation.
In a case of "emperor's new clothes," Clinton's promotion turned formaldehyde-
ridden trailers from the same contractor sued for poisoning residents in FEMA
trailers into "hurricane proof" shelters.*

*Haiti Grassroots Watch, a collective of Haitian grassroots media, probes
the Cash-for-Work program established in Haiti. More than an analysis of the
short-term impacts and the typical concern of wielding influence, Haiti Grassroots Watch offers a historical analysis of its roots in the rescue of the capitalist*

system overall following the US Great Depression. It is difficult to accept that after 20 years of steady privatization and policies that used to be called "structural adjustment," there were still more gains to be made. However, the swift, multinational, and often jumbled earthquake response privatized the plum of Haiti's public utilities, the telephone company, as Haitian journalist-activist Hervé Jean Michel reports. Together, these analyses sound a devastating warning.

* * *

After the Quake, a "Gold Rush" for Haiti Contracts

Ansel Herz and Kim Ives

DISASTER CAPITALISTS WERE FLOCKING TO Haiti in a "gold rush" for contracts to rebuild the country after the January 12, 2010, earthquake, wrote US Ambassador Kenneth Merten in a secret February 1, 2010, cable obtained by WikiLeaks and reviewed by *Haïti Liberté* in June 2011.[4]

"THE GOLD RUSH IS ON!" Merten headlined a section of his 6 p.m. situation report—or Sitrep—back to Washington. "As Haiti digs out from the earthquake, different [US] companies are moving in to sell their concepts, products and services," he wrote. "President Préval met with Gen Wesley Clark Saturday [January 30] and received a sales presentation on a hurricane/ earthquake resistant foam core house designed for low income residents."[5]

Former US presidential candidate and retired general Wesley Clark was promoting—along with professional basketball star Alonzo Mourning— InnoVida Holdings, a Miami-based company that had pledged to donate 1,000 foam-core panel-built houses for Haiti's homeless.

AshBritt, a Pompano Beach, Florida–based disaster recovery company, "has been talking to various institutions about a national plan for rebuilding all government buildings," Merten continued in his dispatch. "Other companies are proposing their housing solutions or their land use planning ideas, or other construction concepts. Each is vying for the ear of President in a veritable free-for-all."

One man who had the ear of Préval, perhaps more than anyone else, was Lewis Lucke, Washington's "unified relief and response coordinator," heading up the entire US earthquake relief effort in Haiti. He met with Préval and Prime Minister Jean-Max Bellerive two weeks after the quake, and at least one more time after that, according to the cables. Lucke, a 27-year veteran of USAID, had overseen multibillion-dollar contracts for Bechtel and other companies as USAID's mission director in postinvasion Iraq.

Lucke stepped down as Haiti relief coordinator in April 2010, after only three months, telling his hometown newspaper, the *Austin-American Statesman,* "It became clear to us that if it was handled correctly, the earthquake represented as much an opportunity as it did a calamity. . . . So much of the china was broken that it gives the chance to put it together hopefully in a better and different way."[6]

But in December 2010, Lucke sued AshBritt and its Haitian partner, GB Group (owned by Haiti's richest man, Gilbert Bigio), for almost $500,000. He claimed the companies "did not pay him enough for consulting services that included hooking the contractor up with powerful people and helping to navigate government bureaucracy," according to the Associated Press.[7] Lucke had signed a lucrative $30,000-per-month agreement with AshBritt and GB Group within eight weeks of stepping down, helping them secure $20 million in construction contracts.

Before the lawsuit was settled, Lucke had already joined masonry product supplier MC Endeavors. The firm sent out another of its many press releases in May 2011 advertising its ability to build homes and applauding Haiti's newly inaugurated President Michel Martelly's declaration: "This is a new Haiti that is open for business now."

AshBritt and Lucke weren't the only gold seekers to end up in lawsuits. Just over a year after InnoVida's benevolent gesture, the company's CEO, Claudio Osorio, and his ex-wife were in court being sued by another NBA star, Carlos Boozer, for having "intentionally, maliciously, fraudulently" squandered a $1 million investment in the company by the basketball player, according to an article in the *Chicago Sun-Times.*[8] "Boozer and his former wife, Cindy," the article reported, "say the Osorios promised 1,000% returns from projects that benefitted disaster-stricken areas." The article further noted, according to Boozer's suit, "InnoVida is a defendant to at least 14 known lawsuits, including a blanket lien on the operating factory's assets," and that the company "was taken over by a court-ordered receiver March 3, 2011."

Ambassador Merten's announced "gold rush" began as Haitians were still being pulled from the rubble. Since then, USAID has doled out nearly $200 million in relief and reconstruction contracts. By April 2011 only about 2.5% of the money had gone to Haitian companies, according to the CDEPR.[9]

Lucke, for one, justified making money off disasters. "It's kind of the American way," he told *Haïti Liberté*. "Just because you're trying to do business doesn't mean you're trying to be rapacious. There's nothing insidious about that. . . . It wasn't worse than Iraq."

* * *

Building Illusions
A Case Study of Bill Clinton's Photo-Op Philanthropy

Isabeau Doucet and Isabel Macdonald

IN THE AFTERMATH OF HAITI'S earthquake, "disaster capitalism" has taken a more avant-garde form than the usual course of privatization, deregulation, and cuts to social services. In post-earthquake Haiti, disaster relief and reconstruction are outsourced to foreign companies, governments, and NGOs, as well as to the UN, alienating Haitians from ownership over their own tragedy. One of the first IHRC projects to be announced, as well as one of the few to be completed, was the Clinton Foundation's million-dollar effort to build hurricane shelters that could also be used as schools. This project, proposed, funded, and executed by the Clinton Foundation (CF), offers a compelling case study in the dynamics of disaster capitalism in post-earthquake Haiti, raising worrying questions about procurement and project oversight, while also highlighting a lack of local consultation in recovery efforts.

While the CF told the IHRC that the shelters are "hurricane proof" and a "decent place" for schoolchildren, our investigation for *The Nation* found them to consist of shoddily constructed trailers fit neither for use as hurricane shelters nor schools. Purchased from a US company being sued over formaldehyde, the imported, prefab units also created few local jobs, and children using them as classrooms complain of chronic headaches, dizziness, and eye irritations.

Yet like the fable of the deluded emperor who paraded before the town showing off his fine linens even though he was naked, the dual-purpose hurricane shelter–classrooms were represented as a successful project in two CF videos, as well as in the foundation's annual and progress reports, and it remainded showcased on the CF website for a long time. The disproportionate emphasis the CF placed on the optics of the project reflects NGOs' increasing emphasis on public relations and publicity. And in a context in which the most well-resourced NGOs are increasingly shaping humanitarian coverage, the case of the CF shelters also underscores the importance of investigative journalism that seeks to probe beyond press releases.

Questionable Bidding

The CF awarded the contract for the shelters' construction to Clayton Homes, a company that is being sued over formaldehyde in trailers it sold FEMA after Hurricane Katrina. Clayton Homes is owned by Warren Buffett's Berkshire Hathaway. Buffett, who is one of the richest men in the world, is also listed as one of the "prominent private sector members" of the Clinton Global Initiative (CGI), a nonprofit group of which Clinton is president.

The CF claims it went through a bidding process before awarding the contract, but despite repeated requests, the CF did not provide any documentation, and various sources claimed there was no public bidding.

A "Failed Project"

Our interviews with structural engineers, documentary research, and on-the-ground reporting, together with laboratory air tests, revealed that the shelters fell far short of the CF's claims. When a leading structural engineer, Kit Miyamoto, assessed the CF hurricane shelters as part of our investigation, he concluded that they were not in fact "hurricane proof," adding that he had never seen trailers used as such. Indeed, FEMA considers mobile homes so unsafe in hurricanes that the agency unequivocally advises the public to evacuate them when hurricanes strike.

Furthermore, none of the schools were provided with running water and latrines, as was promised in the CF's original proposal to the IHRC—this in a country where cholera, a disease that children are particularly vulnerable to and that is preventable under proper sanitary conditions, has killed some 6,000 people since the epidemic first appeared in October 2010. The teachers we interviewed called the sanitary conditions "unsatisfactory" and added that the children suffered a lot because of the heat and often fell asleep in class.

The pressure-treated wooden trailers, which were used as classrooms by more than 1,000 schoolchildren in 2011, had no ventilation other than windows. After barely half a year in use, many of the trailers leaked and had mold, and one had visibly started to rot, with gaping holes appearing in the walls. By mid-June 2011, two of the four schools had prematurely ended classes for the summer because the temperature in the trailers frequently exceeded 100 degrees, and one had yet to open for lack of water and sanitation facilities. Schoolchildren said they regularly suffered from headaches and red and watery eyes, and that they often asked the teacher to give them painkillers and to take them outside. The news of chronic headaches had made it all the way to the mayor's office.

Laboratory air tests in 12 of the trailers found levels of formaldehyde in one trailer to be two and a half times the level at which the CDC warned FEMA trailer residents they could face adverse health effects such as asthma and chronic lung disease.[10] Randy Maddalena, a scientist specializing in indoor pollutants at Lawrence Berkeley National Laboratory, said this was "a very high level" of the carcinogen and warned that "it's of concern." Studies have shown that children are particularly vulnerable to its respiratory effects.

The scientist emphasized that Haiti's hot and humid climate could well be contributing to high emissions of the carcinogen in the classroom. Indeed, months before the launch of the CF trailer project, Haiti's climate was cited as a key problem with a trailer-industry proposal to ship FEMA trailers to Haiti for shelter, with the chair of the House Committee on Homeland Security saying that concerns over "adverse health consequences" could "blemish" the United States' humanitarian efforts.

When the mayor of Léogâne, Santos Alexis, heard that the new classrooms in his community had been built by a FEMA formaldehyde litigation defendant, he said he hoped they were not the same trailers that made people sick in the United States. "It would be humiliating to us, and we'll take this as a black thing," he said, drawing a parallel between his community in Haiti, the world's first black republic, and the disproportionate numbers of African Americans affected by the US government's mismanagement of the emergency response after Hurricane Katrina.

Lack of Consultation

The technical director of Léogâne's Department of Civil Protection, Philippe Joseph, ascribed the new shelters' "infernal" heat, humidity, and other problems to a lack of on-the-ground consultation, saying the decision to bring in the trailers was made from afar and "from the top down." A former UN official confirmed this, saying, "We all knew that that project was misconceived from the start, a classic example of aid designed from a distance with no understanding of ground-level realities or needs."

While the CF claims that it worked with local government to implement the shelter plan, Joseph disputes this, saying that the CF simply informed him that they were building four schools in his district. "To me this is not a consultation," the local official remarked. "To consult people you have to ask them what they need and how they think it could best be implemented."

He added that people desperate for employment and shelters watched as "the Clinton Foundation came in with all its specialists and equipment, but they didn't give any training," and that "if they use a local firm, they will not only create jobs in a community that has been decapitalized by the quake, but they will also take into account the environmental reality on the ground."

The CF said that "up to 300 local workers would be employed to build the schools." However, the Haitian firm subcontracted said there were only five to eight people hired on a very temporary basis. The CF declined to comment on what additional jobs were created.

Analysis

As one of the first IHRC-approved projects, Clinton's shelters raise worrying questions about procurement and project oversight in Haiti's reconstruction, and highlight a lack of local consultation. The CF hurricane shelter project underscores several general points of weakness in the IHRC structure, including the lack of crucial information about projects (such as the identity of the intended contractor) and the lack of monitoring on the progress on any projects. The project also reflected a growing problem of contracting non-Haitian firms, as well as an increasing trend in no-bid contracts given to US companies.[11]

This failed project also raises concerns about the role of the powerful NGO sources that are increasingly shaping humanitarian coverage.[12] Media scholar Natalie Fenton has faulted this phenomenon for increasingly shallow coverage of serious issues, and the dominance of more powerful NGOs in mediating the narrative that gets disseminated.[13]

Yet the coverage produced and promoted by the CF public relations apparatus was not just shallow. With an obliviousness to reality reminiscent of the emperor with no clothes, a CF webpage headline about the project dubbed the trailers an "emergency hurricane shelter project." In understanding this disconnect, we should consider Clinton's exceptional status in narratives about Haiti's reconstruction. The former US president wears multiple institutional hats in Haiti's recovery, from his position as the special envoy for Haiti at the UN to his seat as cochair at the IHRC—a matter of no small importance when one considers the patterns by which news media legitimize official sources, and the credibility that media accord to those who represent major institutions.[14] Yet the CF shelter project raises questions about the IHRC cochair's leadership in a recovery effort that was supposed to be guided by principles of sustainability and local participation.

* * *

Cash for What?

Haiti Grassroots Watch

———

"CASH FOR WORK" (CFW) IS a term that humanitarian agencies use to refer to short-term jobs meant for unskilled labor in poor countries.[15] A main objective is to get money circulating in order to "relaunch" an economy. The term appears to come from Food for Work (FFW), a kind of program that agencies have been using in Haiti and around the world for decades.

Cash has replaced food. As a March 2010 issue of *Humanitarian Exchange Magazine* explained, "Cash has rapidly become an effective part of the humanitarian toolbox."[16]

A CFW job is typically eight hours a day, five or six days a week, two or four weeks in length, with a daily salary of 200 gourdes (which is Haiti's minimum wage, about $5, except for export-assembly factories, where it's 150 gourdes, or about $3.75). Typical jobs include sweeping streets, cleaning drainage canals, removing rubble by hand, building latrines in camps, repairing rural dirt roads, and digging canals.

Origins of CFW

While "cash for work" is a relatively recent addition to humanitarian literature, the concept has been around for a long time. In fact, British economist John Maynard Keynes (1883–1946) might be considered the concept's father. One of Keynes's key insights was that government-sponsored job-creation programs can have a multiplier effect on demand, meaning that job creation would provide workers with more disposable income, thereby increasing effective demand and spurring employment in industries that depend on consumer spending. During the Great Depression, the Franklin D. Roosevelt administration put Keynes's theory to work. Two New Deal jobs programs—the Civilian Conservation Corps and the Work Projects Administration (WPA)—employed millions at a time.

According to journalist Robert Scheer, "Government regulation of the market economy arose during the New Deal out of a desire to save capitalism rather than destroy it."[17] FDR's New Deal offers a perfect example. With thousands of jobless men and women marching on Washington, and with labor organizations and socialist parties gaining strength, the jobs programs were as much about preventing revolution as they were about jump-starting the economy.

CFW Predecessors in Haiti

Those two goals have also been behind the various jobs programs in Haiti throughout the years. François "Papa Doc" Duvalier had a program of *woy-woy*, or temporary "make-work" jobs administered through his Ministry of Public Works. Duvalier used *woy-woy* jobs—and terror—to help prevent any kind of uprising.

Especially during periods of instability, such as the years immediately following Duvalier's ouster and the 1991 coup d'état against President Jean-Bertrand Aristide, projects funded by the US Agency for International Development (USAID) included massive jobs programs. However, studies have shown that the programs did little good.[18] USAID jobs programs "actively strengthened anti-democratic forces and weakened grassroots, democratic organizations," according to one study, which noted that the programs pulled peasants away from food production, created new, "unsustainable" habits of consumption, hindered "the volunteerism and community spirit necessary for development," and "generate[d] dependency."[19]

Is CFW Working Now?

Haiti Grassroots Watch found that most workers were happy to have a CFW job. But journalists working in the cities of Léogâne, Perèy, and Port-au-Prince found examples of corruption and mismanagement:

- A work crew was managed by a motorcycle-taxi driver who was the cousin of the "peasant leader," and the crew had at least one under-age worker.
- In at least three places, workers reported having to pay a "finder's fee" (that is, a kickback) in exchange for getting or keeping a job.
- Work crews frequently had "*zombi* employees," meaning they had fewer workers than they were supposed to, and they were often seen either not working and/or often knocking off work early.
- An incumbent candidate from the ruling Initè political party con-trolled the hiring of CFW workers for many crews.

But Haiti Grassroots Watch's *other* findings—related to the effects of CFW—are more worrying than these examples of corruption. These ef-fects, perhaps not intended, include the undermining of the concept of work and citizens' belief in government.

Undermining the Concept of "Work"
CFW programs are infamously under- and even unproductive. One foreign CFW coordinator called them "cash for standing around and doing nothing." This phenomenon is not unique to Haiti. In the United States, for example, even though the WPA produced lasting structures and employed hundreds of writers and artists, it had nicknames like We Piddle Around and the Whistle, Piss, and Argue gang because its road crews were not always productive.

Haitian economists and even some CFW implementers are worried about the long-term effects of CFW programs. "I worry that we're creating maybe a bad work ethic, because I think that you see a lot of cash-for-work teams all over the city and the country, and if you watch, those work teams aren't necessarily working," said Deb Ingersoll, CFW coordinator for the American Refugee Committee. "I worry that we're providing . . . a visual association of working with not necessarily working hard."

Haitian economist Camille Chalmers agreed. "They know that they are earning money doing something that is not really work. They are very aware of this. You see it clearly when you see people working on the rubble piles. They pick up one block or rock at a time. . . . It creates a kind of deformation in people's heads about what work should be," he said.

Undermining Government Legitimacy
In an August 2010 report on the first three months of the relief, experts al-ready noted that CFW programs, whose workers often wear T-shirts sport-ing NGO logos, might be undermining "government legitimacy."[20]

In interviews in the capital and the countryside, Haiti Grassroots Watch found a growing disregard for the government (although, to be fair, this disregard predates the earthquake), along with a growing expectation that people's basic needs can and should be met by foreign NGOs rather than the government.

"Our future lies with NGOs! We can't count on the government," said Romel François, a CFW manager at the Terrain Acra camp in the capital, home to 5,000 families. "If it were for the government, we would be dead already."

Wilson Pierre, head of the Perèy Peasant Association, which is running a 600-job program for Mercy Corps, expressed similar sentiments. "Whatever program that comes our way, we'll do it," he said. "If it's work, and we get paid, we'll do it." He added, "I think these jobs should be permanent."

These attitudes are "very concerning," Chalmers noted. "This system of 'humanitarian economy' or 'emergency economy' . . . is locking the country into a 'humanitarian approach' and a dependency on aid. There is a growing disconnect between what people think they can do as citizens, because more and more roles are being played by NGOs and international actors in all domains. . . . It also legitimizes the presence of international actors." And that might be a sought-after result, according to Chalmers.

"Look at the Collier report," he said.

Chalmers was referring to *Haiti: From Natural Catastrophe to Economic Security*, written for the UN by British economist Paul Collier in 2009. The report lays out an economic plan that the Haitian government and UN agencies appear to have used as the blueprint for post-earthquake Haiti. Collier recommends that NGOs and the private sector provide basic health and education services, since "scaling up public provision is not a viable solution: the problems of the public sector are deep-seated and it is not realistic to expect that they can be addressed quickly."[21]

A more recent paper by the RAND Corporation, a frequent US State Department contractor, makes similar recommendations, calling for a state that improves security and an atmosphere conducive to investment, but that regulates, rather than delivers, health and education services.[22]

Did CFW Achieve Its Own Objectives?

Relaunching the Economy

One stated objective of CFW programs is to relaunch the economy by getting people working for cash, which is then spent on necessities. But whose economy is being relaunched?

Although Haiti Grassroots Watch cannot determine what role CFW programs have played in getting the economy moving, one thing is certain: sidewalks and streets in the capital are crammed with vendors hawking mostly imported goods. On its website, USAID appears to define this kind of economic activity—selling castoff shoes and imported underwear—as a "success," but not all economists agree.

"The main impact of CFW is on the circulation of money," Haitian economist Gerald Chéry said. Although giving people revenues creates demand, he said, the question needs to be asked: demand for what?

"We need the money to circulate in Haiti, not leave Haiti to go to another country," Chéry said. "The money needs to stay in Haiti so that it will create work. You don't want to pay someone and the person then buys, but another country, not Haiti, benefits."

And yet that is exactly what is happening in Haiti today. Studies by Oxfam and others indicate that CFW beneficiaries spend about half their CFW salaries on food or goods to resell in the street, with the rest spent mostly on rent, school fees, paying off debts, and other expenses.[23]

If half of CFW money is spent on imported food and goods, the ones getting the boost in this recession-battered world economy are outside Haitian borders. Haiti buys more than half of its food from overseas, so a great deal of CFW cash is going to the country's trading partners, the largest of which is the United States. In 2008 Haiti bought almost $1 billion in goods from its northern neighbor; $325 million was spent on food.

Employing Displaced People Living Outside the Capital

One of the problems with earlier FFW programs in Haiti was that agricultural production suffered because peasants left their plots to work on a crew. In 2010 Haiti Grassroots Watch discovered the same problem, at least in some places.

While journalists did note earthquake refugees in work crews at camps in Port-au-Prince, Léogâne, and Petit-Goâve, they found few of them outside those cities. In fact, by about March 11, 2010, almost half of the refugees who fled the capital after January 12, 2010, were back in Port-au-Prince.[24] But NGOs had funding for CFW in the countryside and proceeded to hire peasants to do "repairs" on roads with picks and hoes that will last through about two rains.

In Maniche, in southern Haiti, agronomist Philippe Céloi supervised the six-month Catholic Relief Services FFW program in which peasants built contours on hillsides and performed other tasks related to managing watersheds. Céloi admitted that his workers ought to have been in the fields.

"After six months there will be benefits—not only have the workers gotten a salary, but the community also benefits," Céloi said. But there was a downside.

"Yes, there are disadvantages also," Céloi said. "For example, these people are not doing the planting they ought to be doing. . . . They aren't planting potatoes or manioc or sorghum, so when this program ends, there is going to be a problem because people won't be able to find real food to eat."

Political Stability

While all CFW programs promote political stability as one of their objectives, only one CFW document—a USAID audit that Haiti Grassroots Watch obtained—spells it out.

The USAID Office of Transition Initiatives (OTI), which spent more than $20 million on CFW programs between January 12 and June 30, 2010, via two subcontractors—Chemonics and Development Alternatives—had as one of its primary goals to "support the Government of Haiti, promote stability, and decrease chances of unrest."[25]

The audit criticized USAID's Haiti office for the slow pace of rubble removal. Robert Jenkins, acting director of USAID-Haiti, wrote:

> OTI's strategic objective in Haiti was and is to support stabilization in a changing and volatile environment. The initial means (tactics) to this end were numbers of workers and rubble removal. The underlying assumptions in this regard were: (1) Workers (particularly young males) were less likely to resort to violence if employed; (2) Infusions of ready cash in the poorest neighborhoods would likely have a salutary effect; (3) Rubble removal, again in the poorest neighborhoods, was highly symbolic because it offered hope of return to some form of normalcy.[26]

Jenkins also noted that the programs were "clearly branded as a Government of Haiti initiative," meaning that, in an election year, the programs lent support to the incumbent party and its candidates.

It Looks Like CFW *Is* Working . . .

If CFW programs in Haiti have various negative effects, do they "prevent revolution" and "save capitalism" in the long run, as Scheer noted when writing about New Deal programs?

Certainly the country has not seen the kinds of major demonstrations like the ones that took place in Mexico after an earthquake in 1985.

Within two weeks of that catastrophe, thousands marched in the streets, demanding decent housing. But not in Haiti.

Perhaps the "stabilization" effect is one reason the Haitian government is asking agencies and NGOs to continue and even augment their programs.

* * *

Teleco, Haiti's State Phone Company, Finally Privatized

Hervé Jean Michel

IN MAY 2010 THE HAITIAN government sold a 60% share of Haiti's national telephone company, Teleco, to Viettel, a subsidiary of the Vietnamese army, based in Hanoi.[27] Teleco now no longer belongs to the Haitian people. The new private company that owns all of Haiti's land lines will be called Natcom.

Teleco was the crown jewel of Haiti's state enterprises, but was sold for the fire-sale price of $59 million.

On April 29, 2010, Viettel directors were in Port-au-Prince, where the deal, reached days before the January 12 earthquake, was consummated. Representing the Haitian government at the signing ceremony were officials like Yves Bastien of the Council for the Modernization of Public Enterprises (CMEP); Charles Castel, the governor of Haiti's Central Bank (BRH); and Michel Présumé, Teleco's director.

"Teleco sustained permanent attacks, its network was sabotaged on several occasions, and the situation was not sustainable," Castel said after signing away the company. (In past years, Teleco union leaders have charged that President René Préval's government has deliberately undermined efforts to modernize equipment and improve service in the company to force its privatization.)

Castel also said that the Haitian government had spent $16.875 million (675 million gourdes) to make improvements to Teleco in order to sell it. If this investment is calculated into the deal, it means the Préval government sold Teleco—which used to bring in many dozens of millions of dollars in revenues annually—for a mere $42.125 million.

"Teleco had over 5,000 employees who weren't doing anything," said Présumé. "Many of them spent more time at radio stations than at their workplace." He was referring to the regular interviews Teleco workers and unionists gave about the company's mismanagement and the pending privatization.

Nguyen Khac Chung, a leading Viettel official, said during the signing ceremony that he wanted to make Natcom "the best telephone company in the region." He said that all current Teleco employees will be kept in their jobs if they prove able to assume their new responsibilities. He added that Viettel has provided leadership in other countries such as Cambodia and Laos, Vietnam's neighbors.

"We are eager to participate in the rebuilding of [Haiti] with reconstruction of a new infrastructure and distribution of telecommunications services," said Nguyen Manh Hung, Viettel's deputy director.

Teleco's privatization is the culmination of a long process that began in 1996, when Préval, in his first administration, legalized the privatization of public enterprises. Two other key state enterprises, the Minoterie, Haiti's flour mill, and Ciment d'Haiti, the state cement company, were privatized in 1997 and soon after closed their doors.

Teleco was always a strategically key state enterprise. During the 1991–1994 coup d'état against former President Jean-Bertrand Aristide, millions of dollars in Teleco revenues in large part financed his government in exile.

Notes

1. Mark Schuller, "Haiti Is Finished!' Haiti's End of History Meets the Ends of Capitalism," in *Capitalizing on Catastrophe: Neoliberal Strategies in Disaster Reconstruction,* ed. Nandini Gunewardena and Mark Schuller (Lanham, MD: Alta Mira Press, 2008), 20.

2. Mark Schuller, "Deconstructing the Disaster After the Disaster: Conceptualizing Disaster Capitalism," in Gunewardena and Schuller, *Capitalizing on Catastrophe.*

3. Fully 93% of USAID funds go back to the United States. See Oxfam America, *Smart Development: Why US Foreign Aid Demands Major Reform* (Boston: Oxfam America, 2008).

4. Adapted from an article originally published in *Haïti Liberté* 4, no. 48 (June 15–21, 2011).

5. From US Embassy, Port-au-Prince, to various recipients, "TFHA01: EMBASSY PORT AU PRINCE EARTHQUAKE SITREP as of 1800" (no. 10 PORTAUPRINCE110), February 1, 2010.

6. Jeremy Schwartz, "Austinite Tapped to Lead Haiti Recovery Comes Home," April 18, 2010.

7. Ben Fox, "Lawsuit Opens Window Onto Ex-US Envoy's Role as Rainmaker for American Contractor," January 14, 2011.

8. Herb Gould, "Bulls' Carlos Boozer Allegedly Ripped Off for $1 Million," March 22, 2011.

9. Haiti Relief and Reconstruction Watch (blog), "Haitian Companies Still Sidelined From Reconstruction Contracts," April 19, 2011, cepr.net.

10. Isabel Macdonald and Isabeau Doucet, "The Shelters That Clinton Built," *The Nation,* July 11, 2011.

11. Mark Weisbrot, "Haiti and the International Aid Scam," *The Guardian* (UK), April 22, 2011. Cf. Martha Mendoza, "Would-be Haitian Contractors Miss Out on Aid," Associated Press, December 12, 2010.

12. Simon Cottle and David Nolan, "Global Humanitarianism and the Changing Aid-Media Field: Everyone Was Dying for Footage," *Journalism Studies* 8, no. 6 (2007): 862–78; Natalie Fenton, "NGOs, New Media, and the Mainstream News: News From Everywhere," in *New Journalism, Old News: Journalism and Democracy in the Digital Age,* ed. Natalie Fenton (London: Sage, 2010), 153–68.

13. Fenton, "NGOs, New Media, and the Mainstream News."

14. Gaye Tuchman, *Making News: A Study in the Construction of Reality* (New York: Free Press, 1978), 83; Mark Fishman, *Manufacturing the News* (Austin: University of Texas Press, 1979): 92–93.

15. This article is excerpted and adapted from reports that were published at http://www.haitigrassrootswatch.org on November 9, 2010, and July 18, 2011.

16. Nicolas Lamade, Dr. Hannelore Börgel, and Paul Harvey, "Cash for Work: Lessons from Northern Afghanistan," *Humanitarian Exchange Magazine,* no. 46 (March 2010), http://www.odihpn.org/report.asp?id=3110.

17. Robert Scheer, "'The Great American Stickup': Is Bush Really to Blame for the Economy?" *Huffington Post,* September 15, 2010, http://www.huffington post.com/robert-scheer/the-great-american-sticku_1_b_715952.html

18. See, for example, Laurie Richardson, *Feeding Dependency, Starving Democracy: USAID Policies in Haiti* (Grassroots International) 1997, http://www.grass rootsonline.org; and Lisa McGowan, *Democracy Undermined, Economic Justice Denied: Structural Adjustment and the Aid Juggernaut in Haiti* (Development Gap for Alternative Policies, January 1997).

19. Richardson, *Feeding Dependency, Starving Democracy,* 23.

20. François Grünewald, with Andrea Binder and Yvio Georges, *Interagency Realtime Evaluation in Haiti: 3 Months After the Earthquake,* Global Public Policy Institute and Groupe URD, August 31, 2010, 12, http://reliefweb.int/node/368079.

21. Paul Collier, *Haiti: From Natural Catastrophe to Economic Security: A Report to the Secretary-General of the United Nations,* 2009, 11, http://www.focal.ca/pdf/haiticollier.pdf.

22. Keith Crane, James Dobbins, Laurel E. Miller, Charles P. Ries, Christopher S. Chivvis, Marla C. Haims, Marco Overhaus, Heather Lee Schwartz, and Elizabeth Wilke, *Building a More Resilient Haitian State* (RAND Corporation, 2010), 161.

23. Oxfam, "Cash for Work Phase 1—February to March 2010," a Power-Point presentation made to the Early Recovery UN Cluster. See also Lutheran World Service, "Cash for Work Activities—M & E Results, May–August 2010," PowerPoint presentation made to the Early Recovery Cluster.

24. Linus Bengtsson, Xin Lu, Richard Garfield, Anna Thorson, and Johan von Schreeb, *Internal Population Displacement in Haiti—Preliminary Analyses of Movement Patterns of Digicel Mobile Phones: 1 January to 11 March 2010,* Karolinska Institutet and Columbia University, May 14, 2010, 7.

25. USAID Office of the Inspector General, *Audit of USAID's Cash-for-Work Activities in Haiti,* Audit Report no. 1-521-10-009-P, September 24, 2010, 1, http://reliefweb.int/node/369300.

26. Ibid., 18.

27. Adapted from an article originally published in *Haïti Liberté* 3, no. 42 (May 5–11, 2010).

Part 2

On-the-Ground Realities
Displacement and Its Discontents

5

Moun Andeyò
Persistent Legacies of Exclusion

*As noted in the Introduction and highlighted in several of the essays so far, the earthquake did not magically transform Haiti, despite Clinton's cheerful slogan of "building back better." By the same token, neither did Haiti's social ills begin on January 12, 2010. Social exclusion—*moun andeyò*—has been woven into Haiti's social fabric since before its independence in 1804. "Big" whites, the landed gentry, competed with the "small" whites and laboring and middle classes. Both groups of whites allied against the* milat *(mixed-race) and the* afranchi *(freedmen), many of whom actually owned slaves. The* milat *in turn excluded the slaves, who were distinguished by their status as "Creole"—island-born and familiar with European culture and language—or* bossale, *from Africa. Officially, prerevolutionary Saint-Domingue (the name before independence) recognized 33 racial or color groups, based on gradations of European or African ancestry tracing back seven generations.*

Independence leader Jean-Jacques Dessalines' constitution officially did away with these racial divisions, claiming Haiti as a "black" country. Writing a century later, repudiating the prevailing "scientific" racism at the time, Haitian intellectual Anténor Firmin cited Victor Hugo: tout les hommes sont l'homme *(all men are men, translated into Haitian Creole using the gender-neutral "people,"* tout moun se moun, *a slogan during the 1990 elections that brought Aristide to power).*

Despite these egalitarian sentiments, Haitian society remained one of the world's most unequal in its two centuries of independence. This is exemplified in education and language: from the 1915 US occupation until the 1987

95

Constitution—a project arising from the democracy movement that pushed out Duvalier—French remained the only official language, despite the fact that only the educated elites and middle classes—10%—can understand French. Economically, Haiti topped the list as the most unequal in the hemisphere in 2006, surpassing even Brazil. Haiti has the most millionaires per capita, while 80% of the population survives on the equivalent of $2 per day. Half of the population ekes out a living on a dollar per day.

As Haitian scholar Gérard Barthelemy[1] and others have pointed out, the term andeyò *literally means "outside." Before the massive rural exodus described in Chapter 1 of this volume, Haiti's traditional urban dwellers, educated French speakers, disparagingly refer to the rest of the country as* andeyò, *and its residents,* moun andeyò: *"outsiders." Peasants have long been excluded from Haitian society, as defined by the Republic of Port-au-Prince, as it has become called. True, the earthquake struck close to the capital, destroying the country's nerve center. Had it not been for policies since the 1915 US occupation, and increasingly so since the application of neoliberalism, the earthquake wouldn't have so crippled the nation. Many people died simply because they had to be in Port-au-Prince to get a birth certificate or ID card.*

The divisions between the Republic of Port-au-Prince and andeyò *only increased after the earthquake. There was an opportunity to "build back better" by supporting the 600,000 people who fled the capital in the days following the earthquake—and their peasant families who saved their lives. The response ignoring Haiti's peasants only deepened the divide, making peasants even worse off and triggering a return to Port-au-Prince of an even greater scale. Chenet Jean-Baptiste, longtime peasant association leader, offers an analysis of these exclusions and missed opportunities for Haitian peasants. Other people continue to be cast outside following the earthquake. As media activist Jane Regan writes, the housing plan passed by the IHRC fails to make any provisions for the majority of the Port-au-Prince population who were renters before the quake. On top of this exclusion, the article originally published after the anniversary stories died down and journalists left decried the slow pace of housing reconstruction.*

This is a situation of abse sou klou, *an abscess on an open wound, a bad situation worsening since the earthquake. This is the title of Haitian professor and creative writer Evelyne Trouillot's discussion of the continued exclusions within Haiti's education system. In addition, the majority are without health care, a situation only worsened in the long term following NGO actions. Radical syndicalist union Batay Ouvriye published a declaration on the heels of the earthquake, offering a scathing critique of the nexus of imperialism, local bourgeoisie, and a state created against the interests of workers, landless peasants, and* timachann—*street merchants. Batay Ouvriye calls for a creation of a state in the interests of the masses. Together, the chapter details how the multiple forms of exclusion have been strengthened by the international response, throwing the gauntlet down for envisioning alternatives that promote inclusion.*

* * *

Haiti's Earthquake
A Further Insult to Peasants' Lives

Chenet Jean-Baptiste

THE JANUARY 12, 2010, EARTHQUAKE was one of the biggest catastrophes that the world has ever seen when we look at how many people died or were injured, and the damage and material losses that occurred.[2] The mobilization all around the world to join forces with the Haitian people went in all directions: imposing foreign military forces, particularly those of the United States, occupied the land right after January 12 to bring humanitarian aid. A bunch of NGOs invaded the country (see Chapter 3, this volume). International conferences were held here, there, and everywhere to discuss the best plan to help reconstruct Haiti. The ensuing debate about the earthquake and its consequences focused on three main areas: life in Port-au-Prince, the causes of the earthquake, and the situation of victims and the responsibilities of the state.

Two fundamental questions are not discussed too often: what was the importance and the cost of solidarity that Haiti's peasantry demonstrated after January 12? What place should Haiti's rural-peasant zone have in today's reconstruction bonanza? It is not really noteworthy that these questions are never asked, because in the economic and social life of peasants, as the Creole proverb goes, *bourik travay pou chwal galonnen* (the donkey works so that the horse can run free). This appears normal in the political sphere, because many have been left empty-handed throughout Haiti's history.

Peasants' Humanitarian Crisis Before January 12, 2010

It seems that many international organizations or NGOs only discovered the country's humanitarian catastrophe after January 12, 2010. It is true that the earthquake aggravated the population's deplorable living conditions, certainly in Port-au-Prince. But the rural environment has suffered the worst consequences of the humanitarian crisis established long ago. To understand the roots of this situation, we need to go back into Haiti's past. Specifically one needs to look at the political and economic changes that the US occupation brought about for the peasantry during the period of 1915–1934. During this period, the occupying forces destroyed the regional economy, which helped establish a host of big cities. In 1891, by itself, Jeremie exported 84% of the cocoa production, Gonaïves and St. Marc 80% of the cotton. Another example: During the 1890–1891 fiscal year, the provincial towns provided more than 70% of the funds collected by customs. This regional dynamic increased the conflict and struggles that existed throughout the nineteenth century between different branches of Haiti's oligarchy.

The 1915 US occupation, however, established a system of centralization that would soon dissolve the agricultural economy. They forced peasants off the land they occupied and worked to the benefit of large US companies. To accompany this logic of economic centralization, they also established a system of political and administrative centralization in which all services became concentrated in the capital of Port-au-Prince. This forced peasants into poor living conditions, so they began migrating to Port-au-Prince and other cities, not to mention neighboring countries (particularly the Dominican Republic).

In the 1980s, USAID decided to accelerate this strategy to encourage a massive displacement of peasants to the cities (see Dupuy, Chapter 1, this volume). The biggest decision adopted was the 1981–1983 massacre of Haitian pigs, which were the pillars of the peasant economy. The Inter-American Institute for Cooperation on Agriculture (IICA) estimated the loss suffered by Haitian peasants at $500 million. But peasants only received $9.3 million in compensation (in other words, less than 2% of the losses suffered). After the September 30, 1991, coup d'état, the peasant milieu would suffer an unrivaled humanitarian crisis during the three-year embargo, receiving no aid or support. On the contrary, when the constitutional government of Jean-Bertrand Aristide returned to power in 1994, IFIs imposed a structural adjustment program that made their lives more abysmal. In 1995 the government removed all the tariffs from almost every agricultural produce. Only corn remained, with a 15% tariff (while the tariff on rice is the lowest anywhere in the region, at 3%). During this period, in least developed countries like Haiti, the mean import tariffs were 17.9%.

In these conditions, peasants came to suffer from two unfortunate problems: produce prices would never cease to diminish because the country was invaded by heavily subsidized foreign produce, and agricultural production bottomed out while food insecurity has never stopped getting worse. Despite these deplorable living conditions, peasants sprang into action.

January 12, 2010: Peasants' Solidarity Was Unlimited

After the earthquake struck, some 500,000 people left Port-au-Prince to seek refuge in the provincial cities. They departed for the peasant areas with empty hands, without any money or state or NGO aid. The peasants welcomed all these people, gave them places to sleep, food, and all kinds of aid. Many peasants were forced to consume a good portion of their seed reserves, along with the minimum that they had in savings. These needs increased after the great bonds of solidarity the peasants created with victims. There has been no evaluation of the amount of money, sacrifice, and infinite solidarity that the peasants paid out. There is no serious program announced to compensate the peasants for their expenses. There was no effort to honor or even recognize the importance of the peasants' solidarity, while NGOs and international institutions are struggling for visibility for their few small and disarticulated actions.

Meanwhile, more trouble was in store for the peasants. Monsanto profited from Haiti's new condition of vulnerability created by the earthquake to distribute genetically modified organism (GMO) seeds to peasants. Minister of Agriculture Joanas Gué said Monsanto did not donate GMO seeds, but rather hybrid seeds and vegetable seeds. But we know that the Haitian government has neither the means nor a good strategy to evaluate the seeds that come into the country. What's more, why did Monsanto choose to give this self-named "gift" or "aid" in secret? Only production with artisanal or heirloom seeds can help Haiti's peasant agriculture survive. January 12, 2010, shouldn't have opened the door to completely do away with this agricultural production.

The problem isn't only the lack of recognition for peasants' solidarity and the lack of any government program put in place to benefit them. In all the talk of reconstruction or "re-foundation" (see Deshommes, Conclusion), there has yet to be any approach that clearly shows any interest in the peasantry. Decisions that have been announced have not offered answers to some very important questions:

- How will peasants be able to gain access to better land to work?
- What kind of support will peasants find to improve and protect agricultural production?
- What minimum social services will be put in place to improve peasants' living conditions (such as education, housing, roads, health care, safe drinking water)?
- How will peasants participate in the necessary debates for the "refoundation" or reconstruction of the country?

Haiti isn't Port-au-Prince. The majority of the population lives in a rural and peasant setting. January 12, 2010, added insult to injury for peasants' lives. January 12, 2010, gave more rope for people to be dragged into the Republic of Port-au-Prince. Only the struggle of the peasants' movement can hope to establish a meaningful alternative.

* * *

Resettlement Plan Excludes Almost 200,000 Families

Jane Regan

———

ONE YEAR AND ONE MONTH after Haiti's horrendous earthquake, the world's eyes are focused elsewhere.[3] Aside from a few updates on ex-dictator Jean-Claude Duvalier, Haiti has fallen from the headlines. Gone are the foreign reporters and news crews pumping out anniversary stories.

Long-forgotten are the one-year reports from UN agencies, NGOs, and watchdog groups, full of self-congratulations or hand-wringing over the lack of progress on Haiti's reconstruction.

But there has been a kind of progress.

Haitian authorities—or, to be more precise, those who have authority in Haiti, but who are not necessarily Haitian—actually do have a plan for Haiti's homeless. The ambitious 30-page "Neighborhood Return and Housing Reconstruction Framework (version 3)," obtained January 2011 by Haiti Grassroots Watch, outlines plans to rebuild neighborhoods with better zoning and better services, help homeowners rebuild safer homes, or relocate homeowners to new homes in less precarious locations.

However, the framework leaves out Haiti's largest group of earthquake victims: the poorest of the poor, the renters. "With a few exceptions, the reconstruction is not going to make people homeowners who were not homeowners before," Priscilla Phelps, senior advisor for Housing and Neighborhoods for the Interim Haiti Recovery Commission (IHRC), told Inter Press Service (IPS) and Haiti Grassroots Watch in January.

That means 192,154 families—more than half of the 1.3 million IDPs tallied last fall—will be left out in the cold. Or, in the case of Haiti, out in the sun, the rain, and the dust. According to the framework, "Return and reconstruction will not change the tenancy status of earthquake-affected households: the goal is to restore owners and renters to an equivalent status as before the earthquake, but in safer conditions." For home- and land-owners, things are moving forward, albeit very slowly.

Humanitarian agencies have over $100 million to build 111,240 "transitional shelters" or "T-Shelters"—small huts, usually 18 square meters. As of February 1, 2011, only about 43,100 had been built, due to the rubble choking poor neighborhoods and Haiti's convoluted land ownership situation. (Most donors want to be sure on land titles before building a T-Shelter.) Agencies and construction firms also have at least $174 million pledged of the $350 million needed—in 2011 alone—for repairing or rebuilding homes and neighborhoods. As of February 1, of the approximately 193,000 homes needing to be repaired or rebuilt, only 2,547 had been repaired and 1,880 rebuilt.

But for the hundreds of thousands of former renters living hunched under tents in camps with few or no services, with an average of 372 residents per latrine, there is no shelter—transitional or permanent—on the horizon. Because they are supposed to rent.

Reyneld Sanon, of the Housing Reflection and Action Force coalition (Fòs Refleksyon ak Aksyon sou Koze Kay [FRAKKA]), which is mobilizing with unions and other groups on the housing issue, is outraged. "This is pure and simple exclusion. You could even call this an official policy of apartheid," Sanon told IPS.

In addition to losing all their belongings, many of Haiti's displaced also lost jobs, as well as the huge sums they had paid out for school tuitions and rent prior to the earthquake. In Haiti, one rents six, 12, and even 24 months at a time. Sanon noted that it will take years for families to save that up again.

"These people are factory workers, day laborers. Many are former peasants forced into the city because their land has given out, or because they can't make ends meet. They are the eternal victims of an economic system that protects big landowners and rich capitalists," said Sanon.

A Typical Example of "Reconstruction"

The way the housing issue is being handled offers a typical example of Haiti's "reconstruction." The framework "is intended to signal what the approach is going to be," according to the IHRC's Phelps, who likely helped author the plan and who recently cowrote a report called "Safer Homes, Stronger Communities: A Handbook for Reconstructing After Natural Disasters" for the World Bank.

But the document has never been approved by the government of Haiti. Not by the parliament, not by President René Préval, and not the Inter-Ministry Commission on Housing, which groups together five ministers. Nor has the document ever been held up to public scrutiny or discussed at fora where local urban planners, construction firms, or other stakeholders—like FRAKKA and the homeless people themselves—could perhaps make their opinions known.

Nevertheless, the framework is more than what the "approach is going be." De facto, it is the plan. Because NGOs are moving forward, according to Jean-Christophe Adrian of UN-HABITAT, which chairs the "Shelter Cluster" of the 200 or so NGOs working on the housing issue. "The document represents the consensus," Adrian explained.

Phelps notes that the Inter-Ministry Commission on Housing has "seen it and made remarks," but they have never openly approved or disapproved of it, nor has it been made public. In fact, national government officials have only gone public on one housing project—a plan for 3,000 to 4,000 apartments in the Fort National neighborhood overlooking Haiti's National Palace. "It's a project of public housing high-rises, respecting building norms for earthquake zones, which will house many hundreds of families," Jacques Gabriel, minister of public works, told Agence France Presse in January 2011.[4] But when Minister of Social Affairs Gérald Germain and his bodyguards showed up to place the cornerstone on January 12, they were chased away by angry, homeless protestors. "We want explanations!" a man who identified himself as Leguenson told AlterPresse.[5]

Haiti's homeless are not the only ones who want explanations. According to Phelps, the project does not yet have IHRC approval. Nevertheless, not unlike the lack of coordination and communication sometimes apparent in other sectors, the first stone for the Fort National project was going to be placed even before it received the IHRC's green light.

Or perhaps the Haitian government has decided to skip the IHRC? But according to a decree, it is "responsible for continuously developing and refining development plans for Haiti." "There are still a lot of questions that have to be worked out," Phelps explained. "The proposal they have made is one that needs some vetting. It's quite expensive." Shelter Cluster authorities are also skeptical. "Our experience shows us that, in all countries, these types of projects end up benefiting the middle classes. They don't benefit the poorest people," Adrian said.

With authorities bickering, with no high-rise in sight, and with construction and reconstruction only planned for the homeowners, 13 months later, Haiti's poorest earthquake victims are left exactly where they were on January 13, 2010—in tents and under tarps, living in subhuman conditions, under constant threat of eviction, facing a depleted housing stock with no savings.

* * *

Abse Sou Klou
Reconstructing Exclusion

Evelyne Trouillot

———

THERE IS AN EXPRESSION IN HAITIAN Creole that states, *abse sou klou.* An already difficult situation rendered unbearable. Oil on fire. The poor became even poorer, more vulnerable. The middle classes stretched a bit more thin, the country more dependent, its infrastructures more precarious than before. *Abse sou klou,* injustice and inequalities have become even more flagrant after January 12, 2010.

For at least 48 hours after the earthquake, Haitians were alone, not because the world did not care but because it was rather difficult to arrive in Haiti. During these two days and frightful nights, many Haitians acted as heroes to save their fellow countrymen. Many lives were saved by perfect strangers; many children taken to their families or somewhere safe by Haitians helping Haitians. Haitian people and our Caribbean neighbors were being excluded, written out of the story. In Haiti, the foreign press was from the start focused on the arrival of international aid and paid little or no attention to the actions of Haitians themselves. Their reporting on international aid managed to minimize the contribution of the Dominican Republic and other Latin American countries. They simply ignored the

Cuban contribution, which was very important, since Cuban doctors were already in place and knew Haitian medical working conditions. When the major foreign press talked about the Haitian population, most of them focused on the images of looting and violence, which described some minor incidents that do not at all characterize the general attitude of Haitians during this tragedy.

The rebuilding of the Haitian education and health-care systems after the January 12, 2010, earthquake highlights continuing legacies of social exclusion in the country—exclusions that the earthquake might have provided an opportunity to change. Instead, however, the post-earthquake exclusion was worse than the status quo ante. In the case of education, only a minority of Haitian children could go to school half a century ago. Most of them were elite, and their schooling was for the most part successful. The teachers were well-trained, and private and public schools in Haiti had the same level of performance. Some public schools were even achieving a higher level of success than their private counterparts, and many great Haitian intellectuals went through the public school system.

When social changes and new political ideas brought more children to school, the school system did not take proper measures to adjust. The children coming from a monolingual Creole background did not know a word of French and their parents were illiterate and could not help with homework. But the school system continued just like it had before. Despite numerous reforms through the years, the system generates mostly failures, and only a small percentage of students make it through the official exams after 12 years of schooling. Furthermore, because the state lacks resources, most schools are privately owned. The private schools reflect a vast diversity, ranging from a few very good, very expensive schools for which entry is often based on social status, and an immense majority of schools in which the teachers lack training and do not master the content to be taught, in addition to not speaking French properly.

Therefore, the school system not only reflects but maintains the inequality and injustice of society. To speak in the terms of French social theorist Pierre Bourdieu, the children from the *bidonville* (shantytown) do not even get near the "dominant cultural values" because the teachers themselves do not possess them well. Those youngsters are doomed from the start. After the earthquake, since most school buildings were affected in Port-au-Prince and three other cities, all schools were closed. Some Haitians thought it would be the opportunity to establish a school system that would function equally for all Haitians, a system that would allow the little girl living in a rural community to have access to the same opportunities and knowledge, to feel as much part of the nation, as the little girl from a well-to-do urban family.

What happened? Several factors converged to prevent that change. After the earthquake, some members of the upper class started to complain that their children were not going to school fast enough, and the Ministry of Education wanted to satisfy their demands. So the international organizations and experts involved in decision making rushed to open the schools before they could improve the system as they had promised. After all, it would be perceived as an accomplishment that would make everybody look good. And also in Haiti the school year generates other parallel economic activities. So in April, schools reopened. The minister of education chose a private Catholic school for girls, L'École du Sacré-Coeur, to make an opening statement on Easter weekend. Most public schools were not yet ready to reopen; some were used as sites for the displaced people.

Lycée Toussaint Louverture, a public high school created more than a century ago, remained a center for refugees until November 2010. The numerous small private schools attended by the majority of Haitian children who were the most affected received the least support from the state. Even two years later, many schools remain closed. There are plans to build new schools, and probably they will be built, but when? No one knows. How will they help improve the system? No one knows.

These are the conditions in which, as promised by the Ministry of Education, and with the blessing of the international community, some children went back to school in April 2011. Pictures were taken, reports were written, and speeches were made. The children of street vendors, the service people, the small shopkeepers, the peasants were not so lucky. But that was not information worth sharing. It would have taken a great deal of courage, and a good vision of the future, to delay the reopening of school, to postpone it until the next academic school year in September and to work diligently to give all or most families the possibility to send their children to school.

It would have taken a sense of purpose, an identification of priorities to make the decision that it was better for the society as a whole to start school together after such a disaster. Instead, the decision to restart school in the prevailing conditions reinforced inequalities, and in that sense the consequences of the January 2010 earthquake were more human-made than natural. The Haitian government and its international partners chose the easiest way.

Health Care for the Few

What happened to the medical system is perhaps more catastrophic. Before the earthquake, Haiti had very few public hospitals and some private hospitals and clinics. A few of them were destroyed, as were other major buildings in Port-au-Prince. After the earthquake, Haitian doctors and foreign doctors worked closely together. Haitian doctors and those of Haitian descent came from Canada, Europe, and the United States to help. Again, in the midst of adversity it was one of those great moments when humanity is at its best, and many lives were saved because of the courage and determination of the medical staff. Organizations like WHO, Doctors without Borders, Doctors of the World, and the Red Cross, together with medical teams from Cuba and other Latin American countries, came with supplies, human resources, and technology. Medical services, surgeries, and medicine were supplied free of charge to the wounded and the displaced, as it should be.

However, continuing with the same approach for several months after the earthquake, without some coordination at different levels with Haitians themselves, put the Haitian health system in jeopardy. The general hospital attached to the state university had collapsed, along with the nursing school, pharmacy school, and other buildings attached to it. But most damages to the medical system were the direct result of the help that we received. How? Most Haitian nurses and medical staff left the public system to work for the NGOs, Doctors without Borders, Doctors of the World, and others that pay better salaries and offer better working conditions. The population itself no longer goes to the private doctors, even the ones who had very modest fees; they want everything to be free, understandably. But what will happen when the NGOs go away? They will not stay forever, and they will not be able to offer free medical services and supplies forever.

French doctor Alain Deloche, the president of the organization *Chaine de l'espoir* (Chain of Hope) and who has been working in Haiti and other developing countries since 1989, was shocked by what he saw happening. In an article in *Le Monde* in July 2010, he said that the NGOs were destroying the economic fabric of the country.[6] After six months, private hospitals had to close their doors or reduce their staff. Most of them could not function properly. Haitian health officials were trying to save them with a system of subsidies, but their resources are limited.

If right after the earthquake it was difficult to plan ahead and the initial actions were to prevent human loss and human suffering, it would have been more productive in the following weeks to think about the future and take actions to help the country reach a state of medical autonomy. WHO, several NGOs, and the Ministry of National Health are supposedly working together within the UN Health Cluster toward revitalizing the health system, but they apparently did not approach the problem with this objective in mind. On the contrary, the actions taken so far have weakened or even helped to destroy the system.

Let the Experts Stop Talking

Haiti does need international help, and most Haitians know that. Unfortunately, so far the actions of the international community have contributed to diminish the state. What the British journalist Rory Carroll has called "a vicious circle of dependence and institutional infantilism" has to be broken.[7] Disaster aid has become the norm in Haiti, replacing the much-needed structural measures that will enable the constitution of a stronger society. Haiti is a very complicated country with a singular history that has put it in a marginal position from its inception. Exporting fixed patterns and making them fit the Haitian context is seldom successful. As Haitians continue to question the so-called experts, maybe it is indeed time to ask the experts to stop talking; rather they should listen, observe, and learn, instead of setting the stage for future disasters.

* * *

Position Statement After the January 12, 2010, Earthquake

Batay Ouvriye

What Was the Conjuncture at the Time of the Earthquake?

A hallmark of this political conjuncture is the continuing crisis of the state, a crisis of legitimacy compounded by a crisis of political representation: sham elections, with diminishing and close to null voter turnout, were being organized (see Chapter 10, this volume; note that this text was written well before November 28, 2010).[8] Numerous conflicts were emerging and erupting around the goal of the executive branch to establish "continuity," in order to extend and perpetuate its hold on power. To do so, it was engaged in a number of discredited political schemes, in the context of a "mafia and criminal" state, which, considering the designated candidates of the "party of continuity," was engaged in entrenching its "mafia and criminal" nature. It is true that, after this catastrophe, they are in a weakened position, but the political race among the dominant classes, between the politicians who are the advocates of ruling-class interests, remains very tight. And imperialism, the behind-the-scenes, true-reigning manipulator of this political charade, was a sponsor of this political process, even if it had reservations concerning the overt "mafia and criminal" characteristics becoming entrenched in the Haitian state. We should not forget the battle around the dismissal of the former prime minister and designation of the new one and the continuing repercussions of this on the relationship between imperialism and the current Haitian leaders. All things considered, we were in an explosive cauldron. The January 12 earthquake, even if it has overshadowed these contradictions, has not eliminated them.

Confronting all these contradictions among the dominant classes and imperialism are the popular masses. The results of the last elections, in April 2009, were very clear. The popular masses understood very well that what was at stake in these elections had nothing to do with their own interests. The political struggle among the dominant classes was being settled on the back of the popular masses, and they were well aware of this. Generally speaking, from the standpoint of the popular masses, even if there were several minor opportunists who were trying to validate this political charade, the elections scheduled for February 2010 were undermined by a major underlying contradiction: on the one hand, the ruling classes and their lackeys at the head of the Haitian state cannot continue to govern as they have been, heading straight toward a "failed state," but on the other hand, the momentum of the turning gears of the political power establishment, compounded by their class project of limitless exploitation, does not give them an alternative. Clearly, they have no solution! They are rotting relentlessly, deeper into their decomposition. They have reached the end of the line. But what concerns us in the popular camp is that their decomposition affects the country as a whole, every day!

Notes

1. Gérard Barthélémy, *l'Univers Rural Haïtien: Le Pays En Dehors* (Paris: L'Harmattan, 1990).

2. Translated from the original Haitian Creole by Mark Schuller.

3. Originally published by Inter Press Service newswire, http://www.ipsnews. net, February 11, 2011.

4. Agence France-Prejre, "No End in Sight for Haiti Rebuild: Minister," January 6, 2011. http://www.terradaily.com/reports/No_end_in_sight_for_Haiti_rebuild _minister_999.html.

5. Alter Presse, "Haiti-Séisme-Un an: Population de fort National en Colère," January 12, 2011. http://www.alterpresse.org/spip.php?article10516.

6. Alain Deloche, "En Haïti, quand le remède peut tuer le médecin" (In Haiti, when the medication can kill the doctor), *Le Monde* (Paris), July 23, 2010.

7. "Save Haiti from Aid Tourists," *The Guardian,* November 16, 2010.

8. Originally posted in Creole on the Batay Ouvriye website on February 7, 2010, with the English translation following.

6

The Camps and Being Displaced

Chapter 5 discussed the continued legacies of exclusion, recalling the French expression plus ça change, plus le même: *the more things change, the more they stay the same. One obvious change to Haiti's social landscape specifically brought by the earthquake serves as its most powerful symbol, a constant reminder of the continued impotence of the Haitian state and failures of international aid. Called "tent cities" or "camps," the city of Port-au-Prince now bears on full public display scars of the extended misery. At the peak in the summer of 2010 the International Organization for Migration (IOM) registered 1.3 million IDPs living in 1,300 camps, with over 800 within the greater Port-au-Prince metropolitan area. As of May 2011, there were still more than 600,000 people living in the camps, according to IOM estimates.*

One shudders to think of this new reality becoming a permanent fixture in Haiti's urban landscape. At their best, camps are planned relocation sites with temporary shelters, "T-shelters," made of treated plywood and social services such as security patrols, water, maintained toilets, clinics, and some simulation of a school. This describes barely a handful, as the contracts for services such as water and sanitation began to run out in the first part of 2011. What remains of the clinics are empty and ripped tents emblazoned with fading NGO or UN agency logos. Unfortunately the residents themselves also remain. According to research conducted by Mark Schuller in the summer of 2011, 90% of camp residents were renters before the earthquake. In addition to the slow pace of rubble removal and house repair or construction wherein the vast majority of the more than 175,000 housing units in need of repair or demolition still await action, a disaster capitalism on an individual level combined with the invasion of NGOs in need of housing has driven rental prices for safe housing through the roof. In other words, Haiti's remaining IDPs, and the thousand camps, are not going away anytime soon, except for those IDPs who are forcibly removed.

Fully describing the myriad realities in Haiti's IDP camps is impossible. The camps differ quite significantly: some are veritable cities well on their way to becoming permanent shantytowns with rows of timachann *selling cooked foods to school supplies, used clothing to plumbing. Others are cobbled together with only people's wit and endurance, with ripped-up tarps not even holding back the torrential rains or tropical sun. This chapter offers several perspectives. We begin with the blog by Haiti State University student Carine Exantus, published on the Conversations for a Better World website. This insider's account details the first terrifying weeks under the tent while families still grieving for their loved ones huddled together and scraped together what little aid came their way. Exantus and her family lived in a camp on the Champ de Mars, the national square surrounding the destroyed National Palace, under the gaze of the statues of the heroes of Haiti's independence.*

Following this eyewitness account is the first dispatch, written six months after the quake, from a grassroots group called Bri Kouri Nouvèl Gaye. Bri Kouri was part of a collective of social movement organizations mobilizing to defend the rights of Haiti's IDPs. This dispatch highlights residents' state of fear and the deplorable state of services. Complementing this collection of residents' stories is a survey of 108 camps within the metropolitan area. Schuller and a team of eight State University students collected data on conditions, on residents' awareness of and involvement in aid distribution, and perspectives from the camp committees. Excerpted here is an account of the sanitation, water, education, and health-care facilities within the camps. Following this study is an analysis of the IOM's communication projects within the camps, by professor and solidarity activist Valerie Kaussen. Kaussen discusses the comic book Chimen Lakay *(Voice for the Voiceless) and Citizen Haiti, two communications and outreach initiatives sponsored by the IOM. In addition to untangling the neoliberal ideology within these official projects, Kaussen discusses how they serve as a safety valve to contain dissent. While we could have selected many other realities and perspectives, these four accounts capture the deplorable conditions within the IDP camps, a baseline for the following chapters.*

* * *

Diary of a Survivor in Haiti

Carine Exantus

PART I (January 12, 2010)

THOUGH IT'S BEEN MONTHS SINCE the January earthquake in Haiti, the afteref-fects still linger for the survivors.[1] Around one o'clock in the afternoon, I witnessed the murder of a professor at the university, named Jean-Anile Louis-Juste (known also as Janil Lwijis; see Chapter 3 for his posthumous contribution to this volume). Two men with motorcycles pulled up at the intersection of the Capois and Lafleur du Chene roads and shot him to death. Students of the Faculty of Human Sciences overcame this sad mo-ment of the death of a sociology professor, but not without a lot of pain. The day was already hard enough to bear when around 4:45 p.m., the violent earthquake of January 12 started.

After the murder of my professor, I had left to go home—disconcerted and downhearted—on the public transport. Suddenly, the van in which I was traveling lost its balance. Panicked, the driver quickly braked, throwing all the passengers into the road. I found myself on the ground, in the road, traumatized. I realized that there had been an earthquake. Lying in the middle of the road, I noticed the collapse of several buildings in the area.

Although I was in shock, I had the presence of mind to look for a shel-ter to protect myself from the concrete that was about to fall on me. Hav-ing seen that the Sylvio Cator Stadium was open and the frightened people taking refuge there, I threw myself into a parking space in the stadium to keep myself out of danger.

Finding My Family

Observing the numerous losses—in human life and in material things—I was worried more and more about my family. My legs felt dead. I couldn't even speak yet. I was stretched out on the ground in the hope of clearing my head. But hearing the sobs of wounded people and of family members of the victims, my anguish grew.

No news of my relatives. Fear seized me. I couldn't walk. So I spent the whole night sitting on the ground, thinking of the fate of my family members, of my mother and my brother in particular. For me, it was the longest night, as long as every aftershock that punctuated the night and terrified me.

Panic

The next day, around five in the morning, I left the stadium in the direction of my home to find out what had happened to my family and our house. On the way I came across dead bodies, wounded people. The people were panicked. All these sights did not ease my anguish. On the way I had the feeling that there would be victims at the house. Arriving at the Place du Marron Inconnu (the statue of the unknown maroon, in the Champ de Mars, just opposite the National Palace), I met a neighbor who told me that my gentle mother had looked for me desperately all last night at the Champ de Mars. All of a sudden I became less worried, knowing that the person most dear to me in the world was alive. A little later, several meters away, I met my wonderful little mother. We hugged like old friends who hadn't seen each other in a long time. We cried out in joy and pleasure.

My mother told me that our house had been destroyed and that we had lost two members of our family. I couldn't contain my tears. I no longer had the courage to go toward my house. We had to find a place where we would be "more calm." It was thus that we became refugees at the Place Pétion. We spent the whole day of Wednesday, January 13, 2010, there. Night fell, and we slept on the wet grass, spreading out just two sheets that a neighbor had offered us.

Our New Life

Thus our new life started, a life to which I must adapt to survive from day to day. It's my duty to start over at zero. I spent the whole weekend of the earthquake sleeping—with my family—under the moonlight and on the wet grass. Thus we started to reflect on how to make a small shelter to protect ourselves from the sun and the rain. We procured some wooden posts in order to make a shelter. Neighbors and friends gave us bedding and shared cleaning and cooking materials with us. Thus, it's with these precious objects that we struggle in our new reality that has imposed itself on us, and we don't know how long it will be until we can get rid of them.

Part II (March 17, 2010)

Life in the refugee camps in post-earthquake Haiti is unspeakably hard, with little being done to meet the needs of the refugees. On the Place Pétion, the need for food is the primary goal of every family living in the camp. Certain families have received coupons for a small bag of rice, but only women are allowed to line up for distribution. According to other families who haven't received these, the committee has given these coupons out to people close to their own families. This distribution took place near the National Palace on Friday, January 29, very early in the morning.

Access to Shelter

From the evening of Wednesday, February 10, to Thursday, February 11, there was some rain, and the families all had to get up to make sure that the water didn't damage the sheets that they were using both as shelter and as a bed. All their things got wet. The next day, the families washed their sheets, spread their belongings out to dry in the sun, and tried to put together their shelters again with wood and plastic. Protests began because no one in charge had foreseen this and taken steps to prevent the shelters from becoming wet.

The families want access to tents. Only the families with greater economic means have bought tents, whose origins no one knows. Often you see people in the camp who chase after people who are rumored to have coupons, but these people have not been identified.

Moving the Refugee Camps

According to rumors going around, the government of Haiti wants to move the people in refugee camps to send them to the Place Cathedrale, located at the Rue Docteur Aubry and Bonne Foi. It's a housing center, and its construction has already started. People have noticed the installation of toilets by the JEDCO company in the back of the camp.

An Atmosphere of Anxiety

In the middle of the camp, near the back fence, shelters have been put up where young girls and boys are living, who are about 15 to 25 years old. Often these young people fight and make a lot of noise, despite their risky situation since the disaster. This creates an atmosphere of anxiety for the families living in the back of the camp. Monday, January 15, 2010, around 11 p.m., police officers came to the Place Pétion and were able to capture two prisoners who had allegedly escaped from prison in Port-au-Prince.

More and More Needs Arise

Days go by, more and more needs arise. The heads of the family—or more precisely, the women—complained of only having rice and that they needed other food to cook with and that rice wasn't enough to feed their families. In terms of health care, Cuban and Haitian doctors provided care to those wounded in the earthquake and to people suffering from illness. They are here almost every day between nine and twelve o'clock. Soon, about a dozen of the JEDCO toilets began working, six for women and six for men. Only two are open at night. JEDCO provides toilet paper and a small tank of water and soap to use.

Shelter From the Elements

Because of the strong rain in the evenings from Wednesday through Friday, the families living in this camp are reconstructing their cloth shelters by digging canals all around their shelters to avoid getting wet. This has sparked protests from families demanding tents so that they can protect themselves from the rain.

Part III (March 19, 2010)

Little has changed for those living in the refugee camps in post-earthquake Haiti. At Place Pétion, a camp situated at a strategic point on the Champ de Mars, near the presidential palace and the Ministry of Culture and Communication, the atmosphere is becoming more and more monotonous. The most vital needs of every family living in the camp remain: food, shelter, and health care.

Food

It's been over a month since the families received a little bag full of nine pots worth of rice. There hasn't been any other food distributed since. Twice they have received, from Brazilian agents of MINUSTAH, portable bottles of water. This distribution took place in front of the National Palace. The families in the camp are complaining that they've been abandoned. They're doing their best to feed themselves with what little they have.

The Need for Shelter

The makeshift shelters grow every day. Everyone is trying to protect themselves from the sun and the rain, and they are resorting to wooden pots, plastic, plywood, and sheet metal. Families have procured these materials—which most people don't know where they got them from—by their own means.

Every time it rains, some families touch up or reconstruct their shelters to better protect themselves. They dig tunnels around their shelters to prevent the water from coming in. No weather condition is favorable to these shelters. When the sun is out, the families complain of the heat, which is very strong inside their shelters. When it rains, it's practically impossible to go around in the camp because of the mud caused by the rain.

Weather Conditions

The families, already vulnerable to the least amount of rain, have become panicked at the news of the hurricane season (June 1 to November 31). Every family on the Place Pétion needs a tent to deal with this way of life.

No one keeps track of the donations, whatever they are: food, shelter, and so on. Some institutions have carried out censuses that were not followed by any concrete action. The IOM carried out a census of families with the goal of identifying people without shelter or families (giving them an identification card). Action Against Hunger (ACF) has also done a census of families and raised awareness about hygiene. Volunteers for National Development has raised awareness among young people in the camp about safe sex. The Ministry of the Interior and the Collective of Territories has also carried out a census whose results we haven't seen.

Keeping Clean

To keep one's shelter clean is one of the biggest priorities for people living there, in order to prevent illness. Each family cleans their own area where they live and collects their garbage in a little bag near their shelter. Certain families throw their bags on a pile of rubbish nearby; others throw them in a big garbage can near the Marron Inconnu statue.

Hygiene and Bathing

During the first weeks immediately following the earthquake, people noticed the presence of a seven-member committee that was trying to organize the camp in its own way. Now it's no longer here. The committee had constructed showers that weren't very convenient. Because the water for bathing—which flowed out of a hole—reached the camp, it stagnated and infested the camp with mosquitoes. Now the showers are in a bad state; people can no longer use them.

Sometimes there isn't enough water in the reservoirs that ACF installed for domestic uses. ACF had also installed JEDCO toilets. These were not cleaned regularly. They smelled bad. This made the people take them far from camp and scattered them in the road.

* * *

The Situation of the Displaced Six Months Later

Bri Kouri Nouvèl Gaye

———

"I AM HERE, JUST AS they have left me." These are the words of Roger Bastien, 67, who lost his wife and a son in the earthquake of January 12, 2010.[2] He took refuge in St. Louis Gonzague, an elite private school, on January 13.

With three children, he has been struggling without any help for more than three months, housed under a tarp with some pieces of dirty sheets. The hope for tomorrow and his family keep him going. Six months after the earthquake hit the country, there are no appreciable changes or signs of improvement in the situation of the poor who suffer through the day in the sun, and the night in the rain, without food and without health care.

The IHRC has been created, is spending money, and NGOs and MINUSTAH are partying, while more than a million people do not know what to do with themselves during this hurricane season. Most of the tents and tarps that were received have nearly completely broken or ripped in this storm season for which meteorological services have predicted more than seven major hurricanes to hit Haiti. These hurricanes could cause immense damage. We are in a country where any level of rains and flooding can cause heavy damage.

However, that does not mean anything to the authorities, because $140 million has already been announced for the reconstruction of state offices in order that these men can continue to waste funds, while less than one penny has been allocated to prepare for the hurricane season, which has already begun to create panic.

Many beautiful promises have been made for rebuilding, which is no different from the USAID pledges made in 1986 after the end of the Duvalier dictatorship.

Marise Desulme is working for money (Cash for Work). She abandoned Gonaïves in 2004, after she had lost her family in Hurricane Jeanne, and came to Port-au-Prince to seek a new beginning. But the earthquake was like salt in her wounds:

> One hundred and eighty gourdes [about $4.50] per day is not enough to eat with my husband who is unemployed, and it is in a camp that we have been living for more than five months now. It rains every day, and

we cannot sleep neither day nor night. We have to watch out so that the floodwaters don't wash us away. I would return to Gonaïves, but it is worse than Port-au-Prince. There hasn't been any kind of authority that has come to ask us, what do we bring to sell? I do not think people will ask me to vote for anyone again—what will be, will be.

The political class and the government have created a political crisis to control the most personal conversations and distract people from the humanitarian crisis, which is the most important issue. President René Préval, the elections, the law declaring a "state of emergency," and the question of who will represent the small group of greedy individuals on the IHRC are the main debates and headlines. There are announcements about the hurricane and insecurity issues, but there are no plans to prevent disaster and reduce crime. And so this prophecy will be fulfilled: "Swim to save yourself" (*Naje pou soti*).

We will leave you with a comparison so you can see the true goal of our leaders and their UN and NGO colleagues: in less than three months, an NGO in Chile has already built more than 20,000 temporary houses. This NGO, called A Home for My Family (Un Techo Para Mi Familia), has less capacity, logistics, and money than the UN, Oxfam, Red Cross, IOM, World Vision—but we will stop naming them there, since there are several hundred large NGOs present in this country to earn big money in the name of the victims. Analyze this comparison and you can understand the situation that your brothers, friends, and family are living in after January 12, and what the authorities are planning for us.

* * *

Unstable Foundations
NGOs and Human Rights for Port-au-Prince's Internally Displaced People

Mark Schuller

———

THIS REPORT FOLLOWS SIX WEEKS of research during the summer of 2010. With a team of eight students and a colleague at the Faculté d'Ethnologie, Université d'État d'Haïti, this study covers more than 100 camps for IDPs, a random sample of one in eight of the 861 in the metropolitan area.³ Students conducted quantitative and qualitative surveys in three interrelated areas: conditions and services within the camps, residents' level of understanding and involvement in the camp committees, and interviews with committee representatives. I followed up with a visit to 31 camps.

The results show that despite the billions in aid pledged to Haiti, most of the estimated 1.5 million IDPs are living in substandard conditions. For example, seven months following the earthquake, 40% of IDP camps do not have access to water, and 30% do not have toilets of any kind. An estimated 10% of families have a tent; the rest sleep under tarps or even bedsheets. In the midst of the hurricane season, with torrential rains and heavy winds a regular occurrence, many tents are ripped beyond repair. Only a fifth of camps have education, health care, or psychosocial facilities on site.

The services provided in the camps vary quite significantly according to a range of factors. Camps managed by NGOs (20% of the sample) were twice as likely to have services. Camps in Cité Soleil have almost no services, while those in Pétionville are better managed. Camps that are not on major roads or far from the city center in Croix-des-Bouquets or Carrefour have little to no services. Camps situated on private land—71% of the sample—are significantly worse off than those on public land.

Although many NGOs empower camp committees to select recipients and distribute aid—most notably food, until the government stopped general distribution in April—most official committees do not involve the population. Less than a third of people living in camps are aware of the strategy or even the name of the committees. Two-thirds of members are men, despite well-documented concerns about gender-based violence. While to most NGOs, managing camps or offering services represents their "local participation," it is clear that the present structure leaves much to be desired.

While many committees sprang up organically immediately after the earthquake as an expression of solidarity and unity in an effort to survive, NGOs' relationships with them have several negative consequences, intended or unintended. First, most NGOs did not inquire about local participation, leadership, needs deliberation, or legitimacy. As a result, in several cases, the NGOs and self-named committees excluded preexisting grassroots organizations. Some NGOs, the government, and even the landowners themselves created these committees. This is the root of several conflicts. In most cases, the camp committees—which were active in the earthquake's immediate aftermath—report not doing anything because of lack of funds, testifying to an increasing dependency on foreign aid.

These failures are not isolated incidents but symptoms of larger structural problems that require immediate, sustained, and profound reflection and attention. Solutions include involving IDP populations in large community meetings, assessing levels of democracy and participation within committees, greater NGO accountability, coordination, and submission to a fully funded local and national government. Housing needs to be recognized as a human right (guaranteed by Article 22 of Haiti's Constitution), with concrete, immediate steps to empower people to return to a safe home and basic services (such as water, sanitation, health care, and education) made available to all, regardless of residency status. All of these require the immediate release of pledged aid, the vast majority of which has failed to materialize.

Physical Conditions of the Camps

One is immediately struck by the physical conditions inside the camps, particularly after a rainstorm (an unfortunately quite common occurrence in the summer months). Without exception, sanitation and drainage for rainwater was a serious issue. On the morning after a rainstorm, it is common to find large pools of standing, muddy water—often stretching 20 yards—over which mosquitoes, flies, and other potential disease vectors circle overhead. While miraculously there has not—yet—been a serious outbreak of malaria or cholera (until October 2010—see Chapter 9, this volume), the state of sanitation is manifested in numerous cases of serious skin problems. In at least one camp, Noailles, the researcher estimated that almost all the children had a rash on their bodies because of the heat that is trapped inside the tents, combined with the other disease vectors. I myself contracted a rash following repeated exposure to these unsanitary conditions.

Bracketing the health consequences, this lack of proper drainage and sanitation still represents serious environmental hazards, most notably the smell. Even in camps with latrines, the standing rainwater and mud are pungent, reminiscent of pig farms. Often, as documented by research assistants and the author, the mud seeps underneath people's tents or tarps, rendering it impossible to sleep or keep personal effects (like voter ID cards, birth certificates, marriage licenses, or photos) dry and intact. "It is also impossible to sleep when the mud seeps in. Imagine; everything around you moves," said one resident.

Those whose houses were destroyed or seriously damaged but nonetheless have their *lakou*, or yard, intact, and more than the average economic resources or other means, stay in tents elevated from the ground by cinder blocks recovered from the houses. But those who have these sleeping berths are the distinct minority.

Sanitation

People staying at or near their houses and not inside one of the 800 camps within the capital do not have to contend with the problems associated with sharing a bathroom with neighbors. At even the best-managed camps, this is a widespread concern. The Sphere Minimum Standards are clear about how many people should share a toilet: no more than 20. These conditions are not even being met right in front of the National Palace, where foreign NGOs, dignitaries like former US presidents, and journalists visit. The toilets line the outside of the camp, presenting the appearance of plenty. Hidden from passersby's view are rows and rows of tarps and tents.

And this is in a camp that is relatively well taken care of. Away from the glaring gaze of foreigners there are camps that are far worse off. In Place de la Paix (Peace Plaza), in the Delmas 2 neighborhood, also lining the perimeter, there was a row of toilets next to the trash receptacles, which was next to the water distribution and the site for the mobile clinic. Strikingly, there were only 30 toilets for 30,400 people. In a small camp in Carrefour, to go to the bathroom people have to ask a neighbor whose house is still standing. Camp leader Carline explains, "It's embarrassing. And even though they are neighbors, it's starting to strain our relationship." They have to buy water and carry it back into the camp.

According to the latest Displacement Tracking Matrix (DTM), 6,820 people live in the soccer field outside of the rectory in Solino. Despite this density, residents had to wait for almost five months for the first toilets to arrive. When asked how people defecate, a resident held up a small plastic bag usually used to sell half cups of sugar or penny candy. "We throw it in the ravine across the street." In the recently discovered camp in Impasse Thomas called CAJIT, housing almost 2,500 people in Paloma, a far-off neighborhood in Carrefour, there were no toilets—either portable or latrines—at least as of August 12, 2010, seven months following the earthquake.

These cases are unfortunately not isolated. According to even the most conservative estimates, with some large camps in which assistants had to estimate taken out of the sample, the average number of people sharing a toilet in the Port-au-Prince metropolitan area is 273 people. Thirty percent of camps (27 out of 89) with verified information did not have any toilets at all. Another investigation by LAMP, IJDH, LERN, and the University of San Francisco Law School found similar results, that 27% of families had to defecate in a plastic container or an open area (see Chapter 9, this volume). This data was collected seven months after the earthquake, despite the persistent narrative that people are swelling the camps—or "faking it," just using the camps during the daytime—primarily in search of services.

Unfortunately residents' needs don't stop with the installation of toilet facilities, and many are not cleaned on a regular basis. While 25 camps report that their toilets are cleaned every day (37%, mostly those with portable toilets), 10 camps (15%) report that they are cleaned less often than once per month, and 17 (25%) report not having the toilets cleaned at all. "They treat us like animals!" said an exasperated resident. She was interrupted by a neighbor: "Worse! Animals live better than us." Some members of the WASH (Water, Sanitation, and Hygiene) Cluster are frustrated at what they see as the irresponsibility of NGOs: "We call and call and write report after report. Some just flatly ignore us."

Water

Arguably even more important than sanitation is the provision of safe, clean water. In several reports the United Nations highlights the distribution of water to 1.2 million people as a success of the ensemble of agencies and NGOs. Like sanitation, there are still—as of seven months following the earthquake—large gaps in water distribution to IDP camps. Take, for example, the case of Bobin, in a ravine outside of Pétionville, in a popular neighborhood off of Route des Frères. As of seven months following the earthquake, the 2,775 residents still had no water. A single PVC pipe that had cracked offers some people a couple of buckets whenever the government turns on the tap for paying clients. Many people use the rainwater in the trash-filled ravine. Some individuals had the opportunity to fetch water from a nearby tap, either privately owned or at a nearby camp. Residents mentioned that NGOs had talked about installing a water system, but seven months after the earthquake, it still had yet to materialize.

Several other camps, particularly in Cité Soleil and CAJIT in the hills above Carrefour noted above, were without water as the research team investigated. Said Olga Ulysse, CAJIT leader, "Carrefour is blessed with many little springs. But the problem is that they are running under the destroyed houses and the decomposing bodies. It's very unhealthy." The other choice is to walk downhill to the adjacent camp, pay for a bucket of water, and carry it back up the hill.

Of the camps where assistants could obtain reliable information, 30 out of 71, or 40.5%, of camps did not have a water supply, and three others (4.1%) had a nearby PVC pipe that was tapped outside the camp. With the notable exception of the WASH Cluster—which is distinguished as the only UN cluster led by the Haitian government, accountable to the people and not the NGOs, and characterized by an activist, hands-on approach to filling the gaps in services—people from all levels of the aid industry repeated the refrain that providing lifesaving necessities encourages dependency.

"People are only living in the camps in order to get the free services," said a particular NGO worker, but it could have been one of many. This discourse has wide currency in aid circles and foreign parliaments, including the US Congress. In addition to this issue, several commentators pointed to the issue of profit making. According to a person who works at a foreign development agency, private water company owners persuaded President René Préval to stop free water distribution because it was cutting into their profits.

Health Care

There are several gaps within the coverage of health-care facilities inside the IDP camps. Only one camp in five has any sort of clinic facility on-site. This number does not account for quality. For example, in one camp, Carradeux, a tent was provided by UNICEF that resembles a clinic, but it was completely empty: no medicines, no first-aid supplies, and no nurse practitioners were present during researchers' five visits to this camp. "I'm a nurse," executive committee member Elvire Constant began. "But we don't have the means to serve the population. I spoke on TV and radio, telling the minister of public health that there are nurses available, and the population is vast [24,161, according to the September DTM]. . . . UNICEF [United Nations Children's Fund] knows the tent is here, but they have never come by, not even one day, to negotiate with us, to tell us whether it could be a mobile clinic or a health center."

Inside the camp a couple hundred meters, a tent from Save the Children, whose purpose eluded everyone I asked, was empty and ripped past the point of providing any shelter. Carradeux is an officially managed, planned relocation site, and supposed to therefore be an example for others.

Indeed, the researcher who visited the camp gave this camp a three out of 10 in overall quality, with one being acceptable and 10 being the worst imaginable. Most other camps were given higher scores, meaning the conditions were worse.

According to residents, the median walking distance to the nearest clinic was 20 minutes, with the mean being 27 minutes. Five camps are so isolated that residents told researchers that it takes 90 minutes to reach the nearest clinic. The same can be said of pharmacies. While in the earthquake's immediate aftermath, medications were given to residents free of charge, this practice stopped early on in most camps' neighborhoods. Nine out of 85 responses, 10%, of camps had some form of a pharmacy on-site. The mean time to walk to the nearest pharmacy was 25 minutes, with the farthest being two hours.

* * *

Do It Yourself
International Aid and the Neoliberal Ethos in the Tent Camps of Port-au-Prince

Valerie Kaussen

IN THE NEOLIBERAL WORLDVIEW, THE ideal state is driven by and protects market interests. As such, populations must be discouraged from appealing to the state as a guarantor of basic medical care, education, housing, security, and so on. Instead, personal responsibility, avoiding risk, and individual rather than collective solutions define the ideal relationship between the neoliberal state and the individual.[4] Haiti, as many authors in this volume note, has been called "the Republic of NGOs," with NGOs replacing the state as the provider of basic services. Neoliberal entities themselves, NGOs inevitably reproduce and disseminate the values that characterize the ideal neoliberal state and citizenry. These values are well-represented in the communications and democracy-promotion projects of the International Organization for Migration (IOM), the international NGO responsible for coordinating aid to the hundreds of tent camps in the quake zone.

The stated goal of the IOM communications project is to empower Haiti's IDPs by giving them better access to information, better tools for communicating their needs to the NGOs that serve them, and ultimately supporting and enhancing democratic participation. The IOM's principal communications project, broadly titled *Chimen Lakay* (the Way Back Home), began in the summer of 2010 and targeted the 1.3 million IDPs left homeless by the earthquake. Today, as the IDPs are being dispersed, often through forced evictions, *Chimen Lakay* is targeting the majority population more broadly. The IOM's communications project includes an illustrated newspaper (which to date has a distribution of 500,000); community and commercial radio broadcasts recorded in the tent camps; *Radyo Tap-Tap*, a radio-style soap opera played on *tap-taps* (Haiti's buses or pickup trucks that serve as shared taxis); open-source mapping; citizen journalism; and a program called Voices of the Voiceless, which placed informational kiosks and suggestion boxes in about 150 tent camps managed by the IOM. All of these programs work with a Haitian crisis response organization, Noula, which maps and tracks gaps in services and requests for assistance communicated through the suggestion boxes, SMS messaging, and a telephone hotline.[5]

The newspaper *Chimen Lakay* transmits information on cholera prevention and hurricane preparedness, uncontroversial content nonetheless buttressed by an overall message of personal responsibility, do-it-yourself, self-management, and even "self-help," as one sympathetic observer describes it.[6] The editorial that inaugurated the first issue indeed stated that the message it has to offer tent camp residents is one of "taking care of yourself." It is a fitting way to usher in an issue that also does its best to provide positive stories of camp relocations: *"Deplasman an ka on bon bagay!"* "Displacement can be a good thing!" The editorial councils its IDP readership not to lose touch with the mode of conduct exemplified in the Haitian proverb *Met Kò ki veye kò* (I'm responsible for myself, for my body).[7] IDPs are then instructed "to begin thinking about how [they] will manage to get a small house that is more solid than a tent and that [they] can call [their] own."[8] It tells readers that they need to remember how they lived before the earthquake, which was "by virtue of our perseverance" (*sou fòs kouraj nou*). Finally, the editorial warns, "If people don't decide to fight for themselves to change their own lives, nothing will change, even if the [humanitarian] organizations and the entire Haitian state were to spend the next thousand years giving out aid."[9]

There is, of course, nothing inherently wrong with encouraging people to be active and take charge of their lives. All the same, *Chimen Lakay's* editorializing must be placed in its very specific and troubling context. The IOM distributed the first issue of *Chimen Lakay* in July 2010, when most of the camps had never received tents (people lived under tarps and bedsheets), only 40% had access to drinking water, and 30% had never had toilet facilities. Only 20% had access to educational or health-care facilities.[10] Alongside NGOs' logistical errors and the outright wasting of resources, promised aid money was not materializing. By July 2010 a mere 2% of the $10 billion pledged by the international community had been spent on relief efforts.[11] Furthermore, while the US Congress passed a $1.5 billion aid bill in May 2010, Haitians had to await the one-year anniversary of the quake before seeing any disbursements, the result of bureaucratic red tape and US mistrust of the Haitian government. As of this writing, there is still no plan to build public housing for homeless earthquake survivors and no plan for dealing with the scores of renters who have no viable "way back home" (see Regan, Chapter 5). Forced evictions are furthermore an ongoing crisis.

In this context of aid failure, *Chimen Lakay*'s counseling of self-reliance becomes an ideological effort to form citizen-subjects who take personal responsibility for the ills that afflict them and who don't expect aid from the state or any other institution. "Do it yourself" is an ethic and ideal that originates in the Global North's neoliberal turn, where dwindling state support for child care, health care, and other services means that such labor falls upon unpaid (or very poorly paid) individuals. In Haiti, there has never been a fully functioning welfare state, and the majority population has always been forced to "do it yourself" if anything is to be done at all. Nonetheless, using traditional Haitian proverbs like *Mèt kò veye kò* naturalizes and universalizes donors' own neoliberal ideologies.[12] It also places the onus for aid failures on the Haitian people. In the summer of 2011, as NGOs were beginning to pull out of the camps, a large humanitarian organization attempted to commission a short informational film for its tent camp screenings provisionally titled *How to Clean Up Your Own Camp*.

The writers and editors of *Chimen Lakay* are well-intentioned pragmatists seeking to disseminate public health information and crisis response quickly and efficiently. When faced with a growing lack of services, common sense would dictate that they disseminate self-help messages, like clean your own camp. But such "common sense," as Antonio Gramsci described, is the mechanism by which dominance and inequality are reproduced, and in this sense, *Chimen Lakay* unwittingly reproduces the dominant ideology of neoliberalism. It must also be noted that *Chimen Lakay* receives its funding from the large NGOs and donor organizations. The program's current focus on "disaster risk reduction" (DRR), for example, was not an editorial decision, but a fiscal one. As part of its DRR project, USAID helped foot the bill for a recent issue of *Chimen Lakay* on hurricane preparedness, while the newspaper's first issue, more focused on IDP self-help, was jointly funded by MINUSTAH and the IOM. It is hard to imagine USAID or any other donor funding an issue devoted to, for example, IDP legal rights. In this sense, *Chimen Lakay*, whose creators hope will eventually became a true forum for citizen journalism, remains an organ of the international aid apparatus. Its content determined by international aid priorities, the print version is not yet a newspaper at all, though it is currently the most widely distributed Creole-language publication in the country.

The Voices of the Voiceless program comprised the other half of the IOM's "two-way" communication and thus democracy promotion efforts. At the time of this writing, the program is being phased out and the IOM is hoping to convince another agency to adapt the suggestion boxes to neighborhoods. Voices promised, as its name suggests, to give the silenced a chance to speak out and have their stories heard. Most of the requests for assistance were entered into a Noula database. Letters were selected to be read on the *Chimen Lakay* radio broadcast or were printed in the newspaper. Letter writers asked for food, schooling for their children, new tents, and most often, the Holy Grail: a job. In the fourth issue of *Chimen Lakay*, Maculène R. asked for "a little help" in the Ratima camp. "We have never received anything," she writes, "except this little water they give us. In my name, I ask you for a little aid, just one more time."[13]

The director of the IOM communications program, Leonard Doyle, likens these written communiqués to "letters to the editor." Indeed, Voices of the Voiceless is part of a much larger trend that views self-expression and self-revelation as an end in itself. All the same, letter writers communicate pointed and specific requests, and it is clear that they expect a response; yet the IOM only attempts to ensure responses to letters that report rapes or other violent acts (and it is unclear whether even these letters are followed up on). An experimental initiative, Voice of the Voiceless will depend upon NGO interest in the "product," which is direct response from aid recipients. Suggesting the conflicting goals of improving NGO-recipient communication vs. promoting democracy, in an interview IOM director Luca dall'Oglio, specifically referring to the *Chimen Lakay* radio show, opined that "of course lots of people want to complain about their situation, but it's also true that they are beginning to understand the merits of communication in a democracy."[14]

Dall'Oglio's definition of "democracy" is a neoliberal one that corresponds to Jodi Dean's analyses in *Democracy and Other Neoliberal Fantasies*.

For Dean, the democratizing potential of the Internet and other new communications technologies—which, like Voices of the Voiceless, extol the virtues of "self-revelation, [and] the expression of intense and/or intimate feelings"—is limited by the fact that no one has a responsibility to respond. Such messages become part of the circulation of content in what she terms "communicative capitalism." According to Dean, communicative capitalism is dangerous because it masquerades as democratic participation, thus disavowing "a more fundamental political disempowerment."[15]

As an employee of the IOM communications project told me, "[*Chimen Lakay*] is a way to let people vent. If they don't vent this way, they will vent in ways that are far more dangerous." Indeed, collective, organized responses to the miseries of post-earthquake Haiti have been equated with criminality and unruliness. As of this writing, IOM's communications unit is faced with the difficult task of assisting government-mandated efforts to relocate IDPs back to permanent structures. We can only hope that the exercise of communicating real demands to an increasingly unresponsive international NGO system will not exhaust the political energies of the hundreds of thousands of tent camp residents who will need to rally all of their forces if they are to continue to resist unfulfilled promises, threats of eviction, violence, and an uncertain future.

Notes

1. Adapted from a series of blog posts at www.conversationsforabetterworld .com. Translated from the original French by the Conversations for a Better World team.

2. Originally posted on July 22, 2010, on the Bri Kouri Nouvèl Gaye website, http://brikourinouvelgaye.com/2010/07/22/the-situation-of-the-displaced-six-months-later/.

3. This is an adapted excerpt from a report published by the City University of New York and the Université d'État d'Haïti on October 4, 2010, ijdh.org/ archives/14855.

4. As Wendy Brown writes, in neoliberalism, "The extension of economic rationality to formerly non-economic domains . . . reaches individual conduct, or, more precisely, prescribes the citizen-subject of a neoliberal order." "Neoliberalism and the End of Liberal Democracy," in *Edgework: Critical Essays on Knowledge and Politics* (Princeton, NJ: Princeton University Press, 2005), 37–59, 42.

5. In its emphasis on new communications technologies, IOM participates in the much larger trend of using new media in disaster response, for which post-earthquake Haiti was something of a laboratory. See Anne Nelson and Ivan Sigal, with Dean Zambrano, *Media, Information Systems, and Communities: Lessons from*

Haiti, CDAC, Internews, Knight Foundation, January 2011, http://www.knight foundation.org/publications.

6. Kimberly Coates, "Q&A: Media in Post-Earthquake Haiti," Tomorrow's News (blog), Ashoka International, October 1, 2010, http://knowledge.ashoka.org/node/4889.

7. "Editoryal," *Chimen Lakay,* no. 1 (July 2010): 2.

8. Ibid.

9. Ibid.

10. See Mark Schuller, *Unstable Foundations: Impact of NGOs on Human Rights for Port-au-Prince's Internally Displaced People,* October 4, 2010, ijdh.org/archives/14855.

11. Nick Owens, "Where's the Money for Haiti Gone?" *Daily Mirror,* May 27, 2010; Dana Milbank, "The Sad Math of Aid in Haiti: 6 months, 2 percent," *Washington Post,* July 13, 2010.

12. Another issue of *Chimen Lakay* uses the proverb "Evite miyo pase mande padon" (avoidance is better than asking forgiveness), i.e., avoid risk (*Chimen Lakay,* no. 3 [November 2010]).

13. *Chimen Lakay,* no. 1 (July 2010): 3.

14. Coates, "Q&A."

15. Jodi Dean, *Democracy and Other Neoliberal Fantasies* (Durham, NC: Duke University Press, 2009), 33.

7

Forced Eviction and the Right to Housing

Ever since IDPs began huddling together for mutual survival following the earthquake, many of them have been under constant threat of forced eviction. As noted earlier, the camps remain visual reminders of the failures within the international aid response, eyesores that get in the way of selling Haiti as being "now open for business," as President Michel Martelly boasted in May 2011. More fundamentally, the people struggling to survive under the heat of the tarps or T-shelters were committing the ultimate indignity: they existed. IDPs' mere existence brought visibility to profound social problems, such as the extreme depravity and deep class hostility that has always beset Haiti but had been swept under the rug. The hypocrisy, misery, and inequality could no longer be ignored now that it was in plain view. In this context of class warfare, middle- and upper-class people claiming to be landowners responded with force. On September 1, 2010, UN Secretary General Ban Ki-moon reported that 29% of IDP camps were forcibly closed, and consistently through the summer of 2011, one in four camps was under the constant threat of forced eviction. The IOM reported that more than a quarter million people had been forcibly evicted over a nine-month period.

In legal terms, the survivors' right to security and even a makeshift home was put in direct conflict with private property rights, for the 60% of camps located on private land. A range of international and national laws, from the Universal Declaration of Human Rights (UDHR) to the Haitian Constitution, guarantee IDPs' rights to shelter, basic services, and security. Despite this, people representing themselves as landowners—usually without any legal proof—often successfully blocked lifesaving aid on the often repeated, and false, belief that people were only living in utter misery in the camps exposed to the elements, without adequate water, toilets, health care, or trash cleanup, for the free services.

Humanitarian agencies, in a perverse interpretation of their principle of "neutrality," backed off. This explains why in Schuller's study excerpted in the previous chapter there were statistically significant differences in services like water, clinics, or toilets between camps on private and public land. Evidence proved this discourse of people only staying in camps for the handouts to be false, since the majority of dwellers had no other options and remained after the shutoff. As human rights activists, including the four authors in this chapter, have noted, a pattern emerged wherein threats or actual physical violence were used to force people out.

This chapter details the many issues involved in the contest over the right to housing for the IDPs. Haitian civil rights attorney Patrice Florvilus begins with a discussion of the various international and national legal instruments guaranteeing the right to housing. The right to housing does not just mean a roof over people's heads, he emphasizes, but a range of characteristics such as safety and access to basic services such as water, sanitation, education, and health. International lawyers Mario Joseph and Jeena Shah recount their experience combating forced eviction, discussing the organizing efforts, difficulties, and strategies to respond to these challenges. In addition to the dimension of inequality and class antagonisms already noted, the organizing effort was challenged by a system of dependency reproduced by NGOs.

Following an individual case to highlight inherent structural problems, solidarity activist Mark Snyder shares an excerpt from a report about forced evictions. Consistently, as Snyder and other activists have documented, the Haitian authorities and NGOs have taken the landlord's side in this ever increasing class conflict. As Haitian activist Etant Dupain reports, this conflict erupts into violence that has claimed people's lives. In May 2011, private security agents at a camp in the Port-au-Prince suburb of Delmas beat a camp dweller, Thelucia Ciffren, to death. The police, Mayor Wilson Jeudy, and Martelly did not prosecute this murder.

The threat of forced eviction has only increased over time. Martelly's inauguration sent a green light to individual landowners and municipal authorities such as Jeudy, who lost the presidential contest to Martelly. With private security details roughing people up and ripping tents, Jeudy kicked out hundreds of families on two public squares. Martelly unveiled a plan to "reclaim" six public areas. The Sylvio Cator stadium downtown was shut down in July 2011 before replacement shelter was prepared, to say nothing of the promised neighborhood revitalization. The UN condemned this action, issuing its strongest statement on the issue and for the first time citing legal language that establishes IDPs' rights to housing. But as documented in this chapter, the damage was already done and the pattern well established.

* * *

Workshop on the Right to Housing

Patrice Florvilus

What Is the Right to Housing?

THE RIGHT TO HOUSING IS a fundamental right that the United Nations recognizes in regional treaties and many national constitutions.[1] There is a right to housing; it is a universal right. More than 100 national constitutions around the world recognize this right. It's a right everyone has. Yet the number of people who don't have anywhere to stay, who are living in bad housing conditions, and who are forcibly evicted from the land they occupy is increasing every day. More than 4 million people were forcibly evicted between 2003 and 2006. Today, 100 million people are without shelter,[2] and more than a billion people are living in substandard conditions. The UN announced that 3 billion people will live in substandard conditions in 2050. Most of these people live in the Global South.

The right to housing does not simply mean having a roof over your head. It is the condition of the housing that demonstrates whether the right to housing is respected. More than a billion people in the world do not have access to clean water, and 2.6 billion people don't have sanitation services. These people live in bad sanitary conditions, with much indignity. Several million people die every year as a result: for example, 1.8 million children die annually from diarrhea. The right to housing is connected with several other rights, like the right to live, the right to education and health, and the right to participate in national decisions.

In other words, demands for quality housing also signify a struggle for a society based on social inclusion. To struggle for the right to housing also means to struggle to live in a society without repression. It's a struggle against all forced evictions, which are illegal and which do not respect international humanitarian rights.

Definition and Elements of Housing Rights

According to the UN Committee for Economic, Social, and Cultural Rights, the right to housing doesn't mean just having a roof over one's head. It's the right to have a quality place to live in security, in peace, and with dignity. A house conforms with international law if these conditions exist: security; protection against eviction; exercising basic services and necessary infrastructure; access to drinking water and sanitation; protection against cold and extreme heat, rain, wind, and illness; and access to services for all vulnerable groups, such as people who live with physical impairments, the elderly, and children.

The UN Special Rapporteur for the Right to Housing, Miloon Kothari, defines the right to housing as "the right of every woman, man, youth and child to gain and sustain a safe and secure home and community in which to live in peace and dignity."[3] The special rapporteur underscores the realization that the right to housing is linked with the realization of other fundamental rights like the right to live, the right to protection of privacy, the right to live in a family, the right to have land, the right to food, the right to have access to good water and good education, the right to have quality health care, and so on. These rights need to be guaranteed for women and men, no matter their origin, color, or social class.

For UN Habitat, "correct" housing means sufficient space for people to live as human beings, respect for privacy, spaces that have security, and space for people to breathe well, where all basic services are present.

The right to housing is recognized in many regional and international texts. In the international arena, the two most important texts are the Universal Declaration of Human Rights (UDHR) of 1948, and the International Covenant on Economic, Social, and Cultural Rights (CESCR) of 1966. The International Covenant on Civil and Political Rights (ICCPR) of 1996 also supports this right.

Universal Declaration of Human Rights
The UDHR was the first international recognition of the right to housing. "Everyone has the right to a standard of living adequate for the health and well-being of himself and of his family," it declares in Article 25, "including food, clothing, housing and medical care and necessary social services. . . ."

International Covenant on Economic, Social, and Cultural Rights
The CESCR, written 20 years after the UDHR, recognizes the right to housing in Article 11. The state in all countries is required to take all necessary

measures to guarantee that all people can exercise their rights and have an adequate standard of living for everyone and their family.

International Covenant on Civil and Political Rights
The ICCPR recognizes that everyone has the right to live (Article 6) and be protected from mistreatment (Article 7). People have the right to privacy and protection (Article 17). These international covenants have a legal status that subjects the entire administration to enforcement (laws 156 and 160 in January 2007) for those countries that ratified the 25 articles. The San Salvador Protocol completes the American Convention, clearly stating that everyone has the right to live in a healthy environment (Article 11).

What Does Haiti's 1987 Constitution Say?

In Article 22, it is crystal clear: "The State recognizes the right of every citizen to decent housing, education, food, and social security."

The Question of Private Property

The 1987 Constitution guarantees in Article 36 the right for everyone to have private belongings. People who defend private property rights in the abstract never tried to take a little time to read Article 36-3, which clearly states, "Ownership also entails obligations. Uses of property cannot be contrary to the general interest." In the context after the January 12, 2010, earthquake, we need to ask ourselves the question of how to define private property: Is it only to respect the rights of private land for people who have land? Or is it to look toward the interest of the victims of the *goudougoudou*[4] who need a place to stay after losing all they had? Many of the victims of the *goudougoudou* who stay in public plazas or on private land are people who come from Haiti's poor majority, people who are exploited in subcontracting factories, or small peasants who left the rural areas to come to Port-au-Prince.

How Does Haiti's Civil Law Explain This Situation?

Everyone who thinks others are occupying the land they claim to own must respect what the law says regarding the repossession of this property. The legal process is the only means for people to reclaim property they think belongs to them. In other words, everyone after January 12 who would like to reclaim the belongings that the victims occupied or that they continue to occupy needs to consult the justice system. Only the courts can decide this. In this case, the person claiming to be the landowner needs to fill out an "action of eviction." If the courts rule in favor of the person claiming to be the landowner, a clerk is charged with executing the decision.

In other words, purported landowners must be able to prove the land actually belongs to them (either through purchase, inheritance, or a legal mandate that they are legally able to bring people to court or otherwise take action against people who are occupying the space). If they can't prove this, they have no legal right to forcibly evict anyone. It is worth recalling that most of the land in Haiti doesn't have a formal legal claim or title. This is why, in many cases, people claiming to be landowners do not want to go to the courts. They prefer to hire bandits, armed thugs, police, or the mayor to pressure, sometimes with arms, the IDPs to leave the spaces they have occupied since January 12.

IDPs need to use the formal justice system to defend themselves against forced evictions. The classic bourgeois legal system says that people who have the right to exercise legal action are people of "quality." In other words, someone who cannot prove the land belongs to them, or that they have the mandate to act in the name of the landlord, cannot force anyone off the land. The first approach IDPs should take when they are threatened with eviction is to ask the purported landowner or their legal agent to use the justice system. Anyone who does not work within the justice system regarding evictions is a bandit. Therefore, an individual from any social position does not have the right to use his authority to destroy people's tents. When people act like this, they are bandits. The justice system needs to punish these people for destroying people's property.

The True Sense of Housing Rights

The obligation to respect the right to housing means that the state needs to stand up to all the bullies preventing this right from being exercised. The government violates the right to housing when it uses its power to force people off the land they're living on, or when it accompanies people who claim to be the landowner in pushing people off the land they're occupying in the moment of, or following, a natural disaster. The Haitian state has an obligation to protect all Haitian citizens' right to housing.

The obligation of the state is to construct provisional housing to guarantee housing for everyone victimized by a natural disaster or anyone in an extremely precarious situation. It's a state obligation to take all necessary measures, to put in place a good strategy to turn the right to housing into reality in the rural as well as urban sectors, certainly in the most vulnerable zones.

Forcibly evicted people who have no means to find another house to live in need to file a complaint against the state in national and international courts. These people have the right to reparations as well.

Conclusion

The following is a summary of some fundamental elements for us to use to determine if the right to housing is respected.

Security
Citizens have the right to be protected against all forms of evictions or other threats and the right to healthy environmental conditions. This requires basic services and infrastructure to be established in reality, without demagoguery; quality, clean drinking water is required, as well as energy to cook, electricity, space to wash clothes and to store food, a system to clear garbage, quality drainage, and first-aid services and medical installations.

Habitability
A quality house needs to provide adequate space to protect people from cold, heat, humidity, and rain.

Easy Access
A quality house needs to give access to basic social services, like education, health care, food, clean drinking water, and technology. This requires easy access for children, the elderly, and disabled people to these services without difficulty.

The right to housing will become a reality if these conditions are met:

1. The state treats people's lives as important.
2. The state is not a *restavèk* [child servant], serving neoliberal economic policies.
3. The state cuts ties to the system of brute force established on exclusion and discrimination.

4. We are able to mobilize to compel the state to respect our rights.

5. We organize ourselves to undo the capitalist system.

6. We stand up to recuperate Haiti's rights to sovereignty.

Defending our rights to quality housing is our responsibility!

* * *

Combating Forced Evictions in Haiti's IDP Camps

Mario Joseph and Jeena Shah

THE JANUARY 12, 2010, EARTHQUAKE rendered more than 1 million Haitians homeless. Hundreds of thousands of these people, referred to in legal parlance as IDPs, ended up living in squalid tent camps. To make matters worse, government agents and purported landowners began evicting homeless families from the camps within weeks after the earthquake. According to the IOM, between June 2010 and March 2011, there were at least 247 cases of evictions from IDP camps, affecting an estimated 233,941 individuals.[5]

Forced eviction is defined under international law as the involuntary removal, permanent or temporary, of individuals, families, or communities from their homes or lands, which they occupy, without the provision of or access to appropriate forms of protection, legal or otherwise.[6] Forced evictions are also illegal under Haitian law.[7] Only in rare circumstances are evictions of IDP communities lawfully permitted, and even then the government must provide them with an alternate place to live that meets international standards, as well as due-process protections such as consultation and adequate notice (as stipulated by Principle 7 of the UN Guiding Principles on Internal Displacement).[8]

Despite these legal requirements, government agents and purported property owners who have been evicting residents from camps have often used force and coercive strategies that exploit the IDPs' vulnerability. In most cases, the Haitian government has not provided alternate living quarters. Some municipalities began paying evicted IDPs small sums of cash, but these payments were not coupled with any other housing assistance and were shown to be insufficient to secure sustainable housing, or any housing at all. And often, IDPs were told or made to believe that they would be evicted regardless of whether they accepted the payments.

Because of a long history of fraud and coercion regarding land titles, and the fact that only 5% of Haitian land titles had been recorded by the government before the earthquake, it is uncertain whether the alleged landowners who attempt to evict IDP communities really have legal rights to the land. And because those purporting to own the land usually come from Haiti's tiny but powerful elite, their word itself is generally feared among IDPs.

Sa N'ap Fè Pou Nou? (What Are You Doing for Us?)

Recognizing the extent of these forced evictions, the Bureau des Avocats Internationaux (BAI) began working in September 2010 with grassroots partner organizations like Bri Kouri Nouvèl Gaye, Force for Reflection and Action on Housing (FRAKKA), Invèsite Popilè, Batay Ouvriye, and Asanble Vwazen Solino, to create an advocacy coalition for the constitutional right to decent housing, which includes protection from forced evictions.[9] We called our coalition the Inisyativ Rezistans Kont Ekspliyson Fòse (the Resistance Initiative against Forced Evictions).[10] By pushing for housing rights to be respected, the coalition's activities would not only help prevent forced evictions but also push for a reconstruction plan that includes IDPs' participation and ultimately provides them with access to adequate housing.

At first, we wrote a letter to the prime minister with our demands. We held press conferences. We organized protests. But we failed to pick up any real momentum. We sat in our meetings trying to understand why fewer than 300 people turned up at demonstrations when more than a million people had been living in dilapidated camps for more than six months.

While many of us were becoming discouraged, we reflected on the reasons behind the lack of mobilization and considered the role of the international humanitarian aid community. One clue was to be found in the Asian Coalition of Housing Rights' *Tsunami Update,* which had noted that humanitarian aid agencies created a culture of passive dependency in Southeast Asia after the 2004 tsunami: "In this formula, the victims of calamities are considered to be helpless 'target populations,' and rehabilitation is something that is to be done for them, not by them."[11] We began noticing something similar in the camps, where many would ask, "Sa n'ap fè pou nou?" "What are you doing for us?"

From our perspective, this question resulted from the manner in which assistance had been provided to camps: aid was delivered as charity, not the realization of the IDPs' right to humanitarian assistance, and what help they received was often too little, too late. A study conducted in July 2011, for example, found that the "overwhelming majority of [IDP] families interviewed . . . felt that aid distribution was arbitrary, chaotic, and insufficient to meet their basic needs."[12]

The cash-for-work (CFW) programs implemented by humanitarian aid agencies in camps further served to discourage mobilization (see Haiti Grassroots Watch, Chapter 4, this volume). Humanitarian groups offered CFW jobs to members of camp committees—the very persons in the best position to lead and organize their communities to defend their human rights. Based on interactions with some such members of camp committees, we concluded that once these committee members obtained CFW jobs, one of two things tended to happen: either those committee members would work to ensure passivity among their community so that they could hold on to their CFW jobs, or the population would come to believe that the committee members no longer shared their interests and begin to distrust them.

We also saw a similar lack of transparency and inclusiveness in the way humanitarian aid agencies attempted to respond to forced evictions. Based on interviews with camp residents and humanitarian aid workers, we found that humanitarian actors, ostensibly acting in the name of IDP camp communities, appeared to have made deals with purported landowners without asking for proof of ownership and often without camp residents' true participation (many did not know the terms of the agreements made on their behalf). When camp residents were consulted, often only camp committees were spoken to, some of whom were handpicked by the purported landowner. Even when camp committees represented their communities, not wanting to bite the hand that fed them, they would agree with the terms proposed by aid representatives, regardless of whether the agreement respected their communities' rights. At least once, a committee agreed to an aid agency's proposal that a camp leader organizing the community to defend their rights be removed from the camp in order for the rest of the families to stay on the land for six months longer.

Since IDPs had no part in planning aid distributions, discussions of how and where they should be rehoused, or in negotiations with purported landowners, they did not expect to have any role in the advocacy we were describing. Moreover, the mobilization that we were expecting but that did not materialize also required solidarity among the communities living in more than 1,000 camps in and around Port-au-Prince. Efforts at solidarity were stifled by the arbitrary manner in which aid was distributed among camps and the manner in which the media reported on these aid distributions. Because of the advertising by humanitarian aid agencies heard on the radio, camps that did not receive any aid believed that other camps were receiving abundant resources from humanitarian aid actors and therefore were not living in the same misery as they were. In reality, studies showed that aid was not delivered to most camps, and where it was delivered, the aid was insufficient.[13]

Additionally, the IDP communities had a hard time believing in the efficacy in calling on the government to act. The media and aid community's constant use of the phrase "poorest country in the Western Hemisphere" to describe Haiti—along with the international community's history of undermining economic and social policies the Haitian government has tried to implement for the benefit of Haiti's poor—created a mentality that the Haitian government would never have the capacity to take care of its people and that the only institutions to turn to were aid groups. In turn, by not visibly pressuring the Haitian government to respond to forced evictions and instead appearing to take on the matter themselves, humanitarian aid workers reinforced the notion that the IDPs could only turn to them.

Men Anpil, Chay Pa Lou
(Many Hands Lighten the Load)

Recognizing these obstacles, the coalition decided to begin at square one. We started a series of trainings on IDP rights and solidarity in camps to mobilize IDPs to engage in public advocacy as a unified force. We aimed to get people to stop thinking of themselves as beneficiaries of charity but instead as holders of rights; to stop thinking that the varying levels of misery in the camps meant that they were not all seeking the same thing (adequate housing); to stop thinking that their needs must be addressed by unaccountable humanitarian aid actors, but instead by the government, which is charged with this duty by the Haitian Constitution.[14]

In our trainings, we would pose a series of questions to get IDP communities thinking about the rights, roles, and responsibilities of different actors in society, including the government, private landowners, humanitarian aid agencies, and their own communities—all determined by Haitian law and the design of democracy. We would raise questions about accountability and the motivations of different actors to encourage critical thinking. We would also share stories of solidarity in different periods of Haitian history and in other impoverished or disaster-hit countries. Our pedagogical approach was to provide only guidance and a show of solidarity while participants arrived at solutions to the problems they faced on their own.

We also shared our successes before international and national tribunals as a pole for organizing camp communities. In November 2010 the Inter-American Commission on Human Rights (IACHR) issued directives to the government of Haiti explaining the protections that must be afforded to IDPs from evictions based on a request we filed on behalf of five camps. In July 2011 the national prosecutor agreed to prosecute the mayor of Delmas for his spree of illegal evictions after we submitted a complaint on behalf of three camps.

We began to see small successes from these "Know Your Rights" trainings, as these events demonstrate:

Joseph, a self-identified leader of a camp off of Airport Road in Port-au-Prince, took advantage of the training program to organize a well-attended sit-in in the camp against the purported landowner's violent threats of eviction on the day of the deadline set by the landowner for them to leave. (Joseph's real name, like the others below, has been changed to protect him.) The deadline passed without a forced eviction. The purported landowner later sent armed men to intimidate the camp, but Joseph was armed with a weapon of his own—the IACHR's directives to the Haitian government. The directives made their way through the hands of the armed men to the landowner and eventually to the Ministry of Interior. The next time the landowner contacted the camp, it was to ask them to negotiate a solution wherein the landowner could use part of the land while the camp remained.

Pierre, a committee member in a camp off the main road of Delmas, a suburb of Port-au-Prince, organized his community more easily after they participated in a training. When the community was sent notice by the purported landowner to come to court, much of the camp showed up with the committee leaders and the BAI, along with leaders from other camps. Outside the courthouse, camp residents staged a demonstration, demanding that the judicial system protect their rights as IDPs. While no decision was handed down, the judge explained to the purported landowner that only a proper action for eviction, following Haitian civil procedure and the protections it offers to the defendants (in this case, the camp community), would be permitted.

Despite these small victories, it was clear for these communities and others like them that the threats of eviction would remain. As long as they were not living on property that was theirs or identified by the government as a place where they could live, they would continue to fear threats of eviction.

They would also continue to face threats by local mayors who were determined to display their power before their constituents to "clean up" their towns of the homeless, as the mayor of Delmas demonstrated when he began his campaign of unlawfully and forcibly evicting IDP camps in May 2011.

But by mid-summer 2011 we were starting to see the signs of mass mobilization we had anticipated for nearly a year. Camp leaders, witnessing a change in the mind-sets of the populations they serve, began mobilizing their own communities when other camps were facing threats of eviction to demonstrate their solidarity.[15] We hoped that the start of this mass mobilization would eventually lead to something big enough to put real pressure on the government to realize the right to housing for the hundreds of thousands of persons still living in displacement camps.

* * *

Vanishing Camps at Gunpoint

Mark Snyder

———

ON MAY 27, 2010, 10 well-armed men entered a camp of Haitian IDPs called Centre Regroupment 5 (CR5). Wearing uniforms similar to those of the Haitian National Police (HNP), though without any identifying badges, they pointed rifles and shotguns at the camp residents, demanding their names and that they agree to leave the privately owned property that the camp had been on since January 13, 2010. None resisted, and even those who were only visiting family at the camp were forced to give their names, which were recorded by one of the attackers.

The invasion left the displaced terrified. Most of the children who lived in the camp witnessed the attack, since they were unable to attend school. One member of the camp, Pharrah, a 46-year-old mother of three, described being unable to sleep at night for fear of violence against her family. She said the displaced could not leave their shelters without leaving someone present, because they were afraid of returning to find all of their belongings destroyed in an effort to push them out.

Less than two weeks after the armed men invaded CR5, the camp was visited by the HNP, this time in proper uniforms, accompanied by the local justice of the peace, who prepared and served a document stating that IDPs were occupying private land and had agreed to vacate the property by June 25. On the list were those individuals who had been forced at gunpoint to give their names and consent to leaving. This was the first step in a long process of legal evictions of IDPs from private property in Haiti, though the method of obtaining their names and consent violates Haitian and international law.

Forced evictions of IDPs after Haiti's earthquake were a foreseeable issue, given that 60% of the IDP camps were located on private land[16] and that Haiti has a history of sharp class conflict. While Haitian social movements have successfully worked alongside the displaced populations to resist the evictions, the GOH and international community, including the UN, have largely failed to protect the IDPs' human rights. This failure has allowed private landowners and municipal governments to illegally evict IDPs from both private and public lands.[17]

From Blocking Aid to Bribery

The eviction process at CR5 did not start with the armed threats in May. Before the earthquake, none of the displaced in camp CR5 had lived in the upper-middle-class neighborhood that the camp was located in, a neighborhood whose large residential buildings remained mostly unscathed. Many of the displaced were from lower-class neighborhoods that suffered extensive damage. They had lived across the street in the *bidonvil,* a patchwork of small houses cramped together along the steep mountainside. When they crossed the road to seek shelter from the earthquake damage on the open land in the adjacent neighborhood, they crossed the class divide that has a long history in Haiti.

In a June 29, 2010, interview, the purported landowner, whose residence was on an adjacent lot separated from the camp by a high concrete wall, said that he first told the IDPs to leave in early March 2010. He denigrated the displaced families, saying that they represented a sanitation issue and were "poor and thieves" who were disturbances to the community. He said their presence prevented him from living in his house and made it difficult for the neighborhood to rent apartments.

During the same interview, he said he did not and would not allow aid organizations or the IDPs to install latrines or sanitation. Nor did he want water or shelter materials distributed. He furthermore barred the IDPs from opening *ti mache*—little stores, where family members, often women, earn a small income by selling drinks or food. This was because permitting such activity, the landowner said, would encourage the displaced to stay, just as providing them such "comforts" as water, sanitation, secure housing, or other necessities would also keep them from leaving.

The landowner's statements echoed those made at the UN Office of Coordination of Humanitarian Affairs (OCHA) camp coordination/camp management (CCCM) meetings attended by representatives of international NGOs and coordinated by the International Organization for Migration (IOM). During these meeting it was repeatedly stated in one form or another that "we don't want to make it too comfortable for people in the camps or they'll never leave."[18]

A pattern of acceptance and complacency on the part of those with access to disaster-response resources emerged, leading to the use of violence against the IDPs. Private landowners' restriction of aid pushed the already vulnerable displaced population into increasingly precarious situations. Even before the forced evictions, the Hatian government and international NGOs did not interfere with the blockage of aid and allowed for the further deterioration of IDP support structures, with the NGOs then moving on to less complicated camps where the statistical requirement from donors and board members could be more easily met. This left the displaced in camps facing eviction without observers or partnerships that would advocate for their rights.

By May 2011 nearly one-quarter of all IDPs who remained in Haiti's camps faced eviction.[19] From June 2010 to April 2011, 233,000 IDPs are known to have been threatened with forced eviction.[20] More than 44,000 people have been evicted, with 165,000 still under immediate threat.[21] As the camp population gradually decreased, the year 2011 saw the rate of eviction cases significantly increase. Well-documented evictions of the displaced on public lands are being perpetrated by the mayor of Delmas, Wilson Jeudy, with the use of force and violence.[22] Jeudy openly stated that he would continue to evict the displaced, arguing that the camps harbor criminals. Threats of violence against IDPs continue in other instances, while in others bribes are being offered, from 500 gourdes ($12.50) to several thousand gourdes (with an upper limit of $250) per family.

Where Are They Going?

Although the highest offices of OCHA and the IACHR began using strong language against evictions in 2011, the stage had been set by more than a year of general inaction and acceptance. Camp committees and members organized repeatedly to compel MINUSTAH, the United Nations High Commissioner for Refugees (UNHCR), the Office of the High Commissioner of Human Rights (OHCHR), and the international organizations to provide the various protection measures and projects they said they would, to no avail. Relocation programs to move the displaced back to their own property, though helpful, offered a solution in certain camps to as few as 7.5% of the IDPs.

By December 2010 the IDP population had begun to decrease, which Luca Dall'Oglio, the Haiti chief of mission for the IOM, called "hopeful signs that many victims of the quake are getting on with their lives." He added, "We finally start to see light at the end of the tunnel for the earthquake affected population."[23] Yet according to the same IOM, only 4.7% of those who left the camps "did so because their homes had been rebuilt or repaired," as the *New York Times* reported.[24] And one in four of the registered displaced people are now facing eviction from the camps, also according to the IOM.[25]

So where are these displaced families going when they are evicted or flee because they cannot cope with the deteriorating conditions? In the case of the families of CR5, who were finally evicted, many now live in houses with substantial physical damage. According to a USAID study conducted in January 2011, "64% of houses designated as 'totally unsafe'" had been reoccupied, as Agence-France Presse reported.[26] Others found shelter in different camps and are now once again facing eviction. Pharrah, who gave her name and consent to leave the private property when a 12-gauge shotgun was drawn on her, secured permission to stay on a small plot of land in the *bidonvil* where she had lived before the earthquake, along with two other families. However, the landowner said the families had to leave by August 15, 2011. They will be redisplaced, and left to find solutions without the assistance that the international community pledged to provide.

* * *

New Threats of Eviction After One Death in a Port-au-Prince IDP Camp

Etant Dupain

THE ORPHE SHADDA CAMP HAS been under threat of eviction since July 2010.[27] Camp Shadda can be found on Delmas 1 across from Delmas 5, adjacent to the Toyota HINOTO S.A. establishment. Two hundred families have lived there since the earthquake on January 12, 2010. The victims are accustomed to receiving visits each day from Jean Mark Saliba, who claims to be the landowner and one of the owners of HINOTO S.A.

When I met with camp residents, they explained to me, "We want to go and leave this land because this is not where we lived before January 12. We just want another space where we can go because at the moment we have nowhere else to go."

The president of the camp committee, Terrier Merion, explained that the security agents of HINOTO S.A. often come to pressure the residents to leave, but the residents always talk to them without letting them put them out.

On the day of May 12, 2011, one of the men who represents the landowner, and who is chief of security, named Rosevelt Cheri, showed up with four security agents who were wearing uniforms from HINOTO S.A. They came with a padlock and a chain to close the only gate to enter the camp and prevent the displaced people from entering or leaving. It was 8 a.m. when this representative of Saliba arrived in the camp, where people had started to resist. One of the security agents from HINOTO S.A. hit Thelucia Ciffren, a 51-year-old mother of three, in her head. She fell on the spot, began to bleed, and died a few minutes later on the way to the hospital.

The people in the camp were very angry and so they held the three security agents. They handed them over to the police, but Cheri escaped.

Three days later, when Walies Jean Baptiste, Thelucia's husband, went to bring a complaint with the justice system, to demand justice for his wife, the security agents had already been released. They returned to work even before Thelucia's funeral.

"I felt humiliated in my own country because I have already been the victim of a natural catastrophe," Walies said. "And now I am continuing to be a victim of injustice under the hand of the landowner and the Haitian state, which doesn't respect the rights of internally displaced people."

Walies and his three children, accompanied by several hundred others from the camp, organized a sit-in at the HINOTO S.A. building. They protested and showed how frustrated they are to see the same criminals who killed someone from their camp free and working. As a response to this demonstration, Saliba came into the camp on June 3, 2011. Accompanied by the police, a representative of the Port-au-Prince courthouse, and two justices of the peace, he gave the people eight days to leave the camp, despite the fact that these people don't know where else to go.

Walies is asking for justice and reparations for the death of his wife at the hands of the HINOTO S.A. security on May 12, 2011. He is asking the Haitian government to give them another place to go so they won't continue to be victims at the hands of Saliba, who promised the camp residents he would evict them.

Notes

1. Translated from the original Haitian Creole by Mark Schuller.

2. In the United States, the term most used is "homeless," whereas "persons without shelter" is more correct and does not define people for what they lack, but rather focuses on the lack of housing.

3. Quoted in Miloon Kothari, Sabrina Karmali, and Shivani Chaudhry, *The Human Right to Adequate Housing and Land* (New Delhi: National Human Rights Commission, 2006), 9.

4. The term for "earthquake," mimicking the sound of the earth shaking. Many people do not want to state out loud the word *tranbleman tè a,* the Creole word for "earthquake."

5. IOM, *Displacement Tracking Matrix V2.0 Update,* March 16, 2011, 13, http://www.cccmhaiti.info.

6. See Committee on Economics, Social and Cultural Rights, General Comment 7, Forced Evictions, and the Right to Adequate Housing (Sixteenth Session, 1997), in Compilation of General Comments and Recommendations Adopted by Human Rights Treaty Bodies, U.N. Doc. HRI/Gen/1/Rev.6 at 45 (2003).

7. The ways in which evictions may be carried out are described in the Haitian Code of Civil Procedure.

8. The UN Guiding Principles are available at http://www.brookings.edu/projects/idp/gp_page.aspx.

9. Article 22 of the Haitian Constitution recognizes the right to adequate housing, which "at the very least . . . places a negative obligation upon the State and all other entities and persons to desist from preventing or impairing the right

of access to adequate housing" (Jayna Kothari, *Right of Housing: Constitutional Perspective on India and South Africa,* Lawyers Collective, June 2001). Although the tent camps by no means constitute adequate housing, forced evictions violate Article 22 since camp residents are not provided with adequate housing to which to relocate.

10. The membership of the Initiative changed continuously throughout the first year of its existence, with groups leaving and joining, and subsets designing and implementing separate advocacy activities not mentioned in this article.

11. Asian Housing Rights Coalition, *Tsunami Update,* no. 1 (June 2006).

12. The Institute for Justice & Democracy in Haiti and the LAMP for Haiti Foundation, "We've Been Forgotten: Conditions in Haiti's Displacement Camps Eight Months after the Earthquake," 2010, 14.

13. Mark Schuller, "Unstable Foundations: Impact of NGOs on Human Rights for Port-au-Prince's Internally Displaced People," October 4, 2010, City University of New York and Université d'Etat d'Haïti, ijdh.org/archives/14855.

14. 1987 Constitutions of the Republic of Haiti, Article 19: "The State has the absolute obligation to guarantee the right to life, health, and respect of the human person for all citizens without distinction, in conformity with 'The Universal Declaration of the Rights of Man.'"

15. Trenton Daniel, "Protest over Evictions in Haiti Blocks Traffic," *Miami Herald,* August 2, 2011, http://ijdh.org/archives/20488.

16. USAID, "Haiti—Earthquake," Fact Sheet no. 58 (June 11, 2010): 2, http://reliefweb.int/node/357794.

17. IDPs' right to remain is grounded in the freedom of movement established by the Center for Civil and Political Rights, ratified by the Haitian government. IDP children's rights to a standard of living suitable for normal development and free education are also legally binding on the Haitian government by ratification of the CRC.

18. International Action Ties meeting minutes, CCCM and Protection Cluster meetings, March and April 2010.

19. UNHCR, Protection Cluster, "Expulsions forcees: contexte, enjeux, fonctions" (Forced Evictions: Context, Challenges, Functions), April 12, 2011, http://www.cccmhaiti.info/evictions/SOPs-forcedevictions.pdf.

20. CCCM, "Haiti—Nearly One Quarter of Those Still Homeless in Haiti Threatened With Eviction," press release, April 1, 2011http://www.cccmhaiti.info/z_nearly_one_quater_of_those_still_homeless_haiti_threatened_eviction.php.

21. UNHCR, Protection Cluster, "Expulsions forcees."

22. Bri Kouri Nouvèl Gaye, "Violent and Destructive Eviction at the Kafou Ayopo, Haiti," May 23, 2011, available at http://brikourinouvelgaye.com/2011/05/23/violent-and-destructive-eviction-at-the-kafou-ayopo-haiti; Mark Snyder and Mark Schuller, "Between the Storms? Thousands of Haitian IDPs Are Still at Risk of Forced Eviction," Common Dreams, June 18, 2011, available at http://www.commondreams.org/view/2011/06/18-7.

23. IOM, "Dramatic Fall in Haiti's IDP Population," press release, December 9, 2010.

24. Randal C. Archibold, "Haitians Forced Out of Tents to Homes Just as Precarious," *The New York Times,* April 23, 2010.

25. IOM, "Haiti—Nearly One Quarter of Those Still Homeless in Haiti Threatened with Eviction," press release, April 1, 2011, http://www.iomhaiti.com/ft/page.php?id=40.

26. More controversially, the USAID study questioned the official UN death toll numbers from the earthquake. See Emily Troutman, "US Report Queries Haiti Quake Death Toll, Homeless," Agence-France-Presse, May 27, 2011.

27. Originally posted on June 4, 2011 on the Bri Kouri Nouvèl Gaye website, http://brikourinouvelgaye.com/2011/06/04/new-threats-of-eviction-after-one-death-in-port-au-prince-idp-camp/.

8

Impacts on and
Participation of Women

To comprehend the realities that Haitian women face, it is critical to first understand what black feminist scholars have called "intersectionality," the multiple forms of oppression based on distinct but overlapping identities, such as those of race, class, gender, sexuality, age, and parental status.[1] This intersectionality occurs in the context of what activist scholars have called "structural violence,"[2] the long-term, often invisible system of inequality and poverty, which in Haiti's case comprises the legacies of the country's 1825 independence debt, the 1915 US occupation, and neoliberalism (see Chapters 1 and 2, this volume). As heads of household responsible for the education and health care of their children, women disproportionately pay the price of neoliberalism's privatization and reduction of social services.

The earthquake fractured Haitian society along existing sociocultural cleavages, such as the interlocking systems of oppression of gender, poverty, and kouch sosyal, *roughly translated as "socioeconomic status."[3] As a result, Haitian women's condition, particularly among Port-au-Prince's poor majority, markedly deteriorated,* abse sou klou. *As in other contexts, these preexisting gender inequalities rendered Haitian women more vulnerable to disasters. After "natural" disasters like Hurricane Katrina or conflicts like the war in Kosovo, women's bodies are increasingly targeted for acts of violence. Generally speaking, disasters disproportionately impact women who have greater vulnerability as a result of traditional cultural roles, social policies, and persistent inequalities.[4]*

Only through understanding intersectionality, structural violence, and vulnerability can a post-earthquake epidemic of sexual violence make sense. In the months that followed, international news, legal, development, human

*rights, and solidarity agencies highlighted the issue of gender-based violence
(GBV), which has by all accounts increased since the earthquake. Despite activists' nuanced understanding and efforts, official responses have been inadequate
while reproducing troubling, albeit familiar, discourses that tend to trigger either denial or demonization. As women's groups throughout the world have
warned, patriarchal structures often turn to overt forms of violence in situations
of economic distress when men's status as "providers" or "breadwinners" have
been challenged. This is fueled in the context of the camps, where there is no
privacy to bathe and no space between tents that are all too easy to rip.*

Despite demonstrated inequality, women are said to be poto mitan, *pillars
of the family, community, and society, respected for their central role as heads of
household responsible for raising Haiti's next generation. Women have also been
actively organizing to improve society, including the establishment of women's
organizations. The Ligue Féminine d'Action Sociale (Women's League for Social Action) played an instrumental role in ending the 19-year US occupation
in 1934, and women were active leaders in the democratization movement
leading up to and following Duvalier's ouster in 1986. Since this time, women's
groups like Solidarité des Femmes Haïtiennes (Haitian Women's Solidarity;
SOFA) and Kay Fanm have waged a struggle against violence and legal discrimination, opening safe houses and writing laws. They continue this struggle
today, as Haitian American literary scholar and author Myriam J.A. Chancy
documents. Women from Haiti as well as the Diaspora, and from all* kouch
sosyal *and political positions responded to the earthquake in the ways familiar to women who had always been active, on issues as diverse as the women
themselves. Chancy's beautiful tribute documents the continuity of struggle and
corrects the record that Haitian people, especially women, are merely victims.*

*Including and especially in the camps, women have been actively confront-
ing the wave of violence. Members of groups like* Komisyou Fanm Viktim Por
Viktim *(Commission of Women Victims for Victims, KOFAVIV) and* Famn
Viktim, Leve Kanpe *(Women Victims, Stand Up, FAVILEK) offer legal, moral,
medical, and sometimes material support to other victims of violence sleeping
under tents. This struggle, which includes an injunction to the Inter-American
Tribunal of Human Rights, is documented by a report coauthored by international women's groups like MADRE and Haiti solidarity groups like the
Institute for Justice and Democracy in Haiti (IJDH). Taking its title from a
blog by solidarity activist Beverly Bell, quoting a KOFAVIV activist, this July
2010 report and January 2011 follow-up study (excerpted here) have made a
powerful impact in policy circles.*

*New York University's Center for Human Rights and Global Justice, which
had published analyses critical of the situation of water and food aid, conducted
a study exploring the link between food insecurity and GBV, an excerpt of which*

follows. An alarming 14% of families living in the camps told the researchers that one or more of their household members had been subject to GBV during the first year after the earthquake, and that reports of "transactional sex" and GBV increased when food aid stopped. KOFAVIV cofounders Eramithe Delva and Malya Villard-Apollon, on the front lines in the struggle against GBV in the camps, reflect on the larger meanings of this violence, pointing to Haiti's loss of sovereignty and its continued socioeconomic crisis. Delva and Villard-Apollon also directly challenge the stereotypes that too often accompany the international attention to the GBV epidemic.

* * *

Hearing Our Mothers
Safeguarding Haitian Women's Representation and Practices of Survival

Myriam J.A. Chancy

IN THE AFTERMATH OF THE January 12, 2010, earthquake, Haitian women's voices stood the most silenced and neglected.[5] Such lack of audibility was underscored by the news that prominent figures in Haiti's women's movement, including Myriam Merlet, Magalie Marcelin, and Anne Marie Coriolan, had perished, as well as women leaders in the government and in journalism, including Nicole Grégoire (in public administration), Gina Dorcena (of Radio Tropic), Mirland Dorvilus and Bernardine Bourdeau (both of the women's group Solidarité Fanm Ayisyen, or SOFA). Some died days after the quake—Merlet five days later, after continuously using her cell phone to call for rescue from beneath the rubble.[6]

Merlet, Marcelin, and Coriolan were the leaders, respectively, of Enfofanm, Kay Fanm, and SOFA, women's groups that emerged after the end of the Duvalier regime and that sought to give women a voice across class differences—especially under military rule, be it under the Haitian military (in the 1990s) or as a result of US or UN occupation (in 1994 and intermittently from 2004 to the present). In these periods, women suffered disproportionate bodily harm, ranging from dismemberments in the late 1990s[7] to systematic rapes designed to intimidate and desecrate women's lives, as groups vied for power at the national level. These women's organizations provided radio, print, and scholarly outlets to record what was happening to Haitian women, using first-person interviews and disseminating the information beyond Haitian borders and, in some instances, providing legal recourse to victims.

Elaine Zuckerman, president of Gender Action and a former program officer for Haiti of the Inter-American Development Bank (IDB), notes that before the earthquake, "Haitian women and young girls were victims of rampant rape and violence [and that] individual rape by export-processing factory managers was often a condition for continued employment in jobs that paid a pittance."[8] Aid and loans from the IDB, International Monetary Fund (IMF), and World Bank came with conditions that "required Haiti to remove agricultural tariffs which swamped the country with cheap US rice." This, together with Haiti's loss of agricultural tariffs, "decimated" the livelihoods of poor Haitian farmers, most of whom are women, Zuckerman asserts. Thus, she concludes, "When you aid a nation's women, their children and communities will rise."

Today, post-earthquake, numerous global women's crisis organizations have made clear that women and children are once again disproportionately affected, suffering from lack of access to food and health care, as well as vulnerability to violence. This includes rape in urban areas that lack electricity at night and in overcrowded shelters and tent cities. As Colette Lespinasse, director of the Groupe d'Appui aux Repatriés et Refugiés (GARR), reported at a UN side event related to the Commission on the Status of Women meeting of March 3, 2011, there is also increasing concern "about the protection of orphaned children, who [are] at risk of being sold into forced work or prostitution, especially girls."[9]

The challenge today is to assist Haitian women in re-creating the structures and archives that will result in equal political representation, equal civil protection, and equal economic access to goods and services. Many organizations, such as the UN-affiliated UN Women (formerly UNIFEM), the Huairou Commission,[10] and female heads of state like former Chilean president Michelle Bachelet and former Canadian governor general Michaëlle Jean, recognize this obvious equation, but governmental and international organizations have been slow to follow through. The world's population is almost equally divided by gender, yet its resources are not.[11] In most countries of the Global South, including all the Caribbean nations—and Haiti in particular—women slightly outnumber men and yet, as UNIFEM's former director Inés Alberdi noted, "Women are still outnumbered 4 to 1 in legislatures around the world; the proportion of women's work in vulnerable employment is increasing in almost all parts of the developing world, reaching 85 percent in some regions; women's wages still lag behind those of men; and millions endure some form of gender-based violence, often on a daily basis."[12]

What, then, are some solutions to the problems of insecurity, political, and economic invisibility? First, Haitian women's political representation must be ensured at all the meetings being planned in, outside, and on behalf of Haiti. I am also very certain that those of us outside Haiti—whether Haitian or not, born in Haiti, or descendants of Haitians—must lend our resources and voices to Haitian women *inside* Haiti, since they know best what their true needs are. This does not mean that those of us who are not Haitian or those of us who are but witnessing events in Haiti at a distance must not take part in the rebuilding efforts, but that we must be aware of our privileges as we do so, whatever our respective and personal losses might be in Haiti itself. We are among the survivors whose privileges can make a difference; we can be strong enough to have the difficult conversations that will place our needs beneath those of Haitians on the ground, for their efforts are many and can provide a blueprint for organizing.

We must support and sustain collaborative ventures like the mobilization efforts of Haitian Women for Refugees, which partnered with Lakou Radio New York and the Santo Domingo–based Movimiento de Mujeres Dominico-Haitiana (MUDHA), headed by Sonia Pierre. Shortly after the earthquake, in only their first of several planned convoys, these groups moved more than a ton of supplies from the United States through the Dominican Republic and into areas beyond Port-au-Prince as remote as Léogâne. In short, what I am speaking of is the need to sustain grassroots organizations as well as what the Huairou Commission calls "funds for south-south community to community transfer."[13]

This statement means supporting South-South coalitions and collaborative efforts such that the North-South dynamic that we have seen at play in past aid to Haiti is curtailed; this approach means providing the resources to transmit and store data, whether in the form of images or of broadcasts as they come out of and are restored to Haiti; the intent is to facilitate connections between groups on the ground—for example, linking the isolated Haitian women's art collective Atis Fanm Matenwa, located in a remote mountainous region of the island of La Gonav situated in Haiti's bay, to the larger women's groups in Port-au-Prince that requested arts training shortly after the earthquake.

In efforts to assist women's autonomy, some aid groups like the World Food Programme (WFP) have set up food distribution sites throughout the capital exclusively for women. Smaller organizations like the local Association for the Promotion of Integral Family Healthcare (APROSIFA), reports Beverly Bell, "[have] contracted with . . . *timachan[s],* small food vendors with roots in the community . . . [to serve] one meal a day to the same ten or fifteen families, usually with upwards of seven members per family."[14] Though Bell does not expressly say so, undoubtedly the majority of these *timachans* are market women. The food distributed at the grassroots level is all locally grown, giving lie to the myth that food aid to Haiti must be subsidized from without: Haiti can feed itself and Haitians each other, given the chance. Ironically, the current lack of post-earthquake in-routes for imported food have given initiatives like these half a chance of continuing.

In her International Women's Day piece, Bell also reports that, as in previous periods of insecurity, "Women have taken the initiative in protecting each other, as well as children, from rape and other violence." These efforts include intervening in rapes in progress, paying bus fares for girls to return to countryside families, and offering services of "accompaniment" to record instances of rapes and other violence, as well as to seek necessary aftercare.[15] Given these examples of perseverance and resistance, perhaps now is the time to observe and learn from those in Haiti who have always sustained themselves in an often unrecognized, parallel economy where sharing what one has with one's family, friends, and even strangers is more important than being recognized—where feeding one mouth and then another, and then another, down through the generations, speaks louder to survival than words.

Observing a scene in a damaged kindergarten building turned into a shelter, Bell writes,

> The walls are lined with stacks of bundles tied in sheets. Above the bundles, white banners read "love," "solidarity," and "respect." . . . A two year old dressed only in a t-shirt toddles towards a photographer's camera, beaming and calling. "Photo. Photo." One woman in response to whether she wants her picture taken, replies in perfect English: "No. I don't want my family to see [me] in a shelter."[16]

Such a scene reminds me of my own beginnings and ancestry, of two women three generations removed who did everything in their power to shelter their families, my great-grandmothers: Euphosia Vilmé Chancy, a laundress who also gardened and raised small livestock to make ends meet, and Aricie César Lamour, a market woman. In the black-and-white studio photographs they have left behind, both are unsmiling, dressed simply but soberly, respectably. Unlike the stereotypical images of market and working-class Haitian women with enormous loads upon their heads or half-clad, images that abound in today's media, they represent themselves as the women they are away from their stalls and work, women with private lives that have little to do with the work they must bear.

They both had single children, my grandparents, whose children (my parents and their siblings) they helped to sustain and to raise by sheer will and daily, bone-hard work. Their women's labor ensured a future prosperity that paved the way for women like me to voice their lives, name their names, so that they, like so many Haitian women before them and since, shall not be forgotten. Their photographs remind me of the lives that today's commercial and journalistic images of Haitian women hide, of the great depth of feeling and individuality we should all seek to acknowledge.

But what is different today than some 80 or 30 years ago—when my great-grandmothers were alive and still toiling, their children following in their footsteps in blue-collar trades only a few steps removed from their own (a seamstress, a jack-of-all-trades who ultimately became an undertaker)—what is different today than even some 10 years ago is the degree to which Haiti's infrastructure has been eroded, as well as our ability to establish South-South connections. Today, after the earthquake, we stand a chance of making a difference, but it is a difference that could have been made before January 12, 2010, and that will not be solved by UN-sponsored plans for more factories in a country whose workforce has suffered crippling amputations: it was not a solution for yesterday, and it will not be a solution for tomorrow.

The images coming out of Haiti these days are mixed: they are of hope and despair, of shame as well as joy. Let us ensure that we respect how Haitians, and Haitian women in particular, choose to represent themselves before the camera eye in fullness of self or to tell us, in no uncertain terms, what needs to be done, and how—just as our grandmothers did.

* * *

Our Bodies Are Still Trembling
Haitian Women Fight Rape

MADRE, CUNY School of Law, BAI, IJDH, and Lisa Davis

———

ONE YEAR AFTER THE DEVASTATING earthquake, the government of Haiti, the UN, and the international community have failed to effectively respond to gender-based violence (GBV) against Haitian women and girls living in the sprawling network of IDP camps blanketing Haiti's capital,

Port-au-Prince.[17] With scarce resources and under brutal conditions, women in the camps have organized a breathtaking array of ad hoc services for rape survivors, including community-based security patrols and psychosocial support, legal advocacy, and medical care. But their capacity is limited, and the rapes continue unabated. In fact, over the year, deteriorating conditions in the IDP camps, a deadly cholera outbreak, political upheaval, and persistent impunity for rape have increased insecurity and the risk of sexual violence for women.

Rape and sexual violence are extreme violations of universal human rights and compromise the ability of women to access the full panoply of their civil, political, economic, social, and cultural rights. The deprivation of these rights, in turn, causes a downward spiral leading to further deterioration of human rights.[18]

For example, a young woman who is injured and traumatized by rape may be unable to exercise her human right to attend school, work, or participate in public life. In the wake of disaster, women generally have less access to resources and are excluded from decision making. This discrimination makes women and girls more vulnerable to the impact of disasters, including the specific conditions that give rise to sexual violence. Disproportionate vulnerability in times of disaster also exacerbates the consequences of sexual violence, such as disease, disability, and depression.

Women and girls are put at increased risk of rape by the collapse of social infrastructures, the erosion of family and community networks, inequitable access to social services, absence of law and order, lack of secure housing or safe neighborhoods, and dependence resulting from economic dislocation. All of these conditions have been rife since the earthquake in Haiti, creating a perfect storm of sexual violence that has raged across the camps.

The government, facing constrained capacity resulting in part from international policies that predate the earthquake, only recently issued a strategic plan for housing for the estimated 1 million to 1.3 million residents of some 1,000 IDP camps. The plan will not be implemented for months, if not years.[19] Quite simply, there is no end in sight for the dangerous conditions in which Haitian women and girls live.

Persistent Crisis of Rape in Haiti's IDP camps

In May, June, July, and October 2010, delegations of US lawyers, community researchers, and a women's health specialist investigated the prevalence and patterns of rape and other GBV against IDPs in Port-au-Prince in the aftermath of the earthquake as well as the governmental, intergovernmental, nongovernmental, and grassroots responses to the violence. In May and June alone, members of the delegation interviewed more than 50 women who had survived rape or attempted rape since the earthquake. These women and girls were referred to the delegations by KOFAVIV and FAVILEK.

The investigation revealed striking patterns among the rapes. In particular, a majority of the reported rapes occurred at night and were perpetrated by strangers wielding weapons. Gang rape was not uncommon. Although most survivors were unable to identify their attackers due to the lack of lighting in the IDP camps, others recognized their attackers as escaped convicts or gang members. Patterns also emerged regarding survivors' post-rape experiences. Many women, including grassroots women's organizations working in the camps and poor neighborhoods within Port-au-Prince, were told by their perpetrators to expect retaliation if they reported the rape. Those who did have the courage to report their rapes to the authorities were typically met with indifference. Further, women reported a lack of access to adequate health-care services and facilities.[20]

As of January 6, 2011, KOFAVIV has documented more than 640 cases of rape since the earthquake. Similarly, SOFA, a well-known Haitian women's health organization, documented in its clinics 718 cases of GBV against women and girls from January to June 2010. According to SOFA's assessment report issued in November, sexual violence targeting women is a growing emergency.

International Legal Case

On October 21, 2010, attorneys from MADRE, the International Women's Human Rights (IWHR) Clinic at the City University of New York (CUNY) School of Law, the IJDH, BAI, Morrison and Foerster LLP, the Center for Constitutional Rights (CCR), and Women's Link Worldwide submitted a Request for Precautionary Measures to the IACHR.[21] The petition called on both the Haitian government and the international community to take immediate action to ensure security, lighting, and access to medical care in camps, as well as meaningful participation by grassroots women's groups in planning sessions for addressing GBV in camps. Advocates asked the IACHR to grant the request as an urgent measure to address the multiple acts of sexual violence that women in the displacement camps are facing.

The IACHR's decision includes the following legally binding recommendations:

1. Ensure that medical and psychological care is provided in locations available to victims of sexual abuse of 22 IDP camps. This precautionary measures decision, in particular, ensures that there be privacy during examinations; availability of female medical staff members, with a cultural sensitivity and experience with victims of sexual violence; issuance of medical certificates; HIV prophylaxis; and emergency contraception.
2. Implement effective security measures in the 22 camps—in particular, provide street lighting, an adequate patrolling in and around the camps, and a greater number of female security forces in police patrols in the camps and in police stations in proximity to the camps.
3. Ensure that public officials responsible for responding to incidents of sexual violence receive training enabling them to respond adequately to complaints of sexual violence and to adopt safety measures.
4. Establish special units within the police and the Public Ministry investigating cases of rape and other forms of violence against women and girls.
5. Ensure that grassroots women's groups have full participation and leadership in planning and implementing policies and practices to combat and prevent sexual violence and other forms of violence in the camps.

Building on Successes
Within Haiti's Women's Movement

The success of the IACHR decision rests on its implementation, and that, on participation by women's organizations. In recent decades the Haitian women's movement has achieved considerable success, including the establishment of shelters and support structures for survivors of sexual violence, the adoption of a 2005 law on violence against women, improved rights to women's education and bank credit, and the accession of a few women to government positions and parliamentary seats. Among the movement's important achievements has been the creation of the Ministère à la Condition Féminine et aux Droits des Femmes (Women's Ministry or MCFDF).

In light of Haiti's current crisis, the Women's Ministry should be recognized as a key body in designing strategies to enhance and protect women's rights and in implementing the IACHR's recommendations, which provide a clear starting point for such strategies. Unfortunately, the exclusion of grassroots organizations from key decisions, programs, and policies impacting women's human rights is ongoing to date.

In December 2010 the UN GBV Sub-Cluster[22] released its list of strategies for 2011 for combating GBV in Haiti, a simple one-and-a-half-page, bullet-pointed summary of objectives and goals. Unfortunately there is still no specific mention of including grassroots women's organizations in meaningful participation in the coordination of efforts to address and prevent sexual violence in Port-au-Prince IDP camps, as mandated by international law. This continued exclusion by Sub-Cluster members not only violates their obligations under international human rights law but also undermines strategies to combat GBV, including the IACHR mandate noted above.

This said, in a positive step, the Sub-Cluster did relocate its meetings to the Women's Ministry, a more central location in Port-au-Prince, which helps provide better access to meetings. Under pressure from advocates, the Sub-Cluster leadership met with one out of the several grassroots organizations operating within the IDP camps to address sexual violence.

However, the GBV Sub-Cluster has continued to refuse to provide Creole translation, the primary spoken language of the vast majority of Haitians, at its meetings, making meaningful participation by grassroots groups impossible. The GBV Sub-Cluster coordinator recently stated that providing translation would be "tedious" and that holding the meetings in French is important because the international groups would otherwise be incapable of communicating with one another.

Recommendations

To meet its obligations to combat GBV and fully implement the commission's requests, the government of Haiti needs adequate resources to provide for its own citizens.[23] Pledged funds must be spent effectively and transparently.[24] Moving forward, policies and practices of the UN, donor states, and NGOs in Haiti should uphold the Haitian government's sovereignty and the IACHR's recommendations:

1. Ensure adequate and accessible medical and psychological care.
2. Implement effective security measures.
3. Ensure appropriate and adequate response to complaints of GBV.
4. Investigate and prosecute instances of violence against women.
5. Ensure meaningful participation of grassroots women's groups in leadership and planning of policies to combat and prevent violence.

* * *

Sexual Violence in Haiti's IDP Camps
Survey Results

CHRGJ, NYU School of Law,
Margaret Satterthwaite, and Veerle Opgenhaffen[25]

In October 2010 UN Special Rapporteur Rashida Manjoo denounced the vulnerability of Haitian women to sexual and domestic violence in the country's post-earthquake IDP camps. "In the aftermath of an emergency, pre-existing vulnerabilities and patterns of discrimination and human rights violations are often exacerbated," she said before the UN General Assembly.[26] The following November, the IAHCR granted a request for precautionary measures to be taken that would focus on Haitian women's participation in efforts to combat gender-based violence and to establish health measures and security.[27]

As Manjoo noted, sexual violence often increases in postdisaster settings, in which infrastructure is damaged, security services are overstretched, and living conditions are poor. After the South Asian tsunami in 2004, for example, studies reported an increase in sexual violence.[28] Likewise, in the aftermath of Hurricane Katrina, reported cases of sexual violence more than tripled.[29] In the case of Haiti, sexual violence has been studied both before and after the earthquake, but the studies gathered data using different techniques and varied definitions of sexual violence, making them incomparable. It is therefore impossible to determine with certainty that sexual violence has increased in Haiti since the earthquake.

However, a household survey conducted in January 2011 by the Center for Human Rights and Global Justice (CHRGJ) at NYU School of Law in four IDP camps in and around Port-au-Prince appears to confirm the dire concern expressed by both grassroots and international NGOs: that sexual violence in IDP camps is occurring at alarming rates.[30] The survey found that an alarming 14% of respondents reported that one or more members of their household had been victimized by rape, unwanted touching, or both (referred to together here as "sexual violence").[31] Nine percent of all respondents reported that one or more household members had been "raped or forced into having sex when they did not want to" since the earthquake.[32] Eight percent reported that one or more had been "touched in a way you or they did not want to be touched, not including rape or forced sex."[33]

Not all respondents who reported an incident of sexual violence provided the gender and age of the victim. However, of those who reported gender, the vast majority (about 86%) were women and girls. Notably, men and boys made up about 14% of victims whose gender was reported ("girl" and "boy" were defined as under age 18). Most sexual assault victims whose gender was reported were women in their early twenties, although a number of female victims were in their early teens. The youngest victim whose age was reported was a four-year-old boy.

Findings concerning the pervasiveness of sexual violence must be interpreted with caution, given the problem of underreporting. There are many reasons for underreporting. In Haiti, studies have suggested that shame, fear of retaliation, and very low prosecution rates for sexual violence contribute to the problem.[34] In addition, respondents may not have known about all acts of sexual violence inflicted on their household members, leading to accidental underreporting. Even if they had complete knowledge of such incidents, some respondents may have been reluctant to report them, perhaps especially to male interviewers.[35] Other studies have suggested that intrafamilial sexual violence likely goes unreported in Haiti[36] and may be particularly prevalent in households where other forms of domestic violence are taking place. Finally, while studies—including the CHRGJ study—often survey only respondents over age 18, at least one report indicates that significant numbers of victims of sexual violence in Haiti are under 18,[37] meaning that data collected from respondents over 18 may tend to understate the full extent of the problem.

The full results of the CHRGJ study, including analysis of additional survey data, data collected through qualitative methods, and detailed recommendations, will be explored in a report to be published at the end of the project in autumn 2011. Preliminary analysis of the survey data suggests at least three pressing issues for further research and discussion. First, there is a correlation between food insecurity and sexual violence. Survey respondents who reported having experienced sexual violence themselves were also notably less likely to report having eaten every day in the past week than those who were not victims of sexual violence.

Second, there was a strikingly high level of agreement among respondents about the prevalence of girls and women trading sex for food, money, protection, or shelter since the earthquake—a phenomenon often called "transactional" or "survival" sex, and a difficult issue to address given issues of stigma. The survey results suggest that camp residents believe that trading sex for basic needs has become a more common survival strategy for women and girls in the camps since the earthquake.

Finally, CHRGJ's preliminary data indicate that sexual violence may be worse in camps that lack official management agencies than those that have them. For example, 18% of surveyed households in one unmanaged camp, Champs de Mars in Port-au-Prince, reported experiencing sexual violence, compared with 10% in Terrain de Golf, a managed camp. This may be a particularly significant finding given that as of January 2011, more than half of all camps still lacked official NGO management.

* * *

Women Say, Enough Is Enough!

Eramithe Delva and Malya Villard-Apollon

AFTER JANUARY 12, 2010, HAITI has traversed a difficult impasse where fathers lost their children, children lost their fathers, mothers lost their children, brothers lost their sisters, and so on.[38] Since the earthquake, many families were forced to live in a very degrading situation in camps that are unacceptable for human occupation. As in other countries, good human principles and protocols that humanitarian organizations and the state need to apply have been established. But we observe that in Haiti up until today, these principles are being trampled on, causing women and young girls to be ever more exposed to rapists.

This is a worrisome situation in which the violence does not spare even a one-year-old child. Today, despite Haitian women's shouting in the government's ear, it appears that their ears are blocked shut because nothing really has yet changed for women and girls who have yet to have any relief from the rapists. Study after study, condemnation after condemnation from the Haitian government, from the minister of justice, and from the HNP, but we have yet to see a true plan for security to save the lives of the most vulnerable people. This enables the rapists to continue, and in fact they are increasing their violent and ganglike acts because they know they won't be arrested, or if a victim files a complaint they will have the chance to sneak away. Several bandits have been let out of prison who are committing these acts while the justice system hasn't decided to do anything.

Wherever the Haitian government has set foot, it sees the people piled on top of one another in the camps, stuck in abject misery, while the national and international bigwigs negotiate on their backs to supposedly "get them out of misery." All the while they are putting people in even greater misery.

If we talk about the consequences of extreme poverty on society, we will never be able to stop talking: people living in ever greater suffering turn to theft; women and young girls turn to prostitution, and the number of rapes never stops going up every day; our young men get used, earning a little money to engage in dishonest acts such as kidnapping, killing people, and prostituting themselves to other men.

If the Haitian state fulfilled its responsibility the same way other countries do when disasters occur, the people would never fall into this kind of suffering. Up until today they still can't find a house to live in. They're under a little piece of fabric or tarps. They do not have security where they live.

That clearly shows that the Haitian government has failed in its responsibilities regarding the people's living situation, because today people are stuck in the same situation. There is no change. All the while they say that we have received aid from the whole world, and negotiations for the people are taking place here and everywhere. We will never find a solution. It looks like a conspiracy to fill their pockets on the backs of the people. My friends, how long will we have to wait for a real state that can negotiate in favor of the Haitian people?

After much analysis we have made about the situation in our country, we can observe that January 12, 2010, equals misery, rape, kidnapping, violence against women, juvenile delinquency, and unemployment.

The Haitian people are a very courageous people, because there are no other people in the world who could accept to live the way Haitian people live. The usual image promoted of Haiti is of a savage people or even cannibals, but it's not true. We are a people who have a lot of courage and tolerance.

Notes

1. See, for example, Patricia Hill Collins, *Black Feminist Thought: Knowledge, Consciousness, and the Politics of Empowerment,* 2nd ed. (New York: Routledge, 2000); Kimberlé Williams Crenshaw, "Mapping the Margins: Intersectionality, Identity Politics, and Violence against Women of Color," *Stanford Law Review* 43, no. 6 (1991): 1241–99; Angela Yvonne Davis, *Women, Race, and Class,* 1st Vintage Books ed. (New York: Vintage Books, 1983).

2. Paul Farmer, "An Anthropology of Structural Violence," *Current Anthropology* 45, no. 3 (2004): 305–25; Faye Venetia Harrison, "The Gendered Politics and Violence of Structural Adjustment: A View from Jamaica," in *Situated Lives: Gender and Culture in Everyday Life,* ed. Louise Lamphere, Helen Ragone, and Patricia Zavella (New York: Routledge, 1997): 451–68.

3. J. A. Gracien Jean, in *Sociétés Civiles en Mutation,* ed. Philippe Fils-Aimé (Port-au-Prince: Centre International de Politologie Appliquée-Haïti, 2002), 1–55.

4. For a couple of resources, see Elaine Enarson, "Through Women's Eyes: A Gendered Research Agenda for Disaster Social Science," *Disasters* 22, no. 2 (1998): 157–73; Jane M. Henrici, Allison Suppan Helmuth, and Jackie Braun, *Women, Disasters, and Hurricane Katrina* (Institute for Women's Policy Research, Washington, DC), 2010.

5. This essay is excerpted and modified from a presentation solicited by the Human Rights Project at Bard College for a colloquium titled "Beyond Silence: Meaning and Memory in the Noise of Haiti's Present," March 12, 2010. The essay will appear in its entirety, together with other select colloquium presentations, in a forthcoming volume of the same name (ed. Winter Schneider, Caribbean Press).

6. Information relayed January 17, 2010, via e-mail by Haitian American poet Lenelle Moïse, who received firsthand information from playwright and activist Eve Ensler.

7. For more information on this political juncture in Haiti, see the conclusion of my *Framing Silence: Revolutionary Novels by Haitian Women* (Piscataway, NJ: Rutgers University Press, 1997).

8. Elaine Zuckerman, "To Help Haiti, Upend Aid Habits, and Focus On Its Women Center for Economic and Policy Research," CEPR Relief and Reconstruction Watch (blog), February 8, 2010, http://www.cepr.net.

9. Quoted in UN Women (formerly UNIFEM), "Voices of Haitian Women Highlighted," March 3, 2010, www.unifem.org/news_events/story_detail.php?StoryID=1046.

10. The group's mission statement reads as follows: "The Huairou Commission is a global coalition of networks, institutions and individual professionals that links grassroots women's community development organizations to partners. The networks seek access to resources, information sharing and political space. At the same time, it links development professionals to on-the-ground practice. Currently, the network focuses its joint efforts on five campaigns: Governance, AIDS, Disaster, Land and Housing and Peace Building" (http://www.huairou.org/mission-and-description).

11. See "World Population Prospects: The 2008 Revision" (data sheet), http://www.xist.org/earth/pop_gender.aspx. The table is drawn from the UN Statistics Division, Department of Economic and Social Affairs. Not surprisingly, the population ratios are summarized with emphasis on the male gender (see note at bottom: gender ratio = males per 100 females).

12. Inés Alberdi, "Accountability for Gender Equality Commitments Vital," Inter Press Service, March 1, 2010, http://www.ips.org/TV/beijing15/account ability-for-gender-equality-commitments-vital.

13. See the reports filed under Haiti at http://www.huairou.org.

14. Beverly Bell, "Haiti: Putting 'Humanitarian' Back in 'Humanitarian Aid,'" *World Pulse,* February 15, 2010, www.worldpulse.com/node/17677.

15. Ibid.

16. Ibid.

17. Adapted from *Our Bodes Are Still Trembling: Haitian Women Continue to Fight Against Rape. One-Year Update,* January 2011, http://www.madre.org/images/uploads/misc/1294686468_Haiti_Report_FINAL_011011_v2.pdf. The title was inspired by Beverly Bell, "'Our Bodies Are Shaking Now'—Rape Follows Earthquake in Haiti," *Huffington Post,* March 24, 2010, quoting a woman with the grassroots women's organization KOFAVIV.

18. See Catherine Albisa, "Economic and Social Rights in the United States: Six Rights, One Promise," in *Bringing Human Rights Home,* vol. 1, ed. Cynthia Soohoo, Catherine Albisa, and Martha Davis (Westport, CT: Greenwood Publishing Group, 2008), 26.

19. CIRH, *Plan stratégique, Commission Intérimaire pour la Reconstruction d'Haïti* (Strategic Plan, Interim Haiti Reconstruction Commission), December 14, 2010.

20. A detailed discussion of the findings of this investigation was published as part of the initial July 2010 report, *Our Bodies Are Still Trembling.*

21. See KOFAVIV, FAVILEK, KONAMPAVID, International Women's Human Rights (IWHR) Clinic at the City University of New York (CUNY) School of Law, MADRE, IJDH, BAI, Morrison & Foerster LLP, the Center for Constitutional Rights (CCR), and Women's Link Worldwide, "Request for Precautionary Measures Under Article 25 of the Commission's Rules of Procedure," www .womenslinkworldwide.org/wlw/bajarFS.php?tl=3&per=109.

22. The UN Gender-Based Violence Sub-Cluster in Haiti (the "GBV Sub-Cluster") is coordinated by UNFPA and UNICEF, and includes UN and NGO membership as well as Haitian government ministries. The Sub-Cluster takes the lead on addressing gender-based violence in complex emergencies, natural disasters, and other such situations (GBV Area of Responsibility Working Group, "GBV Coordination at the Local Level," One Response, July 4, 2010), http://one response.info/GlobalClusters/Protection/GBV/Pages/Gender-Based%20Violence %20Working%20Group.aspx.

23. US aid to Haiti, for example, has followed a pattern of undermining the Haitian government. Since the 1995 Dole Amendment, all USAID funds go through NGOs instead of through the government (Mark Schuller, *Unstable Foundations: Impact of NGOs on Human Rights for Port-au-Prince's Internally Displaced People,* York College, CUNY, and Faculté d'Ethnologie, UEH, October 4,

2010, 3. See also BBC News, "Haiti PM Criticises Post-Earthquake Rebuilding Efforts," December 27, 2010, http://www.bbc.co.uk/news/world-latin-america-12082047).

24. Countries and organizations from all over the world pledged more than $10 billion for Haiti relief at the UN-backed donor conference in March 2010, including more than $5.6 billion pledged for fiscal years 2010 and 2011 (CEPR, "Have Rich Countries Forgotten Haiti? Key Facts on International Assistance," Haiti Relief and Reconstruction Watch [blog], August 27, 2010, http://www.cepr. net; Jonathan M. Katz and Martha Mendoza, "Haiti Still Waiting for Pledged U.S. Aid," Associated Press, September 29, 2010; Marisol Bello, "Much of Aid for Haiti Is Still Unspent," *USA Today*, November 30, 2010).

25. Primary investigator: Margaret Satterthwaite; coinvestigator: Veerle Opgenhaffen; NYU Research Team, academic year 2010–11: Isabelle Bourgeois, Farrell Brody, Greger B. Calhan, Kelly Geoghegan, Ellie Happel, Susan Hu, Giulia Stella Previti, Leah Seldin-Sommer, and Emerson Sykes; Haitian Research Team Leaders: Jean Roger Noel and Daniel Tillias; Haitian Field Team: Michel-Ange Dagrain, Jean Dider Deslorges, Mackenzy Dor, Manassé Elusma, Jean Rony Emile, Junior Jean François, Gloria Germain, Jules Indieu, Robenson Jean Julien, Rose Mercie Saintilmont, Pierre Anderson Soulouque, Saint Hubert Talino, and Jude Wesh; NYU Research Assistance: Francesca Corbacho, Isabelle Figaro, Heather Gregorio, Trina J.P. Ng, and Harya Tarekegn.

26. Statement at the 65th Session of the General Assembly, Third Committee, October 11, 2010, http://www.un.org/womenwatch/daw/documents/ga65/vaw.pdf.

27. IACHR, "IACHR Expresses Concern Over Situation in Camps for Displaced Persons in Haiti," press release, November 18, 2010, http://www.cidh. org/Comunicados/English/2010/115-10eng.htm. The petition for precautionary measures was filed by the Women's Human Rights Clinic of CUNY Law School, MADRE, the Institute for Justice and Democracy in Haiti, Bureau des Avocats Internationaux, Morrison & Foerster LLP, the Center for Constitutional Rights, and Women's Link Worldwide.

28. See Madhavi M. Ariyabandu, "Gender Issues in Recovery From the December 2004 Indian Ocean Tsunami: The Case of Sri Lanka," *Earthquake Spectra* 20, no. S3 (2006): S759, S765; Eileen Pittaway, Linda Bartolomei, and Susan Rees, "Gendered Dimensions of the 2004 Tsunami and a Potential Social Work Response in Post-Disaster Situations," *International Social Work* 50, no. 3 (May 2007): 307, 309–11.

29. Michael Anastario, Nadine Shehab, and Lynn Lawry, "Increased Gender-Based Violence Among Women Internally Displaced in Mississippi 2 Years Post-Hurricane Katrina," *Disaster Medicine and Public Health Preparedness* 3, no. 1 (March 2009): 18.

30. See, for example, Malya Villard Apollon (cofounder, KOFAVIV), oral intervention at the 14th Session of the Human Rights Council, June 7, 2010, http:// ijdh.org; MADRE, CUNY School of Law, Institute for Justice and Democracy in

Haiti, and Bureau des Avocats Internationaux, "Our Bodies Are Still Trembling: Haitian Women Continue to Fight Against Rape," 2011, http://www.madre.org (and excerpted in this volume); Amnesty International, "Aftershocks: Women Speak Out Against Sexual Violence in Haiti's Camps," 2011, http://www.amnesty.org; Refugees International, *Haiti: Still Trapped in the Emergency Phase*, field report, October 6, 2010, http://www.refintl.org.

31. Sample size is 365 unless otherwise noted. Statistics presented here were rounded to the closest percent. Detailed data is on file with CHRGJ.

32. This phrasing was based on a question developed and tested in Haiti by Partners in Health. See M.C. Smith Fawzi et al., "Factors Associated With Forced Sex Among Women Accessing Health Services in Rural Haiti: Implications for the Prevention of HIV Infection and Other Sexually Transmitted Diseases," *Social Science and Medicine* 60, no. 4 (2005): 679, 681.

33. The research team chose this phrasing for the question regarding sexual assault outside the parameters of rape based on discussions with partner organizations that work directly with sexual violence survivors.

34. See Kimberly A. Cullen and Louise C. Ivers, "Human Rights Assessment in Parc Jean Marie Vincent, Port-au-Prince, Haiti," *Health and Human Rights* 12, no. 2 (2010): 67n25.

35. See Athena R. Kolbe and Royce A. Hutson, "Human Rights Abuse and Other Criminal Violations in Port-au-Prince, Haiti: A Random Survey of Households," *The Lancet* 368, no. 9538 (September 2, 2006): 871n23.

36. Ibid.

37. Ibid., 294n24: "More than half of [victims of sexual violence whose age was reported] were 17 or under."

38. Translated from the original Haitian Creole by Mark Schuller.

9

Rights and Public Health

With Paul Farmer, a world-renowned physician-anthropologist and fierce advocate for the poor, in a key position within the reconstruction effort as deputy UN special envoy, early progress was made on public health in Haiti following the earthquake. The emergency medical intervention saved thousands of lives.[1] While there were missteps, it was a model of cooperation. Funds were directed toward rebuilding the state hospital and later allocated to building a state-of-the-art teaching hospital in Mirebalais in Haiti's Central Plateau, where Farmer's Partners in Health organization has been offering world-class medical care for over two decades. Ironically, just outside of Mirebalais was ground zero for a deadly outbreak of cholera, which as of May 2011 claimed 5,234 lives.

The cholera outbreak in October 2010 represents a systemwide failure, demanding a rights-based approach to disaster relief and public health. Partners in Health is among the pioneers arguing for such an approach, requiring attention to overall structures, including financial commitments, processes such as local participation, and outcomes like specific on-the-ground service delivery. This approach stems from the basic premise that health is a basic human right to be defended. International conventions have backed this up, also discussing the right to water.

Why hasn't Haitian people's right to water or public health been respected? As with other social issues, such as class and gender inequality, that this book has discussed, Haiti's public health system was far from adequate even before the earthquake. In the mid-2000s Haiti had an average of 2.5 doctors per 10,000 people, with a sizable portion coming from Cuba—either Cuban nationals or

Cuban-trained Haitians. Predictably, given the centralization of resources in the Republic of Port-au-Prince already discussed, this figure was even lower in rural areas and provincial towns. This lack of provision had lethal consequences: most recent pre-quake statistics indicate that 74 of 1,000 Haitian children, almost one in 12, die before the age of five (compared to nine for earthquake-battered Chile). Directly linked with public health is the provision of clean water. Seventy percent of Haitian people did not have regular access to water, and this number was higher outside of Port-au-Prince and on the rise overall.[2] Overall, Haiti ranked lowest, 147th, on a 2002 Water Poverty Index.

International agencies and journalists are often quick to point the finger at the Haitian government for the public health failures. While partially true, this discourse hides the very real and deadly consequences of policies and decisions made by international actors. On top of neoliberal measures like the forced reduction in social spending, funds for public health were squeezed out to service Haiti's international debt, most of which ($844 million)[3] was incurred by the Duvalier dictatorship. In 1991, following Haiti's first democratic election, IFIs such as the World Bank and the IMF decided to force Haiti's people to continue to pay the debts owed by dictatorships. This had a direct impact on public health spending; for example, in 2003 Haiti's debt service was $57.4 million, whereas the entire scheduled grants for education, health care, environment, and transportation combined was $39.21 million.[4] As part of the lead-up to Aristide's 2004 ouster, the IDB withheld $535 million in needed loans, much for water and sanitation. As solidarity activist Deepa Panchang notes in her contribution to this chapter, Partners in Health called these a "straight line" to cholera.

The first cases of cholera were just outside a UN base where troops from Nepal were stationed and whose sewage system was leaky. The world's leading expert on cholera, French epidemiologist Renaud Piarroux, led an international team to investigate. While the report was suppressed for months, in July 2011 the Centers for Disease Control and Prevention (CDC) finally published it. The evidence clearly points to the UN troops who were not tested from a country that had a recent cholera outbreak. A later report in August uses genetic evidence, comparing the strain in Haiti and Nepal, confirming Piarroux's conclusion.[5] Partners in Health physicians David Walton and Louise Ivers remind readers of the failures noted above and also the missed opportunity to rebuild Haiti's rural sanitation system even following the reverse migration of 600,000 people out of Port-au-Prince and billions in aid triggered by the earthquake. The article from the New England Journal of Medicine *ends with a series of recommendations to stop the waterborne disease.*

The second in a series of a longitudinal study of eight camps throughout Port-au-Prince, a September report by human rights groups IJDH, LERN, and

LAMP tracks the lack of progress. The selection in this chapter discusses public health issues such as water, sanitation, and lack of food. Like the previous essay, this one includes a series of recommendations, grounded in a rights-based approach. Deepa Panchang summarizes her Harvard master's thesis exploring why this rights-based approach failed to actualize the right to water, focusing on process constraints. Interviews with NGOs and Cluster officials reveal deep-seated prejudices and a self-help worldview discussed in other chapters. Much more conscious effort—and a new model that centers on respecting Haitians' human rights and dignity—is needed not only to stop cholera but also to assure a minimum level of health care after the aid and media attention fade.

* * *

First, Do No Harm
The Haitian Cholera Epidemic and International Aid

*Renaud Piarroux, Robert Barrais, Benoît Faucher, Rachel Haus,
Martine Piarroux, Jean Gaudart, Roc Magloire, and Didier Raoult*

ON OCTOBER 18, 2010, CUBAN medical brigades working in Haiti reported an increase of acute watery diarrhea to the Haitian Ministry of Public Health and Population (MSPP).[6] In the preceding week they had treated 61 cases in Mirebalais, a city about 60 kilometers northeast of Port-au-Prince, and on October 18, the situation worsened, with 28 new admissions and two deaths. The MSPP immediately sent a Haitian investigation team of epidemiologists, which determined that the epidemic began October 14. The first hospitalized patients were members of a family living in Meille (also spelled Méyè), a small village two kilometers south of Mirebalais.

Meille village hosted a MINUSTAH camp, which was set up just above a stream flowing into the Artibonite River. Newly incoming Nepalese soldiers with MINUSTAH arrived there on October 9, 12, and 16. The Haitian epidemiologists observed sanitary deficiencies at the camp, including a pipe discharging sewage into the river. Villagers used water from this stream for cooking and drinking. On October 21 the epidemic was also investigated in several wards of Mirebalais, where inhabitants drew water from the rivers because the water supply network was being repaired. Notably, prisoners downstream from Meille also drank water from the same river and were infected; no other cause was found for the 34 cases and four deaths reported in the prison.

By October 21 the MSPP publicly announced a cholera epidemic in Haiti caused by *Vibrio cholerae* O1, serotype Ogawa, biotype El Tor.[7] This epidemic was surprising since no cholera outbreak had been reported in Haiti for more than a century.[8] Numerous media rapidly related the epidemic to the deadly earthquake that struck Haiti nine months earlier. Meanwhile, a rumor began to spread that recently arrived Nepalese soldiers with MINUSTAH were responsible for importing the cholera, along with accusations that the soldiers had illegally dumped sewage into a local stream.[9] These suspicions were strengthened by the fact that a cholera outbreak had been reported in Nepal's capital city of Kathmandu on September 23, shortly before troops left for Haiti.[10]

Responding to a request from Haitian authorities to the French embassy for the support of epidemiologists, we conducted a joint French-Haitian investigation from November 7 to November 27, 2010, to clarify the source of the epidemic. Determining the origin and the means of spread of the cholera epidemic in Haiti was necessary to direct the cholera response. Moreover, putting an end to the controversy over the epidemic's origins could ease prevention and treatment by decreasing the distrust associated with widespread suspicions that authorities had covered up a deliberate importation of cholera.[11] Demonstrating an imported origin would additionally compel international organizations to reappraise their procedures. Finally, it could help to contain disproportionate fear toward rice growing, a phenomenon responsible for important crop losses in 2011.[12] Notably, recent publications supporting an imported origin did not worsen social unrest, contrary to what some feared.[13]

Our epidemiological study provides several arguments confirming that cholera was imported into Haiti, in addition to other arguments that have been advanced. To begin with, there was an exact correlation in time and place between the Nepalese battalion's arrival from an area experiencing a cholera outbreak and the appearance of the first cases in Meille a few days later. The remoteness of Meille in central Haiti and the absence of report of other incomers make it unlikely that a cholera strain might have been brought there another way. DNA fingerprinting of *V. cholerae* isolates in Haiti and genotyping corroborate our findings because the fingerprinting and genotyping suggest an introduction from a distant source in a single event.[14]

Considering that the MINUSTAH camp's pipes were pouring sewage into the stream, that the disease was rapidly disseminated in Meille and downstream, and that the prisoners were probably contaminated by the stream water, we believe that the Meille River acted as the vector of cholera during the first days of the epidemic by carrying sufficient concentrations of the bacterium to induce cholera in persons who drank it.

Furthermore, our field investigations, as well as statistical analyses, showed that the contamination occurred simultaneously in the seven communes of the lower course of the Artibonite River, an area covering 1,500 square kilometers, more than 25 kilometers from Meille. The abrupt upward epidemic curve in the communes bordering Artibonite dramatically contrasts with the progressive epidemic curve in the other communes of Haiti. In the latter, it took 19 days before the daily number of cases exceeded 1,000. Suspected cholera was diagnosed in 7,232 patients during these 19 days. If the transmission in the communes bordering Artibonite had been similar to that of other communes, a comparable number of cases would have occurred in the days preceding the alert on October 20.

That many cholera cases would not have gone unnoticed, all the more so as several health facilities of these communes were participating in the MSPP epidemiologic watch. The regression model indicates that the spread of cholera during the peak that occurred from October 20 to October 28 was strongly linked to the Artibonite River and not to the proximity to Mirebalais, as would be expected for road-dependent propagation. This result, as well as the simultaneity of the outbreak onset in seven communes of Lower Artibonite on October 19, is in accordance with contamination of the Artibonite River in a way that could infect thousands, and kill hundreds, of people within a few days.

This hypothesis is also sustained by another early investigation during October 21–23 which showed that most affected persons worked or resided in rice fields alongside a stretch of the Artibonite River and that 67% drank untreated water from the river or canals.[15] Cholera incubation varies from a few hours to six days,[16] and the epidemic curve strongly suggests a rapid decrease of the contamination level in the river because the number of new cases and deaths dropped dramatically after only two days. A lasting phenomenon would have induced a continuing increase of incidence and a later peak.

However, even for a few hours, contamination of a river like the Artibonite requires a large amount of bacteria. For instance, to reach concentrations of 10^5 *V. cholerae* bacteria per liter during only three hours in the Artibonite River, which usually flows at more than 100 cubic meters per second in October,[17] more than 10^{14} bacteria are required. This level corresponds to the amount of bacteria in one cubic meter of rice-water stools harboring 10^{11} *V. cholerae* bacteria per liter. Notably, the fact that the peak in Mirebalais occurred later, on October 26, when daily incidence was dropping dramatically in Lower Artibonite also indicates that a specific mechanism was responsible for the onset of cholera in Lower Artibonite, distinct from continuous spread from the primary focus.

As of August 29, 2011, the Haitian cholera epidemic had killed 6,266 people, according to the Haitian Ministry of Health and Population.[18] This epidemic reminds us how critical the management of water and sewage is to prevent cholera from spreading. To avoid contamination or the suspicion of it happening again, it will be important to rigorously ensure that the sewage of military camps is handled properly. Above all else, aid organizations should avoid adding epidemic risk factors to those already existing in the places where they work, which means respecting the fundamental principle of all assistance: first, do no harm.

* * *

Responding to Cholera in Post-Earthquake Haiti

David A. Walton and Louise C. Ivers

THE EARTHQUAKE THAT STRUCK HAITI on January 12, 2010, decimated the already fragile country, leaving an estimated 250,000 people dead, 300,000 injured, and more than 1.3 million homeless.[19] As camps for IDPs sprang up throughout the ruined capital of Port-au-Prince, medical and humanitarian experts warned of the likelihood of epidemic disease outbreaks. Some organizations responding to the disaster measured their success by the absence of such outbreaks, though living conditions for the displaced have remained dangerous and inhumane. In August 2010 the CDC announced that a National Surveillance System that was set up after the earthquake had confirmed the conspicuous absence of highly transmissible disease in Haiti.

However, on October 20, more than 55 miles from the nearest IDP camp, 60 cases of acute, watery diarrhea were recorded at L'Hôpital de Saint Nicolas, a public hospital in the coastal city of Saint Marc, where Partners in Health has worked since 2008. Stool samples were sent to the national laboratory in Port-au-Prince for testing. The hospital alerted Ministry of

Health representatives in the region and in the capital, as well as WHO representatives managing the Health Cluster, a coordinating group formed after the earthquake. In the next 48 hours, L'Hôpital de Saint Nicolas received more than 1,500 additional patients with acute diarrhea.

By October 21, preliminary results from the national laboratory confirmed our clinical impressions: though cholera had not been seen in Haiti in at least a century and may never have been recorded in laboratory-confirmed cases, it had somewhat unexpectedly emerged in a densely populated zone with little sanitary infrastructure and limited access to potable water. As the contours of the epidemic began to take shape, following the winding course of a large river in the Artibonite region, hospitals in central Haiti started recording rapidly increasing numbers of cases of acute diarrhea. Between October 20 and November 9, Partners in Health recorded 7,159 cases of severe cholera. Among these patients, 161 died in seven of its hospitals in the Central and Artibonite regions.

In Port-au-Prince, sporadic cases were reported in the early phase of the outbreak; most were deemed "imported cases." On November 8, 48 hours after Hurricane Tomas caused flooding and worsening of living conditions in Parc Jean-Marie Vincent, one of the largest settlement camps, Partners in Health reported seven clinical cases of cholera within the camp. On the same day, Doctors without Borders reported seeing as many as 200 patients with cholera in nearby slums. By November 9, the Ministry of Health had reported 11,125 hospitalized patients and 724 confirmed deaths from cholera.

Although we responded as quickly as we could, we were hampered by the rapidity with which the epidemic spread, overwhelming our hospitals with hundreds of patients and stretching already thin resources, staff, and materials. Because there was minimal practical institutional knowledge about cholera in Haiti, we worked with other NGOs to design treatment protocols and institute infection-control measures in affected hospitals. Our network of community health workers began distributing oral rehydration salts, water-purification systems, and water filters, and instructing people about hygiene, hand washing, and decontamination of cadavers. Body bags were distributed to community leaders, and rehydration posts were set up throughout the countryside. A network of cholera treatment centers and stabilization centers was established in coordination with the Ministry of Health.

The cholera outbreak took most people by surprise. Unexpectedly, it was centered in rural Haiti and not in the IDP camps that are situated mainly in the greater Port-au-Prince area. But history would suggest that an epidemic outbreak of waterborne disease was just waiting to strike rural

Haiti. It is well-known that Haiti has the worst water security in the hemisphere. In 2002 it ranked 147th out of 147 countries surveyed in the Water Poverty Index.[20] After the earthquake, more than 182,000 people moved from the capital to seek refuge with friends or family in the Artibonite and Central regions, increasing stress on small, overcrowded homes and communities that lacked access to latrines and clean water. In addition, in many areas of Haiti, the costs associated with procuring water from private companies and the lack of adequate distribution systems have rendered potable water even less accessible for those most at risk.

Waterborne pathogens and fecal-oral transmission are favored by the lack of sanitation in Haiti. Typhoid, intestinal parasitosis, and bacterial dysentery are common. Only 27% of the country benefits from basic sewerage, and 70% of Haitian households have either rudimentary toilets or none at all.[21] But the sudden appearance of cholera, a pathogen with no known nonhuman host, raises the question of how it was introduced to an island that has long been spared this disease. Speculations on this question caused social and political friction within Haiti. Early in the epidemic, the CDC identified the cholera strain *Vibrio cholerae* O1, serotype Ogawa, biotype El Tor. Chin and colleagues report on DNA sequencing of two isolates from the recent outbreak, which showed that the cholera strain responsible for the Haitian epidemic originated in South Asia and was most likely introduced to Haiti by human activity.[22] The implications of the appearance of this strain are worrisome: as compared with many cholera strains, it is associated with increased virulence, enhanced ability to survive in the environment and in a human host, and increased antibiotic resistance. These factors have substantial epidemiologic ramifications for the entire region and implications for optimal public health approaches to arresting the epidemic's spread.

As the infection makes its way to the capital city, there is debate about the likely attack rate inside IDP camps, as compared with the rate in surrounding communities. The latter often have worse access to water and sanitation than the former. But 521 of 1,356 IDP camps listed by the UN camp-management cluster reportedly have no water or sanitation agency, and most are far from reaching the established guidelines for sanitation in humanitarian emergencies.[23] The living conditions of most of Haiti's poor, whether they're living in camps or communities, are equally miserable in terms of the risk of diarrheal disease.

The reported numbers of cases and deaths, though shocking, represent only a fraction of the epidemic's true toll. We have seen scores of patients die at the gates of the hospital or within minutes after admission. Through our network of community health workers, we have learned of hundreds of patients who died at home or en route to the hospital. In the first 48 hours, the case fatality rate at our facilities was as high as 10%. Though it dropped to less than 2% in the ensuing days as the health system was reinforced locally and patients began to present earlier in the course of disease, mortality will most likely climb as the disease spreads and Haiti's fragile health system falters.

This most recent crisis in Haiti has reinforced certain lessons regarding the provision of services to the poor. Complementary prevention and care should be the primary focus of the relief effort. Vaccination must be considered as an adjunct for controlling the epidemic, and antibiotics should be used in the treatment of all hospitalized patients. These endeavors should proceed in concert with much-needed improvements to sanitation and accessibility of potable water. More generally, reliable partnerships are essential, especially if local partners are dependable and have practical experience and complementary assets. Long-term reinforcement of the public-sector health system is a wise investment, permitting provision of a basic minimum set of services that can be built upon in times of crisis. And community health workers who can be rapidly mobilized as educators, distributors of supplies, and first responders are a reliable backbone of health care. In Haiti, such workers can bring the time-sensitive, lifesaving therapy of oral rehydration right to the patient's door.

* * *

"We've Been Forgotten"
Haiti's IDP Camps Eight Months After the Earthquake

Nicole Phillips, LAMP for Haiti Foundation, IJDH, BAI,
Lawyers' Emergency Response Network, University of San Francisco
School of Law, and the Center for Law and Global Justice

THIS REPORT PRESENTS FINDINGS FROM a five-month follow-up of 90 Haitian families displaced by the January 12, 2010, earthquake.[24] The initial survey was conducted in February, and the resulting report, *Neglect in the Encampments: Haiti's Second-Wave Humanitarian Disaster,* was presented to the IACHR, a body of the Organization of American States (IOAS) in Washington, DC on March 23, 2010.[25]

A second survey in July compared how living conditions measured against human rights standards set forth under the Haitian Constitution and international law on the treatment of displaced persons. Fifty-two of the original 90 families surveyed in February were located and interviewed, yielding the following evidence of systematic human rights violations:

- Food: 75% of families had someone go an entire day without eating in the past week, and over 50% indicated that their children did not eat for an entire day.
- Clean water: 44% of families primarily drank untreated water.
- Sanitary environment: 27% of families defecated in a container, a plastic bag, or on open ground in the camps.
- Housing: 78% of families lived without enclosed shelter.
- Health: There were 245 independently listed health problems among 45 families.
- Protection from and during displacement: 94% of families felt they could not return home, while 48% had been threatened with forced eviction since the earthquake.
- Self-sufficiency: 37% of families did not have a single family member with a full-time job, a part-time job, a cash-for-work arrangement, or self-employment.

The Right to Water

Clean, safe water for drinking, cooking, and hygiene is as basic to human survival and human dignity as the air that we breathe and the food that we eat.[26] Additionally, access points should be close enough to enable regular household use.[27] Fundamental tenets guarantee the human right to potable water and demand that those in need have regular and ready access to such water.[28]

The right to water cannot be understood in isolation; it is a keystone right upon which other rights, such as the right to life and the right to a basic standard of living, are built. Indeed, the right to clean, safe water is important for all people, but as our data shows, it is essential to the health of the young and enfeebled.[29]

Our survey found that potable water was only available to residents who could pay for it, and 61% of our survey respondents listed purchased bottled water as their main source of drinking water. This finding begs the questions: (1) How are families able to generate sufficient funds to purchase bottled water, and (2) what other basic necessities are neglected as a result? Some of the 39% who did not have access to bottled water described drinking water from cisterns or tanks, even though they feared the water might be contaminated.

These respondents stated that they drank nonpotable water out of necessity, treating the water when they had the money to buy chlorine tablets or fuel to boil before drinking it. Many families complained that the water they drank made their families sick.

Children faced particular hardship. A mother of a newborn child stated that, soon after the quake, she received tablets to treat water; however, this aid ceased in March, and consequently she had difficulties buying water to give to her child. In [Camp] Acra, the families said the water provided by the International Red Cross made them sick.

Despite this widespread contamination, aid agencies failed to provide any means for treating the water since February. In [Camp] Champ de Mars, the families surveyed stated that the water stations were difficult to access, and on the occasions that the water could be reached, children suffered diarrhea and skin infections as a result of drinking it.

The survey results also establish that, independent of the risks posed by consuming nonpotable water, the simple act of collecting water presents a safety threat. Thirteen families independently agreed that women and children should not attempt to collect water without accompaniment. Accompaniment is not easy, since women and children are traditionally the water carriers in Haiti. In Parc La Couronne, one family stated, "It is not safe for women or children to go collect water alone. They are bothered and picked on."

When asked to comment on the state of their families' drinking water supplies, survey participants provided four primary responses: (1) agencies provided untreated water, (2) clean drinking water had to be purchased or treated, (3) families did not always have money to treat or buy water, and (4) untreated water made respondents sick.

As with post-earthquake access to basic sustenance, the lack of access to clean, safe water imperils the basic security of the Haitian people, from waterborne parasites to physical assault. The denial of clean, safe water is a denial of life, dignity, and health. The continued deprivation of these basic human rights warrants greater attention.

The Right to Health and Medical Care

The earthquake has exacerbated existing health problems and created new health concerns, including mental and physical trauma. A right to health is universally recognized in the Haitian Constitution, Article 23, and under international law, including the right to those factors that determine good health, such as access to potable water and adequate sanitation, a sufficient supply of safe food, nutrition, and housing, as stipulated in the UDHR, Article 25. Furthermore, the Guiding Principle 18 recognizes the right to "essential medical services" as a part of the right to an adequate standard of living, and according to Principle 19, women in particular have a right to female health-care providers and services, including reproductive health and counseling for victims of sexual and other abuses. Any failure to meet the reproductive, psychological, or physical medical needs of IDPs is a violation of their right to health.

Investigators suspect that the respondents underreported their health conditions. For example, only 29 families reported "hunger or malnutrition" as a health problem, yet 39 families said that someone in their family had gone an entire day without eating in the past week. Similarly, only 16 families reported "stress or depression" as a health problem, yet 41 families described their living situation as "very bad" or "terrible" due to heat, overcrowding, mosquitoes, mud, lack of food, lack of water, lack of income, general malaise, or some combination thereof—this more than six months after the earthquake. The conflation of these factors suggests that camp conditions have deteriorated to the point that unacceptably poor health has become indistinguishable from daily life.

Eight of the 45 respondents reported not receiving any medical care, with one citing cost, two citing the lack of an available clinic, and the other five not giving a reason. To some extent, families had "choices" in that they could go to a pay hospital or go without. In Champ de Mars, one family stated that they now had to pay for care at the health center where it used to be free. Another family in the same camp stated, "The local police were providing free medical care for children but stopped providing this service just this week."

Access to care appeared infrequent and unreliable: mobile clinics came once a week, sometimes once a month; consultations cost 100 gourdes ($2.50); or hospitals were located as far as five kilometers away.

Thirty-four respondents described how their poor health affected their life in the camps, including how lack of money and lack of medical care affected their ability to obtain employment and cope emotionally. A woman in Croix-des-Bouquets summarized the cascading effects on her family: "My husband died in the earthquake. I am the sole provider, and when I get sick the whole family suffers."

Overwhelmingly the families expressed concern for the future. They did not know how they would get medical care, pay for treatment, and "live in peace" as a family. Health-care needs are exacerbated in IDP camps, and the failure to meet the needs of IDPs is a violation of the right to health, and ultimately also a violation of the right to life.

Recommendations

Our results indicate that aid has slowed and even stopped in each of the six camps surveyed, making life far worse for most of the families. This report makes the following nine recommendations:

1. Quickly disburse aid necessary to achieve and maintain a life of basic dignity.
2. Follow the UN Guiding Principles on Internal Displacement.
3. Promote participation from camp residents in needs assessment and aid distribution.
4. Require that donors be accountable to aid recipients.
5. Coordinate with the government of Haiti.
6. Encourage self-sufficiency through employment opportunities.
7. Source food aid locally to support local economy.
8. Improve and expand provision of sturdy, safe shelter for camp residents.
9. End the policy and practice of forced evictions.

We encourage the Haitian government, donor states, and aid agencies to allocate more of their resources to meet the basic needs of Haitians living in camps and adopt a rights-based approach to relief and reconstruction.

* * *

"Waiting for Helicopters"?
Perceptions, Misperceptions, and the Right to Water in Haiti

Deepa Panchang

"CHOLERA IS SOMETHING THEY SENT," said graffiti, and people, around town, "to finish killing off the rest of us." Reported cholera deaths in Haiti as of May 2011 surpassed 5,234, with more than 302,401 cumulative cases, although actual numbers could be twice as high.[30] Still, only 37% of the $4.6 billion pledged by donor governments for use in the year following the earthquake was actually disbursed, and surveys indicate that by early

2011, NGOs had only spent a little over half the funds they raised for earthquake response.[31]

However, more than a year after the earthquake, over half of camps had no toilets. As of May 2011, only 48% of people in the camps had access to water.[32] The perpetuation of cholera is a direct result of this. With a solution as simple as clean water, and billions in resources pledged or raised, the dearth of proper services raises serious questions about the humanitarian mechanism itself and its priorities.

Early in 2011 a colleague and I conducted anonymous interviews of camp residents and NGO officials in Port-au-Prince to gauge attitudes toward the work being done, particularly in the sector of water, sanitation, and hygiene (or WASH), with the goal of better understanding the situation. Fifty-one detailed interviews with IDPs and officials working for major NGOs and UN agencies suggested that the perceptions and misperceptions of the people running the aid response were themselves barriers to fulfilling the rights of the earthquake survivors.

"Not Realistic in Haiti"

The Sphere Minimum Standards (SMS) in disaster response provide one way of gauging realization of human rights, with guidelines for the provision of basic needs in disaster settings, such as a minimum of 15 liters of water daily per person, and a maximum of 20 people per toilet.

All of the international agency officials who discussed SMS in their interviews, however, stated that these standards, specifically the minimum indicator of 20 people per toilet, were not applicable or realistic in Haiti. In mid-2010 the WASH Cluster adopted a modified standard for toilet provision, making 100 people per toilet instead of 20 the acceptable goal for NGOs. Not one of the international agency officials who spoke about Sphere Standards expressed opposition to this policy. In fact, the average number of people per toilet from this study (in camps that all had WASH NGOs assigned to them) was 177.

The justifications given for this are illuminating.

"Polluting the Land"

One of the main reasons for the lack of toilets in camps, agency officials consistently reported, was opposition from the owners of land on which camps are situated. Often, landowners find toilets—and frequently even the presence of IDPs—undesirable, in many cases going as far as eviction. However, forced eviction of IDPs and the blockage of humanitarian aid for reasons of land are illegal under provisions of the Haitian Constitution and international human rights law binding on Haiti.[33] Furthermore, 70% to 90% of those claiming to be owners do not even possess title to the land, having obtained it in one of the myriad methods of illegal land seizure in Haiti.[34]

So what do NGOs do when faced with such situations? Most agency officials interviewed absolved themselves of responsibility. None of the respondents interviewed had ever initiated a legal process to support IDPs when faced with an intransigent landowner, despite the proven success of such a route by a local law agency. Some NGO officials targeted most of their sympathy toward landowners. IDPs are "polluting the land," said one IOM official. "If you are a landowner, and you put latrines there, and people come to defecate, piss, shit, on your land, your land is useless now."

"Waiting for Helicopters"?

In March 2011 the WASH Cluster announced free water distribution to camps would cease by the end of the month, since it was "not sustainable in the long term."[35] The cluster would provide guidance on exit strategies from camps, but actual decisions are made on an NGO-by-NGO basis.

With Haiti in the throes of a cholera epidemic, how could such a move be justified? One way was NGO rhetoric about "overprovision" of services as a "pull factor" into camps. In their interviews, many agency officials implied that they believed IDPs would stay in the camps indefinitely if services continued to be extended, providing an excuse for low standards and discontinuation of services. Many speculated about IDP "coping mechanisms" that helped them survive the camp conditions and their ability to leave the camps if they so desired. One NGO official offered the racialized hypothesis that Haitians were "genetically strong" given the "horrendous conditions," such as "slavery and torture," that they had endured. "You or I would not survive one month in one of those camps," she said. IOM officials suggested that a large number of IDPs actually had the means to return to their former homes but were staying in camps anticipating miracles from NGOs. They were "waiting for houses, cars, helicopters," said one, and "visas to Canada," quipped another. One senior IOM official said most IDPs owned land they could return to, and another commented that "we have to be careful because if they had the money to rent it before, why now they don't have it?"

In a not uncommon case of reverse psychology, a high-level official argued that WASH services were sufficient since "people didn't riot and there wasn't mass outbreak of diarrheal disease." Upon a mention of cholera, he responded, "Well, that one didn't happen in the camps, and it hasn't wiped out camps either." Although "I haven't talked to any [IDPs]," this official said, "I think they're pretty pleased."

IDPs beg to differ.

Most camp residents interviewed were emphatic about their need to stay in the camps for shelter and skeptical that they would ever receive better from NGOs. In the majority of camps, respondents said they had nowhere else to go. (The IOM's own statistics state that up to 80% of IDPs were formerly living in rented homes, and rental prices jumped drastically after the earthquake.[36]) One IDP and mother of three expressed her frustration, asking, "Who would like to live under a tent for one year with the heat, sun, and rain falling. . . . Do you think anybody would like to live this kind of life?" Even those IDPs who may be in the camps solely to receive "services" are a testament to the desperate conditions, even outside the camps, that are driving them there. Taking away their source of water hardly seems a humane solution. But NGOs, despite the fact that many among them are still sitting on the funds they raised for Haiti, put the entire onus on the government.

"It's the Structure That Was Supposed to Prevent Cholera That's Complicit"

Rarely discussed in humanitarian circles, however, is the structural undermining of Haiti's government, which led to the country's vulnerability to pathogens like cholera. Beyond the deepening of overall poverty through outside intervention, a legacy of debt and loan blocking has directly affected the water and sanitation sector. Over half of Haiti's debt was odious, having been lent to the money-siphoning, US-backed Duvalier dictatorship.[37] For years following this, Haiti dished out debt payments to its creditors at levels that more than rivaled social-sector spending. In 2003 the government's debt service of $57.4 million far exceeded the combined budget for education, health care, environment, and transportation; as recently as 2006, debt repayment was more than double the $25 million health budget.[38]

Compounding these impacts on social-sector spending was outright denial of approved funding for water and sanitation. Despite the Haitian government's compliance with requirements for the disbursal of an earmarked $54 million loan for water infrastructure from the IDB in 1998, the US government—in an effort to destabilize the elected government of Jean-Bertrand Aristide—was able to block the loan. Although such interference violated the IDB charter, officials continually devised extraneous stipulations to prevent the loan from going through.[39] Given that the designated work had still not begun as of 2010, a Partners in Health doctor asserted that it was "reasonable to draw a straight line from these loans being slowed down and cut off to the epidemic that emerged."[40]

Interviews revealed little historical knowledge of these maneuvers within the very institutions that had engineered or remained silent about them. Instead, in a classic case of institutional amnesia feeding a blame-the-victim discourse, officials most commonly cited the Haitian government for de-prioritizing sanitation or the Haitian people for poor hygiene practices in describing long-term causes for Haiti's vulnerability to cholera.

Among Haitians, however, this historical link is a familiar reality because they live day to day with its effects. If NGOs are to do more than merely plugging holes in the status quo, officials at these institutions will need to combat the misperceptions that keep them complicit in the ongoing denial of the human right to water in Haiti.

Notes

1. Paul Farmer, *Haiti After the Earthquake* (New York: Polity Press, 2011).

2. NYU School of Law Center for Human Rights and Global Justice, Partners in Health, Zanmi Lasante, and RFK Memorial Center for Human Rights, "Wòch Nan Solèy: The Denial of the Right to Water in Haiti," New York, 2008.

3. Mark Schuller, "Break the Chains of Haiti's Debt," Jubilee USA Network, Washington, DC, 2006.

4. International Monetary Fund, "Haiti: Selected Issues," Washington, DC, 2005, 88; World Bank, "Haiti: External Financing Report: October 1, 2000–September 30, 2001," Washington, DC, 2002, vii.

5. Rene S. Hendriksen, Lance B. Price, James M. Schupp, et al., "Population Genetics of *Vibrio cholerae* from Nepal in 2010: Evidence on the Origin of the Haitian Outbreak, *mBio* 2, no. 4 (August 2011): 1–6.

6. Excerpted and adapted from "Understanding the Cholera Epidemic, Haiti," *Emerging Infectious Diseases* 17, no. 7 (July 2011), www.cdc.gov/eid. The authors are grateful to the Haitian Ministry of Public Health and Population authorities, to the Haitian medical teams in each Haitian department, to the Cuban medical teams in Haiti for collecting the data, and to the French Embassy in Port-au-Prince for supporting this study.

7. CDC, "Update: Cholera Outbreak—Haiti, 2010," *Morbidity and Mortality Weekly Report* 59, no. 45 (November 19, 2010): 1473–79.

8. Ibid.; David A. Walton and Louise C. Ivers, "Responding to Cholera in Post-Earthquake Haiti," *New England Journal of Medicine,* no. 364 (January 6, 2011): 3–5.

9. Fred Tasker and Frances Robles, "Source of Cholera Outbreak May Never Be Known," *Miami Herald,* November 20, 2010.

10. Laxmi Maharjan, "Cholera Outbreak Looms Over Capital," *Himalayan Times,* September 23, 2010; Martin Enserink, "Despite Sensitivities, Scientists Seek to Solve Haiti's Cholera Riddle," *Science* 331, no. 6016 (January 2011): 388–89.

11. Haitian Red Cross and International Federation of Red Cross Psychosocial Support Program, "Cholera Outbreak: Note on Community Beliefs, Feelings and Perceptions," December 2010; Équipe Psychosociale de l'OIM, "Liste de perceptions des gens vivant dans les camps vis-à-vis du choléra auxquelles des réponses appropriées sont soumises," 2010.

12. Food and Agriculture Organization of the United Nations, "Cholera Fall-Out Likely to Cause Crop Losses in Haiti," December 30, 2010, http://www.fao.org/news/story/en/item/49044/icode.

13. Imported origin: Chen Shan Chin et al., "The Origin of the Haitian Cholera Outbreak Strain," *New England Journal of Medicine,* no. 364 (January 6, 2011): 33–42. Fear that supporting an imported origin would worsen social unrest: "As Cholera Returns to Haiti, Blame Is Unhelpful," *Lancet Infectious Diseases* 10, no. 12 (December 2010): 813; Louise C. Ivers, Paul Farmer, Charles Patrick Almazor, and Fernet Léandre, "Five Complementary Interventions to Slow Cholera: Haiti," *The Lancet* 376, no. 9758 (December 18, 2010): 2048–51; B. Faucher and R. Piarroux, "The Haitian Cholera Epidemic: Is Searching for Its Origin Only a Matter of Scientific Curiosity?" *Clinical Microbiology and Infection* 17, no. 4 (April 2011): 479–80.

14. DNA fingerprints: CDC, "Update: Cholera Outbreak—Haiti, 2010." Genotyping: Chin et al., "Origin of the Haitian Cholera Outbreak Strain"; Afsar Ali et al., "Recent Clonal Origin of Cholera in Haiti," *Emerging Infectious Disease* 17, no. 4 (April 2011): 699–701. Introduction from a distant source in a single event: Declan Butler, "Cholera Tightens Grip on Haiti," *Nature,* no. 468 (November 23, 2010): 483–84.

15. CDC, "Update: Cholera Outbreak—Haiti, 2010."

16. R.A. Cash, S.I. Music, J.P. Libonati, M.J. Snyder, R.P. Wenzel, R.B. Hornick, "Response of Man to Infection with *Vibrio cholerae.* I. Clinical, Serologic, and Bacteriologic Responses to a Known Inoculum," *Journal of Infectious Diseases* 129, no. 1 (January 1974): 45–52.

17. Bureau des Mines et de L'énergie, Haiti, *Prepetit C. Inventaire des ressources minières de la République d'Haiti. Fascicule IV: département de l'Artibonite,* Port-au-Prince, 1992.

18. CDC, "Frequently Asked Questions About the Haiti Cholera Outbreak," June 8, 2011, http://www.cdc.gov/haiticholera/cholera_qa.htm.

19. This article (10.1056/NEJMp1012997) was originally published on December 9, 2010, at nejm.org. Copyright © Massachusetts Medical Society.

20. C.A. Sullivan, J.R. Meigh, A.M. Giacomello, et al., "The Water Poverty Index: Development and Application at the Community Scale," *Natural Resources Forum* 27 (2003): 189–99.

21. Ministère de la Santé Publique et de la Population, Haiti, *Enquête mortalité, morbidité et utilisation des services (EMMUS-IV): Haiti, 2005–2006*, January 2007.

22. Chen-Shan Shen, "The Origin of the Haitian Cholera Outbreak Strain," *New England Journal of Medicine* 364, no. 1 (January 6, 2011): 33–42.

23. WASH Cluster, *Compte-rendu de réunion #9* (situation report), no. 101112 (November 12, 2010), http://haiti.humanitarianresponse.info/Default.aspx?tabid=83.

24. Institute for Justice & Democracy in Haiti (IJDH) et al., "*We've Been Forgotten": Conditions in Haiti's Displacement Camps Eight Months After the Earthquake,* September 10, 2010, http://ijdh.org/wordpress/wp-content/uploads/2010/09/IDP-Report-09.23.10-compressed.pdf.

25. The LAMP for Haiti Foundation et al., *Neglect in the Encampments, Haiti's Second Wave Humanitarian Disaster,* March 23, 2010, http://ijdh.org/archives/10671.

26. UN *Guiding Principles on Internal Displacement,* http://www.idpguidingprinciples.org/, Principle 18.

27. Sphere Project, Humanitarian Charter and Minimum Standards in Disaster Response (2004), http://www.sphereproject.org/content/view/27/84/lang,english, Water Supply Standard 1.

28. The International Covenant on Economic, Social, and Cultural Rights, http://www2.ohchr.org/english/law/cescr.htm, Article 12.

29. Convention on the Rights of the Child, http://www2.ohchr.org/english/law/crc.htm, Article 24.2.

30. *Health Cluster Bulletin,* no. 25 (May 27, 2011), http://new.paho.org/blogs/haiti/?p=1987.

31. Office of the UN Special Envoy for Haiti, "Analysis Shows 37.2 Percent Disbursement Rate for Haiti Recovery Among Public Sector Donors," press release, April 6, 2011, http://www.haitispecialenvoy.org/press-and-media/press-releases/en/analysis; Disaster Accountability Project, "One Year Report on Transparency of Relief Groups Responding to 2010 Haiti Earthquake," January 5, 2011.

32. DINEPA and UN WASH Cluster, *Indicateurs, Ratios, et Mesures des Performance WASH dans les sites Hebergement Temporaire Mars 2011,* March 2011, http://www.dinepa.gouv.ht/wash_cluster/index.php?option=com_rokdownloads&view=file&task=download&id=769%3Aindicateurs-ratios-et-mesures-des-performance-wash-dans-les-sites-hebergement-temporaire-mars-2011&Itemid=57.

33. Including the Convention on the Elimination of All Forms of Discrimination Against Women, the Convention on the Rights of the Child, and the International Covenant on Civil and Political Rights, which are all binding on Haiti. Also, Haiti's 1987 Constitution guarantees the right to decent housing and to health (articles 19 and 22), and limits the right to private property when "contrary to the general interest" (Article 36[3]).

34. Figure of 70% cited by Housing, Land and Property Working Group: Issues of Renters in the Post-Disaster Scenario 2, 2010. Figure of 90% cited in an interview with a Haitian human rights lawyer.

35. WASH Cluster, Sit Rep, March 23, 2011. Available online at WASH Cluster website, http://www.dinepa.gouv.ht/wash_cluster/index.php?option=com_rokdownloads&view=file&Itemid=41&id=1176:sit-rep-cluster-wash-haiti-23-mars-2011.

36. Bill Sasser, "Haiti's Housing Bubble, More Pressing to Some Than Election or Aristide," *Christian Science Monitor,* March 18, 2011.

37. Jubilee USA Network, "Haiti Resources and Background" (2007), available at http://www.jubileeusa.org.

38. Schuller, "Break the Chains of Haiti's Debt"; IMF, "Haiti: Selected Issues" (2005); World Bank, "Haiti: External Financing Report: October 1, 2000–September 30, 2001" (2002).

39. NYU School of Law, Center for Human Rights and Global Justice, Partners in Health, RFK Memorial Center for Human Rights, and Zanmi Lasante, "Wòch nan Soley: Denial of the Right to Water in Haiti," 2008, www.chrgj.org.

40. Dr. Evan Lyon, quoted in "Partners in Health Physician on Haiti: 'Cholera Will Not Go Away Until Underlying Situations That Make People Vulnerable Change,'" *Democracy Now!* October 26, 2010.

Part 3

Emerging Movements
Political Restructuring in Haiti

10

Politics From Above
Elections and Geopolitics

The earthquake interrupted a process of elections for Parliament and president, forcing a dilemma: whether to hold rushed elections knowing that the conditions would be difficult if not impossible to hold them; to expand the mandate of President René Préval, who demonstrated a spectacular lack of public presence; or to name some sort of interim government with the memory of 2004–2006 still fresh in people's minds. To the people who suffered under ripped tarps, dying from hunger or cholera, facing threats of violence or evictions, none was a good option.

To the international community, which had pledged $10 billion for Haiti's reconstruction, elections were going to happen, come hell or high water—or cholera, for that matter. The US government actually gave millions for the electoral process while waiting until the Democrats lost control of the US House of Representatives after the November 2010 midterm elections to release the $1.15 billion pledged at the UN Donors' Conference the previous March. Either Democrats were afraid to actually disburse the funds, wary of the surging Tea Party, or Haiti yet again fell prey to US partisan politics. Why would the United States spend money on elections but not a penny on emergency aid or reconstruction?

The United States is but one example: collectively, the so-called Friends of Haiti such as Canada and France contributed $25 million to the elections, 76% of the total cost. This question is made all the more urgent given the obvious red flags: The exclusion of Fanmi Lavalas, the party of deposed President Aristide, widely acknowledged as Haiti's most popular and powerful. The endless scandals of the CEP, firmly under Préval's control. The insurmountable logistical obstacles given the near total loss of citizens' official documents and *the ad hoc and informal nature of Haiti's scattered IDP camps, rendering most IDPs unable to obtain official ID cards. The implication of MINUSTAH, already unpopular following a seven-year occupation, driving up rents and stifling citizen mobilization, in every aspect of the elections.*

On Election Day, under MINUSTAH's watch, many observers recorded numerous irregularities. Thousands of IDPs were told their names were not on voter rolls, or that they were in another polling place far away. Some polling stations failed to open at all. Several polling places were sites of bald voter fraud in favor of one or another political party, usually Préval's ruling Inite party. In the end, only 23% of Haiti's registered voters turned out on November 28, the lowest voter-participation rate anywhere in the Americas for a presidential contest. The irregularities were so obvious that 12 candidates, including front-runners Mirlande Manigat and Michel Martelly, took to the streets with their supporters to call for the elections to be annulled and reorganized. From here the situation only became more confusing. Manigat and Martelly withdrew from the protests when they were informed they were likely to join the second round. The official results, supposedly available December 7, were delayed, showing Préval's hand-picked successor edging out Martelly by a fraction of a percent for second place.[1] The international community bullied the Préval government into naming Martelly as the second-place winner. When the "Arab Spring" was in its first blossom in Tunisia and Egypt, US Secretary of State Hillary Clinton made a stop in Haiti before visiting North Africa, threatening to withhold aid and revoking US visas.

This chapter grapples with these issues, what Haitian political anthropologist Jean-Yves Blot called yet another disaster to befall Haiti in 2010. Blot frames this discussion within a cultural analysis, a context of underdevelopment, and the MINUSTAH occupation. He describes numerous contradictions and double-speak on the part of the international community and discusses the reaction of the worn-out populace, taking money from the most expensive campaign in Haiti's history while in the end "vomiting" the entire traditional political structure.

CEPR published research by Mark Weisbrot and Jake Johnston analyzing the voter irregularities and the US State Department's and OAS's official reversal of Martelly and Célestin. With painstaking statistical analysis, CEPR concludes that there was no justification for this action that ended up selecting Martelly. Given the stakes, the close margin, and the lack of any kind of systematic analysis, CEPR concludes that the November 28 elections should have been annulled.

Picking up on themes in both essays, Haitian American writer and scholar Patrick Sylvain discusses Martelly's manipulation of the wave of popular frustration. The actions and discourse of Martelly's campaign, with some of the US

Republican Party's best hired guns, showed warning signs of impending author-
itarian rule, Sylvain asserts. Manolia Charlotin, editor of the Boston Haitian
Reporter, *transitions the discussion into the role that Haiti's vibrant, diverse,*
and growing Diaspora can and should be playing in the political process, in-
cluding lobbying their national governments. Numbering several million in
the United States alone, Haitians in the Diaspora need to flex their political
muscles to hold the US government's feet to the fire when it comes to Haiti re-
construction, Charlotin writes. Any disaster and especially its reconstruction are
inherently political processes, which these readings help to clarify.

* * *

The November 28, 2010, Elections
Another Catastrophe for Haiti

Jean-Yves Blot

———————

THE NOVEMBER 2010 ELECTIONS WERE organized in a context of military occupation by MINUSTAH. In reality, the people call those working for
MINUSTAH "tourist-a."[2] That's what they look like: tourists. They have
beautiful houses and fancy cars, they eat in restaurants, go to the beach,
and hang out all day long. They aren't involved in any way in the country's
social and economic development. On the contrary, in the popular perception, MINUSTAH symbolizes rape (they violate both women and men),
theft (they steal peasants' goats during the carnival season), insecurity (every
time MINUSTAH's mandate finishes, insecurity increases), inflation (since
these people came into the country, rents have skyrocketed, now in US dollars as opposed to Haitian gourdes; see the text in Chapter 2, this volume).
The last deadly, ugly blow MINUSTAH gave the country was cholera
(see Piarroux, Chapter 9, this volume). Despite the hypocrisy and danc-
ing around on the part of the national authorities and a good number of
international ones, *rat konnen, chat konnen* (everyone knows the secret).
In general, MINUSTAH's presence is complicating people's lives in every
sense. Despite all its un-usefulness, MINUSTAH remains a powerful force
in imposing decisions in one sense or another that are not in the interests
of the majority of the population.

Why Do We Call the November 28 Elections a "Disaster"?

A disaster is a tragic event that brings a lot of suffering, misery, sadness, and pain. Mostly, human beings don't directly confront to a catastrophe. They avoid disasters. But why do we call the November 28 elections a disaster? An election is supposed to be a "sovereign" action, an act in which the population exercises its autonomous rights, as people in charge of their own life. Elections should not have any constraints, right or left, like the military in charge. Unfortunately, we see these elections were done under MINUSTAH's command.

Used-Up[3] Elections in a Used-Up Democracy

Generally we use the term *electoral masquerade* because the process wasn't democratic at all, with popular participation at zero. This election was always a game of the imperialists and their domestic servant, Haiti's dominant class. Recall that during the elections, people were beaten down over and over again, already under tents, hit with cholera and hurricanes. Everyone was asking what sense it made to hold elections under these extraordinary conditions.

- Edmond Mulet, civilian chief of MINUSTAH, chose the election date of November 28.
- Experts evaluated the conditions for holding the elections. According to them, everything was "technically" ready for them.
- MINUSTAH was responsible for all election logistics, from bringing the ballots to the polling places to bringing them to the counting centers.
- Foreign experts "recounted" the ballots when the totals appeared too close after the results were available on December 7, 2010.[4]

A Host of Contradictions During the Electoral Process

The facts above strongly suggest MINUSTAH control of the elections. But at times it was convenient to maintain the façade of Haitian sovereignty.

- On one hand, imperialists held all the power in their hands. On the other, national groups clown around, playing the fool, from the CEP to the political parties to the presidency.

- On one hand, candidates like Martelly and Manigat yelled for help because of the games and manipulation on Election Day and even called for the elections to be annulled. On the other, from the time foreigners assured them they would be in the second round, they made an about-face, traitors to the group of 12 candidates who criticized the election's handling.
- On one hand, the CEP couldn't count the ballots well in the first round (that's why they called in the foreign experts). On the other, the CEP could count votes from the second round.
- On one hand, CEP lost its credibility on the first round because of President René Préval's political party, Inite. On the other, it appeared credible when it declared Micky (Michel Martelly) president during the second round.

For all these reasons, we say that this election was another disaster that befell the country. It was an ensemble of catastrophes befalling the entire electoral show. Unfortunately, the press lost its memory, unable to make the links between what happened in the past and what happens today.

Major Historical Lessons

During this great demagoguery committed on the heads of the people between right-wing politicians, a bourgeoisie without any decency, and an international sector without any vision—that together decided to put the country on a straightforward path to death, leaving not even a crumb for the people—the people decided to pull out their little chairs and watch. Others invited them to political meetings, no problem. Can these others buy their conscience with a little bit of money and windy promises?

The people's behavior regarding candidate Jude Célestin [from Inite] clearly shows the change in people's behavior. As the proverb says, *Nou grangou men nou pa saf:* we're hungry but we're not aggressive. Célestin's candidacy demonstrated a lot of extravagance in spending money, big ads on the radio, on all the streets with gigantic photos on the billboards.[5] This candidate had power and a large part of the state apparatus behind him. This candidate also had some pressure groups behind him as well. What happened with the people? The people joined the electoral movement. They took money that was being given, took "cash for work," little contracts right and left (see the Haiti Grassroots Watch text in Chapter 4, this volume). In the end, the people voted following their hearts.

We are facing a people already facing a distressing situation, in the sheer and total misery. National production was destroyed. Haiti's stomach depends on Americans and Dominicans. Struggles are waged to pluck the wealth underground (gold, oil, iridium). The foreigners need to become direct owners in the country and to bring the country down on its knees entirely. The attempt to change the Constitution was to advance the interests of foreigners, not the Haitian people.

It's the same people who already had their neck under other people's feet. People took money from Inite but didn't vote for Inite. People ate Chango's money but didn't pay them with their votes. It is often said that the people know what they want. In this case they knew well what they didn't want. They voted in this sense. They vomited the Lavalas/Préval government. They voted against Inite. They gave Célestin the pink slip despite all the money, the caravans, the big demonstrations in Croix-des-Bouquets, despite all the artists who supported him. Since voting is a personal decision, this is where the final decision was made. Like the proverb says, *Se kouto sèl ki konnen sa ki nan kè yanm:* only the knife knows what's inside a yam. It was clear: the amount of money and the position of power did not influence the people who voted. They took the candidate's money and then told him, "Go away."

Some journalists focused attention on the election campaign in the city of Cap Haïtien. Several presidential candidates went there, and large demonstrations were organized to welcome them. Journalists reported that the same people were in the mobilizations for several candidates. Is getting their hands on a little money more important for them? Since there was never any debate about the political program of x or y, is this how people got started? Changes in the country's direction have another meaning for the people, to the point where they say, "Give me my decaying carcass."[6]

Another special element in the 2010 elections that had nothing to do with any vision or plan for governance was when the people deliberately chose Micky against Madame Manigat. When the elite led the people to a crossroads to say that it needs a decaying carcass to lead the country, that was a pink slip they gave everyone in formal society—hypocritical, two-faced society. Unfortunately many sectors in society act like they don't understand.

The population vomited a model of society. They didn't only vomit a class of politicians, but they tossed all the country's elite in the garbage can, a paradigm shift. The people rejected the elitist society because Micky succeeded in saying what was in many people's hearts. "What is the use for all these plums, all these national or international experts?" This U-turn, is it not a result of arm-twisting because the results remain at zero? Recall that in 1908, Jean-Price Mars wrote a book called *La Vocation de l'Élite* (The Career of the Elite), which clearly shows how the elite has failed.[7]

Conclusion: Creole/*Bosale*

This spectacle that we just survived, the elections from November 2010 to April 2011, is a veritable historical disaster combined with other disasters that appear natural but are based on the country's sociopolitical conditions.[8] In other words, human beings have a large historical responsibility in these catastrophes (see Chapter 1, this volume). But at the same time, we ask if the "Creole" is at fault. The Creoles are creating all the ruckus in the society. The division couldn't be clearer between "Creole" society that picks fights with the rest of the population they call "people underneath," "big toes," "big shoes," or "*bosale*."[9] Jean Casimir gave a good definition of Creole: "It's a way people live when others dominate them, when others put their feet on their necks. It has become habit. . . . Creole culture is a host of knowledge, rules, and principles to show that the master put them into slavery."[10] Whenever there is a lack of popular participation for the majority of the population to say how they think society should be organized, structured, and led, we may find ourselves falling into the same altercation.

* * *

Haiti's Fatally Flawed Election

Mark Weisbrot and Jake Johnston

———————

ON NOVEMBER 28, 2010, HAITIANS went to the polls to elect a new president, 11 of 30 senators, and all 99 members of the Chamber of Deputies. Although the United States, Canada, the Secretariat General of the OAS, the European Union, and other foreign entities supported and funded the elections, the electoral process was mired in controversy long before the first vote was cast.[11] Most important, the very legitimacy of the election was called into question after more than a dozen political parties were excluded from the election—including Haiti's most popular political party,

Fanmi Lavalas—by the CEP, Haiti's electoral authority. The ban on Fanmi Lavalas was analogous to excluding the Democratic or Republican parties in the United States.

Furthermore, no effective measures were taken to ensure that the thousands of voters who had lost their identification cards or their homes following the January 12 earthquake would be able to vote. Despite these fundamental flaws ahead of the vote, then president René Préval, the CEP, key donor governments, and international bodies decided to press ahead with the elections.

As expected, there were also major problems in the conduct of the elections and the tallying of votes. The Center for Economic and Policy Research (CEPR) examined the 11,181 tally sheets from across the country that were posted online by the CEP. These were all of the votes counted by the CEP, and each tally sheet represented one voting booth.

The first finding that raised serious concerns was that the tally sheets for 1,326 voting booths, or 11.9% of the total, were either never received by the CEP or were quarantined for irregularities (see table 10.1). This amounts to about 12.7% of all the votes, which were not counted and were not included in the final totals that the CEP released on December 7 and were reported by the press. This is an enormous number of discounted votes by any measure but is especially so in an election in which the difference between the second- and third-place finisher—which determines who will participate in the runoff election—was just 0.6% of the vote.

This 13% of votes discounted is also much larger than what has been stated by the OAS and CEP in the media. A joint mission of the OAS and the Caribbean Community (CARICOM) that was dispatched to investigate the election announced in its preliminary report that "according to information provided by MINUSTAH, the total number of Polling Stations destroyed did not exceed 4% in the entire country."[12] Albert Ramdin, the OAS assistant secretary-general, was later cited by the Associated Press

Table 10.1 Lost Votes

	Tally Sheets	Votes
Invalidated Due to Irregularities	943	141,427
Quarantined or Not Received by the CEP	1,326	156,656
Total	2,269	298,083

Source: CEP and authors' calculations

using the 4% figure, although somewhat differently: "Nearly 4 percent of polling place tally sheets used to calculate the results were thrown out for alleged fraud at the tabulation center," Ramdin was quoted as saying.[13]

CEPR also found many more tally sheets that had irregularities in the vote totals that were sufficient to disqualify them. Because of how voting centers and voting booths were set up, there is a very simple statistical test that can be applied to the totals to determine their plausibility. Since voters were randomly assigned to the voting booths (alphabetically according to surname), any variation in the percentage of votes received by the candidates between different voting booths should be a result of random variation. We found that for 8.4% of the tally sheets, there were vote totals for the major candidates that would be expected to occur by chance less than 1% of the time.

That most of these implausible vote totals were due to errors or fraud is supported by the large number of clerical errors found on more than 5% of the tally sheets. Examples of clerical errors include tally sheets where zeros were recorded for such categories as total valid votes or unused ballots, where this clearly was not the case. Another example is ballots where the number for total valid votes cast far exceeds the combined votes counted for all of the candidates. We did not count these errors in our tally of irregular tally sheets, because they did not necessarily affect the distribution of votes. However, they are another indicator of the tally sheets' overall unreliability, and especially for the vote totals that lie outside of a 99% confidence interval.

If we ignore the clerical errors and add the tally sheets that were not counted by the CEP (11.9%) to those with irregular vote totals (8.4%)—the latter would be expected to occur less than 1% of the time[14]—we arrive at a total of 2,269 tally sheets that were either uncounted or found to be irregular. This represents almost 300,000 votes, or more than 24% of all the votes. This is an enormous percentage that was not or should not be counted, especially considering the closeness of the vote.

Based on reports from the ground on Election Day, one should expect a high number of irregularities. Ballot-box stuffing, voter intimidation, and the destruction of ballot boxes and even entire polling centers were all reported.[15]

In four of the 10 departments, more than 25% of the tally sheets were either highlighted as irregular or were never reported or were quarantined by the CEP. The problem was not concentrated in one department but spread across the country. These voters actually went to the polls and cast votes, only to have them not counted because of fraud or other irregularities.

Disenfranchisement Not Limited
to Irregular or Discounted Tally Sheets

Overall the participation rate was extremely low: just 22.9% of registered voters had their vote counted. If we remove the additional tally sheets that we have highlighted as irregular, the participation rate drops to 19.9%. As a comparison, Haiti's presidential elections in 2006 saw a participation rate of 59.26%.[16]

This low turnout could have been, and was, anticipated. A former version of the CEP (with many of the same members) had arbitrarily excluded Haiti's most popular party, Fanmi Lavalas, from Senate elections in April 2009. Not surprisingly, most Haitians boycotted the election, which resulted in a participation rate below 5%, according to most independent observers.[17] The legislative elections that took place on November 28, 2010, were originally planned for February and March 2010,[18] before the earthquake threw everything into chaos. In November 2009 the CEP once again announced the arbitrary exclusion of Fanmi Lavalas, as well as 14 other political parties.[19]

Another major concern ahead of the elections was that efforts to register and provide polling centers for more than a million people who were displaced by the earthquake were not very successful, either because of logistical concerns or because of political reasons. In Camp Corail, an official resettlement site housing some 6,000 people, only 39 people appeared on the voter registration list.[20] It quickly became clear that efforts to provide accessible voting centers for the IDPs were grossly inadequate. Many showed up at the polling center they were told to go to, only to find that their names were not on the list. The call center that was set up to inform people of their voting center was quickly overwhelmed and unable to provide much assistance. This problem was foreseen. With so many millions of residents displaced by the earthquake, and many missing most of their possessions, including voting cards, ensuring that all of Haiti's eligible voters could participate in the elections was a gargantuan task.

In CEPR's analysis, these difficulties are apparent in the extremely low participation rate in the capital, Port-au-Prince, and surrounding areas where the number of IDPs is the greatest. Ouest Department, where the earthquake had the greatest effect, had by far the lowest participation rate among the 10 departments. This was not simply due to a high number of irregular tally sheets. Artibonite Department, where 25% of the tally sheets were either never reported or were quarantined by the CEP, still had a significantly higher participation rate than Ouest.

Looking even closer at Ouest Department, the average participation rate in the cities of Port-au-Prince, Carrefour, Delmas, and Pétionville was just 12.4% (11.4% if we remove additional irregular tally sheets). These four cities are home to more than 22% of the country's registered voters, yet they accounted for only 12.3% of the total votes counted. Other factors could have contributed to a lower participation rate in Ouest, but given the large number of IDPs, it is reasonable to conclude that the difference is at least partially because displaced persons were unable to exercise their right to vote.

No Conclusive Results

Given the immense number of unrecorded and irregular vote totals, and the exclusion of the biggest political party, considering this election legitimate is difficult. The election results are very much inconclusive as to who qualified to advance to a second round. CEPR's recount of the CEP tally sheets, without considering irregularities, was very close to the preliminary results published by the CEP: each candidate's percentage of the vote was within two-tenths of a percentage point of the CEP's results. Mirlande Manigat came in first with 31.46%, Jude Célestin was in second with 22.60%, and Michel Martelly was in third with 21.74%. However, as we have pointed out, the CEP counted hundreds of tally sheets that CEPR highlighted as irregular. If we remove those tally sheets from the count, the results change. After removing the 943 additional sheets highlighted as irregular, Martelly and Célestin switch places.

There is another way to look at the vote count. We can assume that all of the tally sheets the CEP quarantined or did not receive were "normal," that is, they followed city-level participation rates and vote distributions. If we project an estimate in this way, Célestin would move back into second place, even after removing the irregular tally sheets that were found with the statistical test. Figure 10.1 shows the results under these different scenarios, as well as the preliminary results from the CEP.

Alternatively, we could project another scenario to take account of the disenfranchisement of displaced voters. In this scenario, Port-au-Prince, Carrefour, Delmas, and Pétionville would have double the participation rate that they actually had. In this fourth scenario, Michel Martelly, who took nearly 40% of the vote in the 15 largest cities, would be the second-place finisher in all of the above scenarios.

The point here is not to determine which candidates should have gone to the second round of the election; on the contrary, this analysis shows

Figure 10.1 No Clear Winner for Second Place

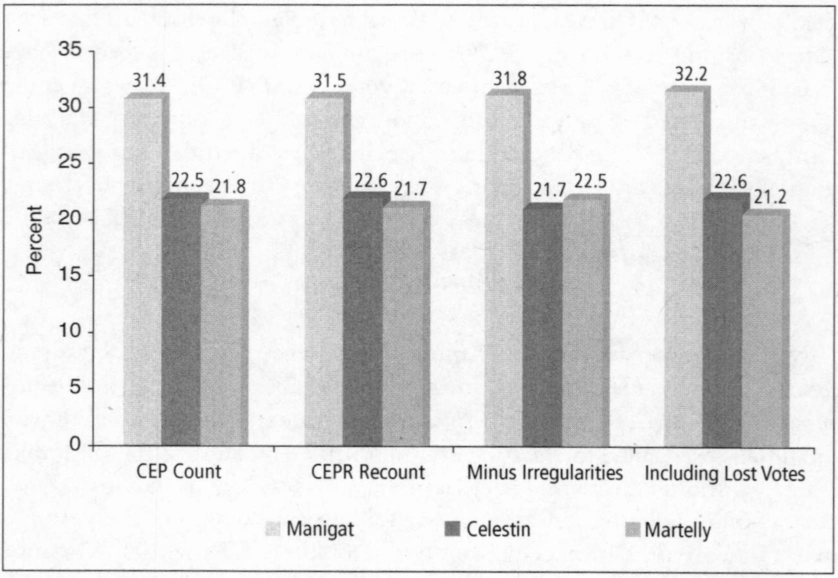

Source: CEP and authors' calculations

that it is simply impossible to determine who should have done so. The second round that did take place in March 2011, in which Martelly prevailed, was based on arbitrary assumptions and exclusions—just as the first round was.

* * *

Martelly's Election
Shades of Populism and Authoritarian Rule

Patrick Sylvain

———

ONE COULD CONSIDER MICHEL JOSEPH Martelly's election to the Haitian presidency in April 2011 as a sequel to Graham Greene's *The Comedians.* [21]

It seems as though everything in Haiti is either a comedy or a tragedy; the political emergence of a popular singer known for his superficial and sexually explicit lyrics is, more than anything, akin to a stage comedy, a momentous farce. Martelly, despite his lack of political experience and education, is now expected to serve as Haiti's head of state and to lead a nation in a perpetual state of crisis, lacking institutions and qualified civil servants.

For the past few decades, the derision of ethics, justice, education, and national character could only produce a political candidate that mirrors the ideals of the society at large. Martelly's ascension to power is a byproduct of the society's ills and entrenched crises, but it is also the repudiation of former president René Préval's failed presidency and the politics of silence that displeased and alienated the already disenfranchised population.

Leading up to the election, much of the population, at least those who voted, carried pictures of Aristide while simultaneously sporting the number 8 (to symbolize Martelly). In any logical realm, those two figures would be incompatible (despite their populist-driven campaigns).

As a matter of fact, Aristide and Martelly represent politically antithetical points of view. After all, Martelly openly supported Aristide's ouster from power in both 1991 and 2004. Also, he is a strong supporter of reestablishing the military that Aristide banned from operation. The intersecting point between these two charismatic figures, however, is the fact that populism resides strongly in the realm of Haitian popular representative democracy.

The writer Lyonel Trouillot recently remarked, "When voting is offered to people who do not feel that they are citizens, in an atmosphere of old regime, they then vote for 'disorder.' From Duvalier to Aristide and ending with the election of Michel Martelly, the Haitian presidency becomes a general state, a free for all." In a savage state of inequity and abject poverty, a virtual free-for-all was what empowered the majority of Haiti's population that voted for Martelly, administering a severe blow to the traditional political class. And as Trouillot states, "The disorder did not change the social order, it has revealed and exploited the squalid."

Although Martelly did sound very presidential during his first prepared national speech, promising to unify the country and do away with sectarian politics, one must also remember that he represents a package that has been tightly made over. The image of the morphed bad-boy-to-politician figure must be sold and projected.

As Martelly emphasized, "Everyone must get behind [his] project, because [his] project is a national project, it is a project for the nation." So far, his rhetoric comes with very little specifics, but the sound bites are exquisitely pleasing, especially his reference to creating "an inclusive nation." Ironically, there is now a nation that must be included when Martelly and his financial backers have in the past rejected the very people they are now embracing.

Why the shift? What is at stake? Are there puppeteers controlling the popular singer who was once a right-wing supporter of paramilitary groups such as the Front for the Advancement of Haiti? Could there be something behind the nudge by the international community for him to assume second place after the first presidential round, and finally be elected as the democratic president of Haiti? It is interesting to know that he has been mandated to lead the country toward recovery along with the IHRC, led by former US president Bill Clinton.

Of course, one can look at Martelly in two ways:

Positively. He is notorious for pushing the sociocultural envelope, as well as for being an ambitious businessman who speaks the language of the people. He claims that "when there is a leader, the people will follow." Plus, his intellectual limitations might push him toward achievement, as he could seek to surpass expectations and prove that the traditional power seekers, the intellectual class in the country, only talks about the people when it is convenient for them. Having already been a millionaire, and comfortably placed above the traditional political class (which translates to being above the customary black color line and also above the middle-class threshold, but associatively below the ruling possessing class), he is in a much better position to mediate and therefore effect change. Last, his affiliation with the military as well as with Duvalierist factions puts him in a milieu where militarism and the security apparatus of the country would not be threatened and might even benefit from his leadership, given his emphasis on the rule of law. With security comes an atmosphere conducive to investment and greater economic prosperity.

Negatively. Authoritarian streaks in two recent speeches he delivered, including the call for "war on war" when it comes to the press, should be taken seriously. While campaigning in Les Cayes on March 6, 2011, he categorically declared that "the country will be marching in the right path, where everyone will be placed under order." He added, "Justice for everyone and the rope for those who deserve it." This is interesting, considering the fact that he has often claimed that the "people are with him and will follow their trusted leader." Haitians should be cautious as his zeal and ambition to succeed might create an authoritative state à la Duvalierism, in which the supremacy of the state becomes law, and the law becomes privatized for the interest of the state.

Certainly, the Haitian military will return, but how much of the budget this institution would consume despite the country's need for health care, education, and agriculture remains unclear. Given the supremacy of the international community in the development strategies and goals under the IHRC, one would have to wonder about the extent to which the country is accelerating further into privatization. After all, the bourgeoisie has not been in direct executive power since 1946, and the international community has been pushing for privatization since 1986.

To project ideals of populism and reinforce symbols used to mirror Aristide while rejecting his politics, Martelly's core agitating team (Richard Morse and Roro Nelson) employed songs that were associated with Aristide by simply changing the name of the target subject. For example, the rally song "Kiyès ki towo a? Se Aristide ki towo a" (Who is the raging bull? Aristide is the raging bull) is now transformed as Martelly as the raging bull. Martelly has been symbolically and linguistically substituted for Aristide.

Additionally, Martelly has become, symbolically, the father of the country since the grandmother/mother (candidate Mirlande Manigat) was rejected. To this end, he recycles a song sung for Aristide by an old peasant man in June 1990: "Lè m'ap pale ak papa m', papa m' rele pa m'" (When I speak to my father, my father calls me his own). Again, Aristide the father has been substituted with a young, newly made-over father who promises order and progress while lambasting governmental waste during the past 30 years. But why only the past 30 years when it was the Duvaliers who squandered the country's wealth? It is because Martelly is a neo-Duvalierist who applauds the order of the old regime.

Most striking in this political ordeal is the fact that Martelly was elected on a political platform that is known as "Repons Peyizan," the peasant response. However, not one peasant or representative of the other organizations that formed the political platform were mentioned during his victory speech. Interestingly, one of the coalition's partners that formed the platform, the Organization for the Safety of the Nation, pulled out due to what the leader, Patrick Henry, referred to as a grave violation of the charter. Once again, a major crisis of party politics must have occurred without the criticism of the media. This is possible only in a country where political institutions are absent and political candidates are allowed to use platforms as launching pads for self-interest rather than for the formation of political parties.

Martelly's populist discourse presumes a harmonized notion of the people, and he tries to show his embodiment through the people by employing his rugged past as transparent currency as well as a societal mirror. He seeks an immediate identification with those he claims to represent—those in the streets, the disenfranchised, and the peasants. His populist leadership and legitimate mandate are touted as a transparency of representation, and thus a translation of popular will to affect orderly, clean, and effective gover-nance. However, populism can easily shift the political horizon and turn order into an authoritarian state.

* * *

The Haitian Diaspora
Supporting Reconstruction From the Centers of Power

Manolia Charlotin

IN THE 20 MONTHS SINCE the earthquake, the Haitian Diaspora community has remained fervently involved in Haiti's recovery and reconstruction. Di-aspora leaders, Haiti scholars, and human rights advocates have held nu-merous conferences, community meetings, and forums. Throughout these efforts, the need for deeper Diaspora involvement in long-term policy ad-vocacy continues to permeate the conversation. It has become apparent that the voices of the estimated 1.5 million Haitians living in the United States need to be heard where policies are developed in key US power cen-ters such as Washington, DC.

Two recent major policy gains in the Haitian community—dual citi-zenship in Haiti and Temporary Protected Status (TPS) extension and re-designation in the United States—should serve as a driving force to build a robust, comprehensive advocacy agenda for better US policies toward Haiti. These wins didn't come easily, nor did they happen without relentless advo-cacy. Dual citizenship remained an unlikely possibility until major political strides were made in the last year, due mostly to the acknowledgment of the immeasurable role the Diaspora played in the aftermath of the earthquake, and that Haiti would need its Diaspora now more than ever to rebuild.

As for TPS, the White House announced three days after the earth-quake it would grant eligible Haitians already living in the United States the chance to remain and work here legally for 18 months. For the Haitian community and immigration reform advocates, this was long overdue. For years, those calling for the humanitarian protection believed that conditions in Haiti—the aftermath of massive hurricanes, political upheaval, and abysmal poverty—should have led the United States to issue TPS to Haitians.

Since the TPS designation was incorporated into immigration law in 1990, undocumented nationals from countries such as Sudan, Nicaragua, and Somalia have been eligible for the status. Six countries embattled with natural disasters and political turmoil have been granted the status over these past two decades. According to the Department of Homeland Security (DHS), about 350,000 immigrants are living in the United States under TPS. The US government has been cautious, to say the least, with policy related to Haiti because of the belief that any type of perceived leniency could result in Haitians flooding onto US shores. And many say because of that, Haitians were passed up year after year for TPS.

Advocates kept up the fight, and on May 17, 2011, more than 16 months after the first designation, DHS Secretary Janet Napolitano announced the extension of TPS for roughly 48,000 Haitian nationals who currently had the designation. Leaders from the Diaspora worked with tireless pro bono legal organizations like the American Immigration Lawyers Association of New York, the Immigration Coalition at the University of Miami School of Law, the Massachusetts Law Reform Institute, and the Immigration Advocates Network. The extension was made effective July 23, 2011, and allowed Haitian beneficiaries to remain in the United States an additional 18 months—through January 22, 2013.

Now Haitians living abroad, particularly in the United States, have access to the political process in Haiti and immigration status that allows many to make a living to provide for their families here and back on the island. This presents a timely opportunity to harness the strength of different stakeholders.

A few notable groups around the country, developed post-quake, are indeed serving as conveners to tackle a myriad of issues. The Washington-based Haiti Advocacy Working Group (HAWG) coordinates advocacy efforts for more than 30 diverse international nonprofits on US–Haiti policy, including MADRE, the Robert F. Kennedy Center for Justice and Human Rights, TransAfrica Forum, Grassroots International, Partners in Health, and Jubilee USA Network. Given that many of these groups have built fruitful relationships on Capitol Hill, this loose collective has pooled together its resources and influence to address issues ranging from aid transparency and human rights of displaced survivors to capacity building of civil society institutions.

In March 2011, HAWG organized a week of events in Washington that culminated in a Lobby Day that brought together many representatives of civil society organizations, women's rights groups, rural peasant associations, and international agencies from Haiti. They also invited many Haitian American elected officials and intellectuals to join meetings with members of Congress, providing testimony to the failing aid efforts and, most importantly, the deplorable living conditions of survivors. These efforts resulted in meetings with 34 different government offices, including USAID, the State Department, and members of the Congressional Black Caucus.

Throughout the spring and summer they continued to work with Diaspora groups such as the Haitian Women of Miami, the Haitian League, Haitian American Grassroots Coalition, and Mobilize for Haiti to advance aid transparency legislation. In May 2011 the Assessing Progress in Haiti Act was passed through the House, intended to guarantee greater oversight and accountability of US relief and reconstruction efforts in Haiti. The accompanying Senate bill has since gained support from key leaders, including Senator John Kerry from Massachusetts (chair of the Foreign Relations Committee), who represents the state with the third-largest population of Haitians in the United States. Through this bill, US agencies would be held accountable for effective use of aid funds that bolsters the Haitian government and functioning of the civil society.

The Haitian Congress to Fortify Haiti—a Chicago-based Diaspora nonprofit that played a key role in dual-citizenship advocacy—in coordination with Lott Carey (a network of African American Baptist churches) has assembled a group of diverse leaders and advocates from the black faith-based community with longstanding interests in Haiti. With an emphasis on maintaining a Haitian-led effort, they are working to craft a new policy advocacy initiative on a host of issues from reconstruction to immigration.

In July 2011 a group of leaders in the Diaspora kicked off a national listening tour in Boston. The Haitian Fund for Innovation (New York), Konbit for Haiti (Florida), the Lambi Fund (Haiti), and Oxfam America (Boston/Washington)—in collaboration with the *Boston Haitian Reporter*—brought Diaspora perspectives on issues they would like to address through advocacy. The tour planned to visit US cities with major Haitian populations, and the *Reporter* was slated to document and report on these listening sessions and the ongoing effort to coordinate disparate advocates, leaders, and groups around the country who work on US–Haiti policy. It is important that the Haitian media tell the story of Haitians coming together, working together to exercise their rights to collectively address decades of failed US policy toward Haiti.

What stands out about these efforts is that they are interconnected. Given the enormity of Haiti's challenges and the depth of US involvement in these chronic crises, US citizens of Haitian descent have an immense responsibility to communicate, coordinate, and remain informed. Building on the work that has been done in the past, it is time that the Diaspora and friends of Haiti become long-term strategic partners of the people of Haiti by engaging policymakers, industry leaders, labor unions, development officials, and agencies by flexing their political muscle.

Notes

1. Haiti's Constitution calls for a runoff in cases where a single candidate fails to obtain a clear majority in the first round.

2. Translated from the original Haitian Creole by Mark Schuller.

3. The original word was *pèpè*, originally describing clothes so used that thrift stores in the United States couldn't sell them, shipped to Haiti in bales.

4. "Le CEP Annonce les Resultats," *Le Nouvelliste*, December 8, 2010.

5. *Nouvelliste*, the week before the election, showed how candidate Célestin had five pages of ads by himself.

6. A play on the campaign slogan for Manigat, *ban manman m*, "give me my mother."

7. Jean Price-Mars, *La Vocation De L'élite* (Port-au-Prince: Imp. E. Chenet, 1908).

8. Myrtha Gilbert, *La Catastrophe n'Était pas Naturelle* (Port-au-Prince: Imprimeur II, 2010).

9. The latter term stems from a longstanding division between island-born, mixed-culture Creoles with African-born slaves, or *bosales*. It has become an insult, an object of ridicule expressed throughout the culture as Uncle Bouki and his contemporary forms of Alcibiade and Tonton Bicha.

10. Jean Casimir. *La Culture Opprimée* (Port-au-Prince: Médiatexte, 2006), 235.

11. This article is excerpted and adapted from Jake Johnston and Mark Weisbrot, "Haiti's Fatally Flawed Election," Center for Economic and Policy Research, January 2011, updated February 2011, http://www.cepr.net/index.php/publications/reports/haitis-fatally-flawed-election.

12. Organization of American States (OAS), "Statement by the OAS-CARICOM Joint Electoral Observation Mission on Haiti's Presidential and Legislative Elections of 28 November 2010," November 29, 2010, http://www.oas.org/en/media_center/press_release.asp?sCodigo=E-461/10.

13. Jonathan Katz, "Haiti Election Results Could Be Delayed for Weeks," Associated Press, December 18, 2010.

14. Between 1% and 3% of these tally sheets could be expected to fall outside of the confidence interval due to random variation.

15. For Election Day observations from CEPR's Alex Main, who was on the ground in Haiti, as well as numerous news reports of irregularities, see Center for Economic and Policy Research, "Election Live-Blog," November 28, 2010, http://www.cepr.net/index.php/blogs/relief-and-reconstruction-watch/election-live-blog. See also OAS, "Statement by the OAS-CARICOM Joint Electoral Observation Mission."

16. International Institute for Democracy and Electoral Assistance (IDEA), "Voter Turnout Data for Haiti," database available at http://www.idea.int/vt/country view.cfm?renderforprint=1&CountryCode=HT.

17. Institute for Justice and Democracy in Haiti (IJDH), "The International Community Should Pressure the Haitian Government for Prompt and Fair Elections," June 30, 2010, http://ijdh.org/archives/13138.

18. At that time, the election for the Senate and the Chamber of Deputies was split into two separate elections, with one to take place in February and one in March.

19. IJDH, "International Community Should Pressure the Haitian Government."

20. See OAS, "Statement by the OAS-CARICOM Joint Electoral Observation Mission."

21. Adapted from an article of the same name originally published in the *Boston Haitian Reporter,* April 14, 2011.

11

Politics From Below
Solidarity, Participation, and Emerging Movements

Haiti was born from a slave revolt incited by religious leader Boukman at'Bwa Kayiman on August 14, 1791—an act that was, in Haitian American anthropologist Michel-Rolph Trouillot's description, "unthinkable."[1] The Haitian Revolution and the radical notion that tout moun se moun—*everyone is a person—smashed the dominant ideology that African people are worthy only of being slaves. Since then Haiti has inspired other freedom fighters in the Americas, including Latin American liberator Simón Bolívar, who received refuge and military aid from Haiti, and dozens of slave revolts across the Caribbean and the United States.*

Haiti's people have had to contend with 200 years of an unholy alliance of foreign powers unified to punish the upstart republic and a local elite only too happy to serve foreign interests to maintain control over the domestic population. This collusion created one of the world's most notorious dictatorships. The Duvalier dynasty received $900 million in foreign aid (not to mention loans) as well as tactical and political support from the United States, United Nations, World Bank, and the Catholic Church, at least until Duvalier's grip became total with help of the infamous tonton makout—*the secret police—toward whom even the IMF knew funds were being directed.[2]*

Despite this, Haitian people have resisted, organizing a quiet revolution finally strong enough to cast off the Duvalier dictatorship in 1986. Not satisfied with what appeared to many to be a US-backed coup d'état, the people continued to push for democratic reform and a society based on inclusion, participation, transparency, and national production. Reactionary elements continued to attack, confuse, infiltrate, divide, and kill Haiti's grassroots movements. But

213

subdued and oppressed, the popular struggle persevered. Haiti put the crisis of high food prices in 2008 on the world map with nationwide food riots. In 2009, despite trigger-happy UN troops and cases of teargas, the movement succeeded in raising the minimum wage, only to be undermined in a backdoor deal between President René Préval and UN Special Envoy Bill Clinton.[3]

The earthquake was certainly not an exception. Throughout this book have been stories of solidarity, of unity, of resistance. For the first terrifying days following the earthquake, when the roads were blocked and the airport destroyed, no external aid came in. During this time Haitian people could have showed the entire world how a dignified people could put aside class and sectarian differences to pull together and collectively survive, if only the mainstream media and agencies would notice. Later, when the official aid came attached with foreign military and agendas, this solidarity was replaced by an increasing dependency and hostility. Social movements reached across bitter partisan lines to work together to defend IDP rights or stop rape. As an inherently fragile formation in an unstable environment beset by numerous layers of political agendas, organizing social movements to respond to the current kriz konjonktirèl—*the "conjunctural crisis"—remains a challenge.*

Longtime solidarity activist Beverly Bell gives voice to many social movement leaders, discussing numerous unsung acts of solidarity and courage, from the Port-au-Prince neighborhoods to the peasantry who opened their homes to their beleaguered cousins from the rubble-covered capital. Bell describes the early steps of organizing formal responses and proposing alternatives before the dust settled and the rubble was removed. As the PDNA was being rushed together to serve as an official blueprint for development, women's organizations within and outside of Haiti persisted in demanding greater participation and inclusion for women, drafting a "Gender Shadow Report" to serve in their transnational advocacy effort. Excerpts here focus on the grassroots level and propose specific economic alternatives.

Discussing her insights inside Haiti's government as the first minister of women, physician and SOFA activist Lise-Marie Dejean recounts the continuities of the women's movement, not only before and after the earthquake but also draws parallels between the first women's organization, Ligue Féminine, *founded in the last days of the 1915 US occupation. In addition to protection against violence and a series of laws to undo discrimination, Dejean proposed housing as a priority demand for the women's movement as early as 1993. The right to housing, of course, remains one of the core struggles following the earthquake.*

We close with a resolution from an international colloquium hosted by FRAKKA in May 2011 signed by hundreds of attendees—including 35 IDP camp committees, 40 Haitian organizations, and solidarity organizations such as the MST, Brazil's Landless Workers' Movement. The resolution offers a roadmap of demands and organizing strategies for the movement for housing rights. These are only four of many other stories of solidarity, participation, and resistance cropping up from under the rubble, some still to receive the sunlight of recognition. To quote Haitian revolutionary leader Toussaint Louverture, just before his execution: "The roots are strong and deep."

* * *

"We Bend, but We Don't Break"
Fighting for a Just Reconstruction in Haiti

Beverly Bell

A POPULAR HAITIAN SAYING GOES, "We are bamboo. We bend, but we don't break."[4] This expression of resolve in the face of adversity has been in wide circulation since the January 12, 2010, earthquake, taking on even greater meaning. The number of Haitians killed by one of the most destructive disasters in world history is unknown; estimates range from 250,000 to 350,000. Just under 2 million people were rendered homeless, displaced, or dispossessed, according to the UN. For those already exiled to the absolute margin of survival, the socioeconomic impacts of the disaster are incalculable. In earthquake-hit areas, the vulnerable almost invariably lost some combination of family members, homes, personal belongings, merchandise, or whatever else might have given them a little protection from hunger, suffering, and death.

Even before the earthquake, Haiti's destitution was a marvel on the planet. The poet Jean-Claude Martineau often says in his public presentations, "Haiti is the only country to have a last name. It's 'the poorest country in the Western Hemisphere.'" But as tenacious as oppression and deprivation have been throughout Haitian history, the country's highly organized grassroots movement has never given up the battle its enslaved ancestors began. The movement is composed of women, peasants, street vendors, human rights advocates, clergy and laity, workers, and others. The mobilizations, protests, and advocacy have brought down dictators, staved off some of the worst of economic policies aimed at others' profit, and kept the population from ever fitting quietly into anyone else's plans for them.

By far the single largest force of rescuers and first responders during the quake's aftermath was ordinary citizens who responded spontaneously and without reward. Neighbors worked together to dig out survivors from collapsed buildings, usually with only their hands or whatever implements they could improvise. They unearthed corpses, set up brigades to clear rubble, and organized security teams in neighborhoods and camps.

"We've shared our pain and our suffering," said Mesita Attis of the market women's support group Martyred Women of Brave Ayibobo. "If you heard your baby in the ruins crying 'Mommy, Mommy, Mommy,' 14 people would run to help you. If you don't have a piece of bread, someone will give you theirs."

The aid and accompaniment responses are based in the long tradition of solidarity that has kept this resource-poor people alive for centuries. Not long after the quake, Yolette Etienne, director of Oxfam Great Britain–Haiti, commented, "The tremendous chain of solidarity of the people we saw from the day of the earthquake on: That is our capacity. That is our victory. That is our heart. From the first hour Haitians engaged in every type of solidarity imaginable—one supporting the other, one helping the other, one saving the other. If any of us is alive today, we can say that it's thanks to this solidarity."

Beyond the immediate aftermath, family members, neighbors, and strangers have assumed the bulk of caregiving for hungry, wounded, homeless, and abandoned survivors. In areas directly damaged, as well as those to which survivors have fled, people have pooled their time, belongings, and funds. They have shared food, sheets, and tarps; looked after the injured and ill; provided child care; given money for medicine; kept a protective eye out for women and children who are at a high risk of being assaulted; and taken in orphaned and abandoned children.

Judith Simeon, an organizer with peasant and women's groups, echoed what many of the others said: "Everyone was helping everyone. What people had, they shared with others. It was truly those who had nothing who did the most. It was our citizen obligation to take care of those who needed it."

But given the magnitude of the disaster, these efforts by ordinary Haitians have not been enough to help everyone. Neither has international aid, which, according to hundreds of interviews and months of observation, has yet to significantly address any of the needs of vast swaths of earthquake-hit populations. Although a remarkable $9.9 billion in aid has been given or pledged by individuals and organizations throughout the world, there is a huge gap between the dollars and international posturing around aid, on the one hand, and the population in need, on the other. As of early June 2010, hundreds of people in refugee camps reported that they had received little—some rice, perhaps a tent—to nothing at all.

In this context, some peasant, student, neighborhood, and other groups have turned the solidarity into more formal, organized programs. They are providing shelter, medical care, community mental health care, food, water, children's activities, leisure activities, security, and support for much-needed agricultural production. To cite just one among many diverse responses, the peasant organization Tèt Kole Ti Peyizan Ayisyen in the rural region of Piatte employs a three-part strategy: taking people into their homes; bringing food to other homes that are housing internally displaced people; and bringing the fruits of their fields, like bananas and peas, to camps in Port-au-Prince.

The outpouring of community-based assistance and support is a useful reminder of the collective resilience and resourcefulness that are key to Haitian culture.

"In Haitian families, the way they socialize children, they give a lot of importance to the capacity of endurance," said psychologist Lenz Jean-François. "They teach children to always be ready for a tough situation, and to struggle to hold their dignity."

The grassroots approaches offer a different vision and practice of what "humanitarian" can mean when it is embedded in aid given with respect, dignity, and a commitment to equity. And the approaches serve as a guide to what a society that privileges mutual aid over profit, and democratic participation over domination, could look like in Haiti.

The Haitian popular movement has set for itself the formidable task of addressing not only the ongoing humanitarian crisis among refugees but also the reconstruction effort as a whole. Yannick Etienne of Workers' Struggle said, "We have the opportunity as a movement to continue our organizational work, to push for social justice, and to unify the people to take change into their hands. We still have the remnants of an organized people; they didn't all die under the debris."

Social movements have moved forward in creating coalitions, shaping their own alternative plans for the country's future, and mapping out their advocacy strategies. Dozens of interviews with social movement leaders and numerous declarations reveal a clearly emerging consensus. First, it includes full participation of those who are usually denied both input into public policy formation and benefit of the fruits of those policies: peasant farmers, sweatshop workers, informal-sector workers, destitute women, and others.

Second, it establishes greater justice and equity as the ends of what grass-roots organizations call "constructing the country," as opposed to re-constructing it, since few are served by re-creating the gross levels of mass poverty and social exclusion that existed before the earthquake.

As early as February 13, 2010, and at least on three later occasions, more than 50 NGOs and grassroots organizations devoted to a variety of issues (alternative development, women's rights) and representing various sectors (rural people, youth) met in Port-au-Prince to advance these ends. Their declaration read in part:

> [We have] decided to launch a national and international campaign to bring forth another vision of how to redevelop this country, a vision based on people-to-people solidarity to develop the opportunity now fac-ing this country to raise up another Haiti. We [want] to build a social force which can establish a reconstruction plan where the fundamental problems of the people take first priority. These include: housing, en-vironment, food, education, literacy, work, and health for all; a plan to wipe out exploitation, poverty, and social and economic inequality; and a plan to construct a society which is based on social justice.[5]

The social movement's priorities are as follows:

1. *Creating participatory democracy.* This has been at the heart of de-mands from the moment Haiti emerged from the brutal 30-year Duvalier dictatorship in 1986; it may be more relevant today than ever. Government must serve the people, be accountable to them, and include their participa-tion. Through many public declarations, press conferences, and, since early April, daily demonstrations, citizens are asserting that it is their right to be formally brought into decision making. Says Julie Desrosiers, a street mer-chant, "We need a true democracy in the country. More than just elections. We need a say in how the millions of aid [dollars] are spent, so that we the people actually benefit instead of just the big shots."

2. *Rebuilding under a new economic paradigm,* one that breaks free of unfair trade rules under which food and many other basics are imported, and a coveted job is in a sweatshop earning $3 per day. Social movements are adamant that Haiti adhere to principles of economic justice, includ-ing trade rules that privilege Haitian producers and Haitian goods, food sovereignty, employment opportunities, workers' rights, and cancellation of its foreign debts.

3. *Protecting the environment.* This is connected to constructing a new economic model, putting people and the earth before capital, and protecting

life from commodification. Central to social movements' advocacy is tough environmental regulations for industry, which are today virtually nonexistent. Also central are solar electricity, solar ovens, reforestation, integrated water-management systems, and an agricultural system that privileges the small-scale production of diverse, organic food.

4. *Putting social needs at the center.* As articulated in a meeting of women from KOFAVIV from their new home in refugee camps, those needs are, in a rough ranking of priority, housing, food, health care, education, and work.

5. *Prioritizing agriculture.* Peasant and other organizations insist that the government must invest in and offer active support to small-scale agriculture, and that foreign food aid must be reined in to give Haitian farmers a chance to compete. They are also adamant that trade policies must protect small-farmer production to create food sovereignty, the right of a nation to produce locally for local consumption. Only 4% of the funds outlined in the Haitian government's PDNA are earmarked for agriculture. "The government is giving away the whole country," said Doudou Pierre of both the Peasant Movement of Papay and Vía Campesina. "We are for family agriculture that respects the environment, but for that we must have government support and we must have land."

6. *Ensuring women's and children's rights.* In the fragile and dangerous post-catastrophe environment, social and economic rights for women and children must be front and center. According to surveys conducted by KOFAVIV, rape and violence are escalating, so increased security is critical. Malya Villard, an organizer with KOFAVIV, said, "The government didn't respect our rights even before the Presidential Palace was destroyed, even before the Palace of Justice was destroyed. We need those rights in the reconstruction."

A corollary of these priorities is generating what Camille Chalmers, director of the Haitian Platform to Advocate Alternative Development (PAPDA), called "people-to-people solidarity, not of that solidarity that nation-states use in order to dominate the people." Horizontal alliances will continue to be important over the coming years to help Haitians ensure full rights for all; gain different trade policy that does not undermine but develops labor rights, environmental standards, and food sovereignty; ensure that government policy privileges human need for all over profit for some; and create space for women's full rights and power. And the voices and energy of people in the United States are especially needed to challenge the neocolonial elements of the US reconstruction plans that are blocking Haitian leadership.

Despite their advocacy, the Haitian people, together with their government, have been bypassed in the planning and oversight of how aid money is spent and in reconstruction policies. The international donors' forums in Montreal (January 25), Santo Domingo (March 17), and New York (March 31), where the large-scale plans were developed, were led by foreign ministers and international financial institutions. UN Secretary-General Ban Ki-moon has touted the process as "a sweeping exercise in nation-building on a scale and scope not seen in generations."[6] But Haitian voices have been lost amid the declarations of the IMF, the UN, the US government, and others.

The Haitian government receives one cent of every dollar that has come in since the earthquake and is not consulted on the rest, according to the Associated Press. "The NGOs don't tell us . . . where the money's coming from or how they are spending it," Prime Minister Jean-Max Bellerive was quoted as saying.[7]

On April 15 the Haitian Parliament formally ceded its powers over finances and reconstruction to a foreign-led CIRH for the next 18 months (see Willems, Chapter 2, this volume). The CIRH's mandate is to direct the post-earthquake reconstruction of Haiti through the $9.9 billion in pledges of international aid, including approving policies, projects, and budgeting. The World Bank will manage the money.

Most members on the CIRH are foreign. The criterion for becoming a foreign voting member is that the institution or country has contributed at least $100 million during two consecutive years or has canceled at least $200 million in debt. Others who have given less may share a seat. The OAS and NGOs working in Haiti do not have a vote.

The CIRH is headed by UN Special Envoy Bill Clinton and Bellerive. The only accountability or oversight measure is Haitian President René Préval's veto power. Few expect him to use his veto, both because his record is not one of challenging the international aid apparatus and because of possible repercussions, in terms of the dollar flow, by the CIRH. According to Antonal Mortiné, the executive secretary of the Haitian Platform of Human Rights Organizations, the CIRH has made Haiti a *restavèk,* or child slave. "This is not the path to democracy," he said.

While the international community excludes the Haitian state from reconstruction and the Parliament even votes to exclude itself, so the Haitian state excludes its people. The government has failed to invoke even token discussions with civil society, except informally with some business-people and a few NGOs that do not represent a base. One indicator is the citizenry's inability to provide input into their government's strategic plan of long-term development based on the PDNA. The government of Haiti granted just one week, March 14–20, for "consultation with civil society and the private sector" on the PDNA. But four of those days were *after* the government approved the draft plan, on March 15.

The agenda for a just Haitian future is monumental in the best of times. Today it is being shaped by people who still may be accommodating themselves to the fact that their child or mother, not seen since January 12, is dead. It is being shaped by people who are living in tents in squalid, dangerous camps. It is being shaped by people who are profoundly traumatized and have no access to mental health care.

It may be that their suffering sharpens the determination to have their needs met in a context of social and economic justice and democracy. That is the perspective, at least, of Ricot Jean-Pierre, director of advocacy for the Platform to Advocate Alternative Development in Haiti (PAPDA). "Sadness can't discourage us so that we stop fighting," he said. "We've lost people as in all battles, but we have to continue fighting to honor them and make their dreams a reality. The dream is translated into a slogan: Another Haiti Is Possible."

* * *

Gender Shadow Report

Women's International Network of the World Association of Community Radio Broadcasters (AMARC), Equality Now, Gender and Disaster Network, Groots International, Huairou Commission, Lambi Fund of Haiti, MADRE, ORÉGAND (Observatoire sur le développement régional et l'analyse différenciée selon les sexes), PotoFanm+Fi: Rebuilding Haiti Initiative, g+dsr

---

This preliminary report was written in consultation with a coalition of women from diverse backgrounds working in grassroots communities in Haiti as well as in the international arena. Released on March 31, 2010, the same day as the Haiti Donors' Conference held at UN headquarters, it highlights gender concerns absent from Haiti's PDNA, the operative blueprint for Haiti's reconstruction. The report offers donors, international agencies, and other stakeholders human rights–based policy guidelines to promote and protect the rights of Haitian women.

Although the PDNA comprises eight themes—governance, environment, disaster risk and management, social sectors, infrastructure, territorial development, production sector, and cross-cutting sectors (including gender, youth, culture, and social protection)—only the last theme addresses gender, and only peripherally so.

Preamble

Recognizing the devastation that the January 12, 2010, earthquake in Haiti, and its aftermath, has caused on the country and its people, in particular women and girls who are disproportionately affected due to the gender-based violence and discrimination they face,

Recalling that the Convention on the Elimination of All Forms of Discrimination Against Women (CEDAW), the Beijing Platform for Action, and the Convention on the Rights of the Child form, respectively, the basis of the international legal framework for the protection and promotion of the human rights of women and girls,

Recalling that the Inter-American Convention on the Prevention, Punishment and Eradication of Violence Against Women ("Convention of Belém do Pará") provides a regional legal framework for the protection and promotion of the human rights of women and girls,

Recognizing that violence against women and girls is a human rights violation that hinders and prevents individual, community, and national development,

Recalling the commitment of governments to the Millennium Development Goals, in particular Goal 3, to promote gender equality and to empower women and girls,

Recalling that Security Council Resolution 1325 (2000), whose 10th anniversary is upon us, "urges Member States to ensure increased representation of women at all decision-making levels in national, regional and international institutions and mechanisms for the prevention, management, and resolution of conflict,"

Recalling Security Council Resolution 1892 (2009) on Haiti, which emphasizes "the need for increased efforts to support the participation of women in the political process," and "[s]trongly condemns the grave violations against children affected by armed violence, as well as widespread rape and other sexual abuse of women and girls," and "[r]equests the Secretary-General to continue to take the necessary measures to ensure full compliance of all MINUSTAH personnel with the United Nations zero-tolerance policy on sexual exploitation and abuse,"

Recalling Security Council Resolution 1820, which "[r]equests the Secretary-General and relevant United Nations agencies, inter alia, through consultation with women and women-led organizations as appropriate, to develop effective mechanisms for providing protection from violence, including in particular sexual violence, to women and girls in and around UN managed refugee and internally displaced persons camps . . . ,"

Recalling the commitment of governments to the Paris Declaration and the Accra Agenda for Action on Aid Effectiveness,

Recognizing the important work already undertaken by the United Nations Gender in Humanitarian Response Working Group in their February 2010 paper on "Gender Mainstreaming in the Humanitarian Response in the Aftermath of the Earthquake in Haiti,"

Concerned that qualified Haitian women and Haitian women's organizations are not given the opportunity or are being excluded from deliberations and decision-making processes related to the reconstruction and economic and political recovery of Haiti,

Welcoming the statement made by former Chilean president Michelle Bachelet during her visit to Haiti in February 2010 that "Haiti's reconstruction will be faster if women are an intrinsic part of the process,"[8]

Underlining the March 18, 2010, Statement issued by 26 Haitian groups, including the women's groups Enfofamn and SOFA, decrying the almost total exclusion of Haitian civil society in the deliberations during the donors' conference in Santo Domingo that addressed the "Plan for Reconstruction of Haiti,"

Underlining the March 22, 2010, statement issued by CONAP, refusing to support the PDNA process and urging that all steps aiming at the construction of Haiti cannot occur without the genuine participation of the populations,

Underlining the March 17, 2010, Plateforme Femmes Citoyennes Haiti Solidaire that aims at ensuring equality between women and men in the vision and plan of action for a new Haiti,

Urges the immediate inclusion of Haitian women's voices and their equal participation in all sectors related to the reconstruction of their country, and

Exhorts the international donors, the government of Haiti, and the UN to fulfill their commitments and obligations set forth in the above-mentioned laws, declarations, resolutions, and statements, as the case may be, without further delay.

Why Haitian Women's Participation Is Critical

Women in Haiti are disproportionately impacted by the earthquake, both because they face gender discrimination, exposing them to higher rates of poverty and violence, and because they are responsible for meeting the needs of the most vulnerable, including infants, children, the elderly, and the thousands of newly disabled people.[9] Women's full participation and leadership in all phases of the reconstruction of Haiti (as mandated by UN Security Council Resolution 1325[10] and other internationally recognized standards) requires that a gender perspective be integrated into ongoing discussions and planning.[11] Such a human-rights-based approach is mandated by international law and crucial to rebuilding Haiti on a more sustainable, equitable, and disaster-resilient foundation.[12]

To overcome discrimination and to fulfill their roles as primary caregivers, Haitian women require and are legally entitled to a policy architecture that upholds the full range of their human rights, including social and economic rights. Women's leadership and caregiving work should be recognized and supported by policy and program mandates and transparent resource commitments that enable women to play meaningful, sustained, and formal roles in all stages of the relief and recovery process.

We applaud the actions of donor states to assist the people of Haiti in this time of crisis, and present the following principles to help guide governments, international organizations, and other stakeholders in providing for the protection and promotion of women's human rights in the reconstruction plan for Haiti. Because disasters amplify existing social inequalities, a gender perspective is critical to avoid recovery policies that inadvertently reproduce discrimination against women.[13] Our detailed recommendations highlighted throughout the report provide specific guidance on ensuring women's rights to participation and consideration in these processes.

We respectfully remind donor governments of their obligation to ensure that policies are nondiscriminatory in outcome as well as intent. The UN Guiding Principles on Internal Displacement call on governments to consult with Haitian women and ensure their participation in decisions that impact their lives. Effective consultations enable participants to actually influence outcomes and are anchored in formal partnerships with Haitian women's groups (particularly local grassroots groups), who are empowered and resourced to take public leadership in the process of reconstruction.[14] The Donors' Conference must ensure Haitian women's effective participation and leadership in all stages of the National Relief and Reconstruction Plan.

Reinforcing the Grass Roots

More than 500,000 earthquake survivors have fled Port-au-Prince to the countryside, where grassroots organizations often make decisions that impact the entire community. As in many countries, women continue to be underrepresented as grassroots leaders in Haiti.

At the grassroots level women often do not know their rights or understand that they have a role to play in shaping the policies that affect their lives.

In Haiti, women's involvement in agriculture is high, and they engage in selling the produce and other goods. They work in the informal sector as vendors; domestic workers thus support the communities' economic activities to a great extent. But their lack of awareness and inferior social position place them in a highly vulnerable position in the post-disaster phase.

Peasant women face many obstacles that include disproportionately high rates of illiteracy, lack of knowledge of backward and forward linkages, social constraints, and an imbalanced amount of familial responsibility.

Despite noble intentions, a perceivable gap exists between huge recovery, relief, and rescue operations and the needs of community at a grassroots level, especially of women and girls who are most vulnerable. This is a result of failure to engage these groups in reconstruction process and operations effectively.

Recommendations

1. The grassroots voice must be heard in the rebuilding of Haiti. The grass roots must lead the efforts in rebuilding and decentralizing Haiti. Not the politicians. Not the elite. Not foreign governments.

2. The participation of women is a well-documented factor for political, social, and economic success.

3. Women must be equal partners in the process of democratic development in Haiti. As activists and leaders, the contributions of women are crucial to building a strong and vibrant society.

4. Women's groups and women's rights advocacy networks at the grass roots have to play a central role in post-disaster reconstruction and relief efforts. To be specific, this includes recognizing and advocating for the differential needs of women and girls be taken into consideration for humanitarian response and early recovery.

5. International aid agencies/humanitarian organizations have to focus on supporting grassroots women's organizations devastated by the earthquake through strengthening their structural and functional capacities. This is crucial given the fact that these organizations have been successful in meeting women's needs in the past and that these organizations have better community outreach to facilitate humanitarian and early recovery efforts, support the ministry at the cutting-edge level, prevent gender-based violence, and boost economic security for women and their families in the post-disaster context.

6. At the grass roots, women have to be made partners in multidonor-funded projects on need assessments and reconstruction plans and provide an opportunity to women to assume leadership roles in deciding their own and their families' future.

7. At the grass roots, high priority is to be given to increasing women's access to essential services, and information has to be made available to women on relief and rehabilitation activities so that they will be able to take benefit of the support being provided and available. Grassroots organizations can be effective networkers in ensuring maximum community outreach of information.

8. Involve women's microfinance groups, women's neighborhood groups, animators [Haitian term for community organizers], women peasant groups, and women's NGOs in vulnerability and capacity assessments to get their knowledge, insights, information, experiences, and resources, and to influence macroeconomic policies and recovery.

9. Engage women's cooperatives in subcontracts.

10. Convene women-only conferences to train women exclusively on their natural abilities as leaders in the community and encourage them to leverage those strengths to create change in the community. Create an environment in which women can advocate on policy, make decisions, be elected as officers, and participate meaningfully in every facet of life.

11. Create literacy, social awareness, and community vigilance programs accessible to and appropriate for grassroots women.

12. Convene gender-equity roundtables for men and women so that men can better understand the need for gender equity and equality in the family, work, and community.

13. Create a decentralized infrastructure that functions through region-specific women's centers for economic development, better roads, public education, health care, social services, and access to potable water and sanitation. If investment in decentralization is a priority, the major cities and towns in the rural provinces are poised to expand and become vital centers

for national productivity. As a result, women can have the opportunity to become leaders in this decentralized growth and access information and infrastructure for a better future.

14. Women's consultations should not be limited to their health and security concerns only; rather, they have to be involved in discussions along with men on matters concerning community welfare in the post-disaster situation. Consultations with women on crucial issues of shelter designing, housing needs, relocation of families, and decisions related to closure of camps is highly essential.

15. Special initiatives need to be taken to network small, community-level organizations with larger institutions to facilitate effective funding and implementation of women's development in a post-disaster context. This is very effective as the local organizations are familiar with local needs of women and children and context-specific design needed for effective response.

* * *

"We Need to Stay Vigilant"

An Interview with Lise-Marie Dejean[15]

The following is a selection of an interview with Lise-Marie Dejean, a medical doctor, longstanding member of SOFA, and the first minister of Women's Condition and Rights, named by President Jean-Bertrand Aristide in 1994.

I returned to Haiti in 1986 [when the Duvalier dictatorship was overthrown, February 7]. We had an ongoing struggle in the Diaspora as well to support the struggle in Haiti. So when we returned in '86, we were happy to see that Haitian women were even stronger than we were. They were organized; there were different women's groups that were organized. There was a big demonstration on April 3, 1986, all over the country, in all major cities, where women took to the streets to demand that the cards were to be reshuffled.

When I returned, I tried to make contact with different women's groups, and I chose one of them, SOFA, where I am until today. As such I can say that I returned to the struggle to change women's condition.[16] It also allowed me to research the women's movement in Haiti.

An organization called Ligue Féminine [Feminine League] struggled for women's rights. When we returned to Haiti we had the chance to meet with a founding member of the league, Colette Pouchol Oriol, who unfortunately died this April [2011].

I joined SOFA in '87, which was founded a year earlier. We knew that the Ligue Féminine had already disappeared because Duvalier had manipulated it. He said he would work on women's emancipation and took women into his so-called government. He set up a bunch of offices, and that divided the women's movement. The movement finally was destroyed by the power he gave self-named women's rights advocates over other women. He crushed the very idea of the women's movement in Haiti. And as he had eliminated the right to free association, people didn't have the right to organize meetings. Three people didn't even have the right to talk while they were standing in the street.

This is why not only the women's movement but all groups were forced to function underground. According to our research, we knew that many women of the Ligue left for exile, others were arrested or tortured, so the movement disappeared. The Ligue was created on February 22, 1934, so SOFA was created on the same date, February 22, 1986, to continue the work.

So, when SOFA was founded, it explicitly followed the model of the Ligue Féminine, which was involved in the movement to force the US military out. There are obviously parallels.
Let's just say that the earthquake is a pretext for the UN troops and the international agencies, because they started working here a long time ago! A key example I always share, not because I was in favor of Aristide when he came to power in 1990: many Haitians came back to serve their country. They didn't need money! They came to work, to develop the country. You see? What did they do? With the [1991–1994] coup, [Raoul] Cédras [de facto military dictator of Haiti until Aristide's return in 1994] killed many people. When [coup leaders and paramilitary] heard that people took to the streets, they eliminated almost 3,000 people. You see? This coup d'état frightened people, which puts us in the condition wherein we accept anything.

Despite this, we are a people founded on resistance. I believe that this tradition of resistance will allow us to stand up to these racketeers.

How does the women's struggle compare to that of the Ligue?
The first thing is the situation of inequality between men and women. For instance, a man has the right to rape a woman, to assault her; he can beat a woman because the society gives men rights over her. That is the condition

of women, very much connected with what they call "gender relations," the social relationship between men and women in the society.

The country's underdevelopment is a factor that augments unequal gender relations. For example, we're an underdeveloped population where 47% of the women work, but look at the working conditions! Women accept bad working conditions because they are heads of household, they don't have a man with them, and that's what impacts their condition. The state doesn't take any measures to ensure that men take responsibility over the children. So women heads of household are forced to work to take care of her children. The woman works to work to give her children a better situation. But when we organize ourselves together in groups, present our demands to the state, we can push them to adopt a series of laws. For example, a law just passed regarding responsible paternity—unfortunately so far only in the Chambre and not yet in the Senate. This could change women's condition.

You just gave an example of a demand from the feminist movement, to change paternity. What are some other demands that the Haitian women's movement brought about?
Well, the existence of the Ministry [of Women's Condition] is the result of the women's demands. This started with SOFA and later an accord with all other women's organizations. We brought this before the president, before Parliament, to have a Women's Ministry, for women to sit at the table where decisions are made. And that's what it is. This is a fruit of the women's struggle to change women's condition.

However, since 1996, every time a government changes, the very existence of the Women's Ministry is threatened.

We had to take off our gloves to explain [its importance]. Haiti signed a number of conventions—for example, the Begin Declaration—calling for women to be represented at the highest state levels. Regarding the rejected prime minister candidate [Daniel Gérard Rouzier, who publicly stated he would shut down the Women's Ministry], we said that he was not aware or pretended not to be aware. He doesn't understand what a Ministry of Women symbolizes. That's why he could say such a thing. Right now we don't know who will come. The threat is still there, and it means that we need to stay vigilant.

And the relationship between the Ministry and the movement?
It is very close with the organizations. If you want to be able to make a change, you'll be able to realize it through these organizations. The people

know that when she comes inside the ministry, she has to make sure every-thing's in order. She needs to organize because it is the only way to find a response to what she needs.

So the Ministry is 16 years old. I believe it is the only Ministry that gives an example of power *with* the people, and that is very important (the Ministry of Agriculture began this way with peasants' movements). It creates an example for how to govern in another way. It's not up to you hiding in your office or sitting behind your computer to decide what the people need.

You talk about how the women's movement has stayed true to its vision. You gave some examples of results: some laws passed, the existence of the ministry. Can you talk about some of the major challenges for women in Haiti before and after January 12? What are women's most core demands?

Before January 12, I remember that while Aristide was in exile, in 1992, 1993—during the first coup d'état, when we had the FRAPH [Paramilitary death squads during the 1991–1994 coup d'état], the army, when all day long people were being violated and women raped—women insisted a lot on two things. First, to have a life free of violence, that the state would protect them against violence. Second, a journalist asked me what the needs for women were, what the coming government needed to do to meet women's needs, to begin getting on with their lives? I said housing. It was in 1993. The person said, "Housing?" I told him yes, that if you ever come to La Plaine, in Martissant,[17] you will see the situation people are living in. I told him that you don't even need to go to Cité Soleil.[18] One of the emblems we had in the 2000 Global Women's March was a cardboard box because people used to sleep on them. They used cardboard to cut it and use them to build houses. It really strikes you when going to "Cardboard City" in Cité Soleil, really testifying to the problem of housing.

January 12 sharpened the focus on the housing problem and violence. Because now women live in a series of conditions one on top of one another, lack of privacy. They are at the mercy of any vagabond who would want to rape them.

What needs to be done?

I always believe in organization. We are made to organize ourselves. Organization permits you to reflect on your situation, on your needs and see how you can, little by little, not only defend your rights but meet your needs and to pressure the state. I believe in solid organizations to allow us, first of all to recover our autonomy as a people and work in solidarity and collaboration with other people who respect the personal and national identity of people to get out of where we are. Because every people has their own cultural characteristics. This is what we are working for, and this is what keeps us alive.

* * *

Final Resolution: International Forum on the Crisis of Housing in Haiti, May 19–21, 2011

FRAKKA

WE, ORGANIZATIONS OF SURVIVORS LIVING in IDP camps, as well as social and grassroots organizations, assembled for three days (May 19–21, 2011) at Fany Villa in Port-au-Prince to reflect on the problem of housing within Haiti's longstanding crisis.[19] Following an exchange around the theme "January 12: Nightmares, Reality and Dreams," we state,

1. We commend the initiative taken by FRAKKA and other partners to host this forum, which allowed us to hear the testimonies of many camp residents and to exchange views on housing and other issues being faced in the camps. This exchange allowed us to better understand the root of the problems we face and to issue resolutions and an action plan that will guide our efforts during 2011–2012.

2. We heard a number of testimonies about the living conditions in IDP camps, which demonstrated that we cannot continue to live in conditions wherein our basic rights as individuals and communities are violated every day. We heard testimonies of the many diseases contracted by people living under tarps, of the pain of women suffering from all kinds of violence, and of children who cannot attend school or plan for their futures in these conditions. We see how the planned camps (like Corail) have become hell and do not offer conditions within which life can flourish.

3. We discovered that most of us in the camps are living in fear. We live under the threat of eviction, as both the government and private landowners are maneuvering (even setting fire to some camps) to force us out, even though we have nowhere else to go. These acts are crimes against our

very lives and violate our fundamental rights. According to an IOM report published in March 2011, more than 47,000 people have already been evicted, and 165,977 more face the threat of eviction. We resolve to fight these evictions and to ask for reparations for those who have been victims of forced displacement, which is a violation of human rights.

4. During this forum, we were pleased to hear the testimonies and analysis of friends from foreign countries like the United States (New Orleans and Miami), the Dominican Republic, and Brazil on the struggle for housing rights and how they are carrying out this struggle in the international context (via the International Alliance for Inhabitants). We learned a lot about the way these friends are fighting and the victories they have achieved. It was with joy and with much respect that we received the Brazilian Landless Rural Workers' Movement (MST), Take Back the Land, COOP HABITAT, and Other Worlds. We salute the determination of our friends and the movements they represent.

5. Throughout the forum, we saw how the Haitian government, ruling classes, and international institutions have not responded to the housing problems that millions of Haitians have long faced and which have become more serious since January 12, 2010. Most of the people who lost their homes in the earthquake do not have the means to rebuild. Sixteen months after the catastrophe on January 12, 700,000 people are living in the streets and many more families are living in horrible conditions in shantytowns. Many people had to return to damaged houses that could collapse at any time. We reject false solutions such as the distribution of tarps or building of temporary shelters—shelters that cannot resolve the issues at stake, that do not protect us, and that do not respect our dignity and the lifestyles of our families.

6. We resolve to continue the struggle to force the state to define a global policy on housing that guarantees the right of all Haitians to have a home to live in that respects their dignity as people. The government should create an office to start housing construction projects to respond to our needs.

Therefore:

• The government must define a land-use policy for the country. We must not forget that this has been poorly defined since long before January 12. Before the earthquake, 80% of the population in Port-au-Prince was living on 20% of the land. We want housing discrimination, in all forms, to end, and for distinctions [in government services and infrastructure] between rich and poor neighborhoods, to end. All neighborhoods should be places where people can live in dignity and security. We reject all the wealth and infrastructure being concentrated in only some parts of the city. We also reject the reconstruction of the nation's land only to create free trade zones.

• The Parliament must draft and vote on a law to guarantee the right to housing in this nation, as outlined in Article 22 of the Haitian Constitution of 1987, as well as in the International Covenant on Economic, Social and Cultural Rights. This law must define the codes that all people must respect for housing construction (soil, materials, distance, basic services, environment, aesthetics, etc.).

• The government must look for and acquire land though expropriation [eminent domain] so that there is sufficient space to respond to the housing needs of the population.

• The population must participate in decision making regarding where new houses and neighborhoods are being constructed. We have to say what kind of Port-au-Prince we want to build. Those who come from other countries, with plans already drawn up, cannot say this for us.

• We are ready to give our contribution (in financing, work, and materials) so that we can create housing that respects people's dignity. However, the government must finance construction projects to let us get housing as soon as possible, even if we pay a reasonable rent over several years. The government must immediately create a special fund to finance public housing. There is a lot of money being wasted that could be invested instead to respect the population's right to housing. The budget of MINUSTAH for only 12 months could allow the construction of more than 77,000 houses and give nearly 400,000 people respectable homes to live in.

• Homes and land are the source of life that allow people to live, grow, be safe, and help families to reproduce. The government and our communities must take all measures for these resources to remain a source of life, instead of turning them into merchandise so the bourgeoisie can make tons of money off our backs.

• The government must hurry so that all those without a lot of means can get housing that respects their human dignity. Institutions like the National Bank of Commerce and the commercial banks should put in place special programs to help the population repair or build good houses, with particular attention paid to those with few economic means and those with disabilities.

• The government must implement rent control, since rents have risen up to 17 times higher than before [the earthquake] and [sometimes] must be paid in US dollars. We must have this law to keep speculators from making millions off of our misery and despair.

• The government must guarantee security as to where we live. We do not want houses built one on top of the other, or houses where we live to crash into each other each time one falls down because they are too crowded. We must find housing where we can breathe easily. They must be guaranteed against all the risks that threaten our country. Land use must be based on preparing for the biggest risks (earthquakes, hurricanes, landslides, floods, tsunamis, and so on). The government must develop education and training programs so we can prepare for these and other risks.

• The right to housing cannot be separated from our other rights: the right to work, the right to health, the right to education, the right to leisure, the right to a clean environment. All of these rights are interconnected. This means that all house construction must be done in a way that facilitates our enjoyment of all of these rights. Camp Corail Cesselesse is the worst example of this, considering how they decided to corral the population like animals, without reflecting on the connection between all economic, social, and cultural rights.

• We ask the Haitian Parliament to ratify the International Covenant on Economic, Social and Cultural Rights, as a tool that can strengthen our struggle to defend our rights.

• In all house construction projects, they must plan for public spaces that allow our communities to have and develop collective activities, such as taking in some fresh air, playing sports, having meetings and assemblies, and carrying out cultural activities such as theater and painting expositions. Public spaces must have a special management. There must be special attention for the use of all coastal land to protect the environment, the mangroves, and carry out cultural activities that are connected to the ocean resources.

• We resolve to create village communities where each family has its own space, and where the community has space to engage in collective activities. We believe that cooperative housing is a viable alternative that can protect the right to housing for those who do not have great economic means.

• We want houses that respect our local architectural style and that use as much local materials as possible, such as clay, marble, and bamboo. We want beautiful houses that represent our culture, houses that give the community life, and that help us maintain dialogue between ourselves; houses that have yards and gardens where we can grow vegetables and medicinal plants, houses that respect the dignity of our bodies with the little bit of privacy that everyone needs. We want houses that provide space for us to live as families with neighbors in the *lakou* [traditional communal court-yard], where we can share food and daily activities. We must defend our local architectural heritage.

• Each neighborhood must have a cultural center to educate children and youth on the values of Haitian culture and the history of the nation. These must have special children's activities. In each neighborhood, there must be space that will aid us in constructing our collective memory as a people. In this sense, it is important for us to construct monuments to remember all our brothers and sisters who perished in the earthquake of January 12, 2010.

• In the houses we are building and in the collective infrastructure, we must remember people with disabilities and facilitate their mobility and daily activities.

• Every housing construction project must give special attention to the rights of women. It is good, whenever possible, for the title to the house to carry the name of the husband and wife. In inheritance (when property is separated), men must not benefit disproportionately to women. In housing law, the government must protect the rights of women living alone or in a family where a husband has multiple wives. Women and men have the same right to housing. Our organizations must struggle against all forms of physical and moral violence that women are subjected to in the home. Work in the home must be shared equally between men and women. We request a special training program to allow women to be integrated into all levels of the construction work being carried out.

• We denounce the corruption scandals in the management of housing programs; corruption in the government, in NGOs, and in the IHRC. They must reinforce all the government offices and structures that address housing.

We resolve that:

• The time is ripe for the right to housing to be respected in our country.
• We will fight against forced evictions and against all forms of intimidation on the part of the government and landowners, who inflict more misery on us when they force us to move without providing alternative sites for housing. We ask all communities to organize in order to rapidly circulate information regarding intimidation and threats, so that those threatening the lives of our families can be taken to court.
• We will strengthen our organizations and reinforce the alliances among grassroots and social organizations. We will build a strong social

movement that has the capacity to defend the interests of the exploited classes.

• We will make the struggle for housing a priority, and support homeless people and those living in camps in this struggle.

• We will disseminate information and conduct trainings across the country on the right to housing, and build organizational tools that will strengthen our struggle to force the government to respect these rights.

• We will join in the fight against all injustice and exploitation. We resolve to remain mobilized in the struggle to change our society and our government. This struggle must be aimed at constructing a new state that gives more importance to people's lives than to money, and that defends the interests of the exploited classes. It is only this kind of government that can respond in a real way to our demands for housing.

• We will join in the struggle for justice because we know the housing issue is linked to issues of employment, education, health, sanitation, electricity, transportation, communication, working conditions, land reform, and environmental policy.

• We have resolved to stop considering housing as an issue that can be resolved on an individual or family basis. Only collective solutions can resolve access to land for us to build on, housing and rent speculation, environmental management, and neighborhood management.

• We will create training programs on the radio, in churches, temples, and schools to make people aware of the importance of housing rights. We will organize trainings and debates in the camps and in popular neighborhoods with children, youth, and adults. We will launch a special newsletter to disseminate information on what is happening in the camps and shantytowns.

• We will support the International Alliance of Inhabitants and other organizations fighting internationally to defend the right to housing. We resolve to participate in a weeklong mobilization in October 2011, and we ask for a national day each year during which we celebrate the right to housing for all.

• We will ask all grassroots organizations and all other movements to mobilize with us on the housing issue so that we can achieve this dream of justice and liberty. We resolve to bring all of our forces together to overthrow the capitalist system, the bourgeois government, the government of landlords, the government that defends imperialist interests. We resolve to regain the sovereignty of our country in order to construct a society in which we can enjoy guaranteed access to housing and all our fundamental rights.

[*There follow hundreds of signatures from at least 40 grassroots groups and NGOs, and at least 35 IDP camp committees.*]

Notes

1. Michel-Rolph Trouillot, *Silencing the Past: Power and the Production of History* (Boston: Beacon Press, 1995).

2. James Ferguson, *Papa Doc, Baby Doc: Haiti and the Duvaliers* (Oxford: Basil Blackwell, 1987).

3. Confirmed by Dan Coughlin and Kim Ives, "Newly Released Wikileaked Cables Reveal: Washington Backed Famous Brand-Name Contractors in Fight Against Haiti's Minimum Wage Increase," *Haïti Liberté* and *The Nation,* May 25, 2011.

4. This article originally appeared in the *NACLA Report on the Americas* 43, no. 4 (July–August 2010: 28–31, 42).

5. "The Position of Various Public Organizations and Institutions After the Catastrophe of January 12," Port-au-Prince, February 13, 2010.

6. Quoted in "Planning the Haitian Renaissance," *Newsweek,* April 1, 2010.

7. Jonathan Katz, "Billions for Haiti, a Criticism for Every Dollar," Associated Press, March 5, 2010. Sources taken from USAID and the United Nations; see also informationclearinghouse.info/haitiaid/jpg.

8. Presented by Equality Now, Gender Action, Gender and Disaster Network, Groots International, Huairou Commission, Lambi Fund of Haiti, MADRE, ORÉGAND (Observatoire sur le développement régional et l'analyse différenciée selon les sexes), PotoFanm+Fi: Rebuilding Haiti Initiative, Women's International Network of the World Association of Community Radio Broadcasters (AMARC) Main Writers: Anne-Christine d'Adesky, journalist and author; Karen Ashmore, executive director of the Lambi Fund of Haiti; Taina Bien-Aimé, executive director of Equality Now; Denyse Côté, professor and director of ORÉGAND, Université du Quebec en Outaouais; Lisa Davis, MADRE; Elaine Enarson, independent scholar/consulting sociologist, University of Denver; Janet Feldman; Sandra Jean-Gilles, Experte Egalité Femme/Homme a l'Unité d'Appui au Programme de la Coopération Canadienne (UAPC); Jennifer Klot, senior adviser for SSRC programs on HIV/AIDS, Gender, and Security; Yifat Susskind, communications and policy director of MADRE; Denisse Temin; Sophie Toupin; Elise Young, gender action consultant. UNIFEM News, February 20, 2010.

9. See Inter-American Commission on Human Rights, "The Right of Women in Haiti to Be Free from Violence and Discrimination," Doc. OEA/Ser. L/V/II Doc. 64, March 10, 2009.

10. UN Security Council Resolution 1325, S/Res/1325, October 31, 2000 (emphasizing the need for women's "equal participation and full involvement in all efforts for the maintenance and promotion of peace and security").

11. For example, UN Guiding Principles on Internal Displacement, UN Doc. E/CN.4/1998/53/Add. 2, February 11, 1998; G.A. Res. 58/214, UN Doc. A/RES/58/214, February 27, 2004; Accra Agenda for Action (2008), http://www .undp.org/mdtf/docs/Accra-Agenda-for-Action.pdf.

12. See, e.g., Guiding Principles on Internal Displacement, Principle 4, UN Doc. E/CN.4/1998/53/Add. 2, February 11, 1998; Organisation for Economic Co-operation and Development, Gender Equality (OECD), "Empowering Women So That Development Is Effective," 2009; Accra Agenda for Action.

13. See n. 3; OXFAM International, Briefing Note: The Tsunami's Impact on Women, 2005 (explaining women's special vulnerability during and after natural disasters).

14. One methodology is available in the UNCHR Tool for Participatory Assessment in Operations, http://www.unhcr.org/450e963f2.html.

15. The interview was conducted in June 2011 by Mark Schuller. Jimmy Toussaint transcribed the interview, and Joris Willems translated the text from Hatian Creole.

16. "Women's condition" is Haitian feminist terminology for common realities, as opposed to individual "situations," similar to C. Wright Mills's "sociological imagination," used during consciousness-raising sessions.

17. A low-income neighborhood of Port-au-Prince, often the site of violence.

18. Often regarded as the worst. According to film *Ghosts of Cité Soleil* (Asger Leth, Milos Loncarevic, dirs., 2006), it is the "most dangerous place on earth."

19. Translated from the original Haitian Creole by Alexis Erkert and Monica Dyer.

Conclusion
Shifting the Terrain

In a volume like this, it is tempting to compile a list of solidarity actions that could unify Haitians living in Haiti and abroad, together with foreigners acting in solidarity. Given the time lag between submission and publication, the tectonic shifts traversing Haiti may be triggering even newer on-the-ground realities. Two years after the earthquake, how many permanent houses have been built? How many people are still living under makeshift tarps or T-shelters? Have the NGOs left? Will the IHRC have handed off its sovereign decision-making power for Haiti's reconstruction to the government? How many new jobs were created, and did this jump-start a vibrant local economy? Are women still facing the epidemic of GBV? Will the solidarity that saved people's lives immediately following the earthquake survive the militarism, the NGO-ization, the dependency, the antagonisms stoked by the inequalities inherent in Haiti, in the humanitarian enterprise, and within the world system?

Even if the time lag weren't an issue, with a collaborative effort such as this book—with more than 40 Haitian, Haitian Diaspora, and solidarity individuals and groups responding to a seismic event of such global and historic proportions—pulling together a single list of propositions does a disservice to the text's diversity of voices. Attempting to synthesize the many diverse identities, issues, and political perspectives is indeed a tall order. Despite our many differences, we contributors share a commitment to Haiti; a belief in collective organizing; passionate defense of Haitian sovereignty; support for participation of local communities and particularly the most marginalized; a vision of democracy and inclusion; advocacy for human rights, solidarity, and justice;

concern that the outpouring of support for Haiti will be a passing fad; and hope for a better future.

This book is a tool for educating students, journalists, solidarity activists, and humanitarians, hopefully inspiring and informing principled action. The range of different perspectives presented herein—from groups not often sitting at the same table—will hopefully inspire readers to get involved in joining the effort, picking up the taptap *(public transportation) en route. Most of these texts have been published before, and those that have not been were written by committed scholars, journalists, and activists working for a better future in Haiti. All authors' royalties from this book are going to support the movements within Haiti just discussed.*

To frame this action, and to end this conversation, we all (Haitian, Diaspora, and solidarity) need to act to change how Haiti is talked about, thought about, and written about. As Gina Athena Ulysse, Haitian American anthropologist and performance artist, repeats, "Haiti needs new narratives, now more than ever." Ulysse interrogates the deep racism within international media against a people who stood up to slavery and colonization, and how these narratives shape international responses to the earthquake. One of the most powerful narratives inspired by the earthquake is the concept of "re-foundation." Historically grounding and offering an alternative reading to what might otherwise be another terra nullius, *a blank slate typical of neoliberal disaster capitalism, Haitian economist and State University research director Fritz Deshommes concludes with the last project of "re-foundation," Haiti's 1987 Constitution. Still in effect, the democratic principles encoded in Haiti's foundational law should be implemented, guiding the process of Haiti's reconstruction.*

* * *

Why Haiti Needs New Narratives Now More Than Ever

Gina Athena Ulysse

———

SOON AFTER THE EARTHQUAKE, MAINSTREAM news coverage of the disaster reproduced longstanding narratives and stereotypes about Haitians.[1] Indeed, the representations of Haiti that dominated the airwaves in the aftermath of the January 12 quake could virtually be traced back to those popular in the nineteenth century, especially after the Haitian Revolution, as well as to the twentieth century during and after the US occupation of 1915–1934. Understanding the continuities of these narratives and their meaning matter now more than ever. The day when Haitians as a people and Haiti as a symbol are no longer representatives of or synonymous with poverty, backwardness, and evil is still yet to come.

As I have discussed elsewhere, Haitians as subjects of research and representation have often been portrayed historically as fractures, as fragments—bodies without minds, heads without bodies, or roving spirits.[2] These disembodied beings or visceral fanatics have always been in need of an intermediary. They hardly ever spoke for themselves. In the academy, they are usually represented by the social scientist. And after January 12, enter the uninformed, socioculturally limited, and ahistorical journalist.

The day after the quake, correspondent Susan Candiotti filed one of CNN's first on-the-ground reports. Clearly overwhelmed by the scenes of death, she commented on the indifference of those roaming the streets, many of them still covered in dust. "In an almost chilling scene, you would see people in some instances sitting nearby [the dead bodies lining the streets], some of them with vacant stares in their eyes just sitting in the middle of the street," she said. "At times, you would see young children walking about as though seeing this horror didn't bother them. And you had to wonder, is that because this country has suffered so much and through so many natural disasters over so many years?"

More than a week later, on January 22, CNN anchor Anderson Cooper appeared on the air with another correspondent, Karl Penhaul, reporting from Haiti. Penhaul related the story of a woman who survived the quake but lost her two young children. Surprised to see her force her way onto a bus to get out of Port-au-Prince, Penhaul said he asked her if she had buried her children before leaving. "And she simply said, 'I threw them—I threw them away,'" Penhaul said, interpreting the woman's reply, "Jete," to mean that *she* threw them out. The only word he apparently understood was *jete* (throw, fling, hurl). He did not mention the prepositions that came before or words that came after the verb, nor did it occur to him that the woman was saying she did not have the opportunity to bury them because they were thrown into a mass grave by others.

"Can you imagine a mother saying in any culture, 'I threw them away'?" the reporter said incredulously. Penhaul was also perturbed that the people he saw weren't crying. "As I put to this lady," he continued, "you know, 'Why don't you Haitians cry?'" Cooper tried to move the conversation toward a discussion of trauma and even mentioned the word "shock," but only at the very end of the segment.

In media coverage of the quake and its aftermath, this dehumanization narrative—portraying traumatized Haitians as indifferent, even callous—took off on what I call the subhumanity strand, which was particularly trendy. It stems from the dominant idea in popular imagination that Haitians are irrational, devil-worshiping, progress-resistant, uneducated, accursed black natives overpopulating their God-forsaken island. There is, of course, a subtext here about race. Haiti and Haitians remain a manifestation of blackness in its worst form because, simply put, the unruly enfant terrible of the Americas defied all European odds and created a disorder of things colonial. Haiti had to become colonialism's bête noir if the sanctity of whiteness were to remain unquestioned.

Haiti's history would become its only defense against these portrayals, although in mainstream media that same history would be used against the republic by historical revisionists. The day after the quake, the televangelist Pat Robertson proclaimed that the catastrophe in Haiti was a result of the country's pact with the devil, a belief that many Protestant Haitians themselves accept as true. The "devil's pact" refers to the ceremony at Bois Caïman on August 14, 1791, said to have sparked the Haitian Revolution. On that day, it is said, rebel leader and Vodou priest Boukman Dutty presided over this ceremony in which those in attendance swore to kill all whites and burn their property. Cécile Fatiman, the presiding priestess, sacrificed a pig to honor the spirits. Robertson's rereading of the ceremony was yet another example of the racialization of Haitians that so often goes unspoken in mainstream accounts.

At issue was a religious practice (Vodou) that is not only African in origin, but maintains an allegiance to that continent in contrast to Eurocentric belief systems. Days later, *New York Times* columnist David Brooks would fine-tune this characterization of a progress-resistant Haiti, leaving aside the question of imperialism, to ask, "Why is Haiti so poor?"[3] His answer: "Well, it has a history of oppression, slavery and colonialism. But so does Barbados, and Barbados is doing pretty well. Haiti has endured ruthless dictators, corruption and foreign invasions. But so has the Dominican Republic, and the D.R. is in much better shape." Never mind historical particularities. Brooks ignores the difference between being in bondage, killing for one's independence, and becoming a geopolitical pariah, on the one hand, and being granted freedom centuries later at a peaceful ceremony where one actually gets to sing the new national anthem, on the other.

This discourse—powerful even in Haiti among religious conservatives—suggests that perhaps those who brought about the revolution should have waited until the great powers saw fit to grant Saint-Domingue its freedom. This aversion to the impact of history would be repeated over and over again. On January 23, CNN's then–chief international correspondent,

Christiane Amanpour, did a short segment on Haiti in which she high-lighted key moments in Haiti's history. She began with the "bloody revolu-tion," skipped to decades of turmoil until President Woodrow Wilson sent in US troops in 1915, then jumped to 1945, when Haitian leaders began a series of dictatorships culminating with the reign of Duvalier the father and the son. She then noted the ascension of Jean-Bertrand Aristide, who was ousted by a military coup in 1991, leading to the surge of Haitian boat people on the coast of Florida and so on.

These superficial glosses on Haitian history did not go uncontested. A reader identified as Danlex posted the following response on the CNN website, dated January 24 at 8:27 p.m. ET:

> Given your penchant for balanced and incisive reporting, I am disap-pointed that this time around your report on Haiti's history leaves much untold. It is shallow and does not help to put this country that has so long been misunderstood in proper perspective. For a start I would rec-ommend that you read a recently published article by Sir Hilary Beckles pro-vice-chancellor and Principal of the Cave Hill Campus, UWI. The article is entitled The Hate and the Quake. Then, you can perhaps get France's view on the whole issue and how would they if they have a conscience respond to Haiti's crisis now. But it is time that the world see Haiti as not merely a country befuddled by voodoo [*sic*] and illiteracy but a victim of a prolonged collusion of the World Powers of the day.

I realize that in focusing on this issue of representation, I am in a sense actually doing Haiti a disservice. After all, the emphasis on deconstructing symbols only reinscribes the dominant narrative, which already gets lots of airplay. So here my activist and academic goals clash. A deconstructive ex-ercise alone cannot fill the lacuna of stories from Haitian perspectives with counternarratives about the earthquake and its aftermath.

Those of us who study Haiti know this conundrum only too well. As scholars, advocates, or just plain concerned witnesses, we know, to put it crudely and in layman's terms, that historically speaking, Haiti has an im-age problem. That remains Haiti's burden. Sometimes I joke that when the first free black republic made its debut on the world stage, Haiti lacked proper representation. A point of clarification: It's not that Haiti did not have a good agent, but that its representation at the time—newly freed blacks and people of color—and even still today was not considered legiti-mate and powerful. Indeed, we know that few colonists or metropolitans considered the idea of a Haitian insurrection even possible.

In a chapter titled "An Unthinkable History," in his *Silencing the Past*, Haitian anthropologist Michel Rolph-Trouillot writes,

In 1790, just a few months before the beginning of the insurrection that shook the French colony of Saint-Domingue and brought about the revolutionary birth of independent Haiti, colonist La Barre reassured his metropolitan wife of the peaceful state of life in the tropics. "There is no movement among our Negroes. . . . They don't even think of it," he wrote. "They are very tranquil and obedient. A revolt among them is impossible." And again: "We have nothing to fear on the part of the Negroes, they are tranquil and obedient." And again: "The Negroes are very obedient and always will be. We sleep with doors and windows wide open. Freedom for them is a chimera."[4]

Chimera: A figment of the imagination, for example, a wildly unrealistic idea or hope or completely impractical plan or perhaps an underestimation.

Both before and after the publication of Trouillot's book, numerous scholars, including C.L.R. James, Mimi Sheller, Sibylle Fischer, and others, have addressed the inconceivability of black freedom in the white imagination during the nineteenth century. One of the most notable examples was *On the Equality of the Human Races* (1885) by Joseph-Anténor Firmin, a Haitian anthropologist, journalist, and politician. Firmin wrote his tome as a riposte to *An Essay on the Inequality of the Human Races* (1853–1855), a founding text in scientific racism by Count Arthur de Gobineau. Firmin sought to debunk the dominant racist ideology of his time using a positivist approach, launching an argument that would be silenced for more than a century in France and the United States.

In the section of his book titled "The Role of the Black Race in the History of Civilization," Firmin recounts the role that newly independent Haiti, which he called "the small nation made up of descendants of Africans," played in the liberation of Latin America through its support of Simón Bolívar. "Besides this example," he wrote, "which is one of the most beautiful actions for which the Black republic deserves the whole world's esteem and admiration, we can say that the declaration of independence of Haiti has positively influenced the entire Ethiopian race living outside Africa."[5] He went on and on. We could read Firmin's work as exemplary of nationalist pride, or perhaps as a call for recognition that, indeed, *Tous les hommes sont l'homme*—roughly, All men are man, as Victor Hugo put it, quoted in the epigraph of Firmin's final chapter. Or *Tout moun se moun,* as we would say in Creole.

In considering the issue of representation and the meaning of symbols, I believe it is imperative that we begin with a simple question: How did the enfant terrible of the region become its bête noire? Enfant terrible. Yes. Many of us were taught that Haiti was an avant-garde in the region, second only to the United States, which had ousted the British. This small territory where enslaved Africans outnumbered their European masters dared to successfully defend itself against three European armies to claim its independence at a time when other nations in the region still trafficked in slaves. Freedom came at a price, the hefty sum of 150 million francs and 60 subsequent years of international isolation. The seclusion fermented cultural practices in ways that rendered aspects of life in Haiti the most recognizably African in the hemisphere.

Haiti's history would be silenced, disavowed, reconstrued, and rewritten as the "Haytian fear"—code for an unruly and barbaric blackness that threatened to export black revolution to neighboring islands and disrupt colonial power.[6] Reading this moment, literary critic J. Michael Dash observes, "It is not surprising that Haiti's symbolic presence in the Caribbean imagination has never been understood in terms of radical universalism [which it actually represented and sought to embody]. Rather, the 'island disappears' under images of racial revenge, mysterious singularity, and heroic uniqueness."[7]

The distortions that emerged in the aftermath of the successful revolution would have impact for years to come. Indeed, the "chimera" of black freedom, and the stereotypes of savagery that go with it, to this day remain central to how we talk about Haiti, represent Haiti, understand and explicate Haiti and Haitians. This, of course, begs us to ask a bigger question concerning the role that these narratives play in more practical matters, in policy papers and so on. For indeed, there are certain narratives that allow us to remain impervious to each other by the way they reinforce the mechanics of Othering. Or as Trouillot puts it, "The more Haiti appears weird, the easier it is to forget that it represents the longest neocolonial experiment in the history of the West."[8]

* * *

The 1987 Constitution
A Lever for the True "Re-Foundation" of the Nation

Fritz Deshommes

UPON BEING ASKED LESS THAN a month after the January 12, 2010, earthquake about the national forecast for recovery, spokespersons for the Haitian state uttered the word "re-foundation," and we could not believe our ears.[9] We supposed that, given the state of their emotions as they were overtaken by events, they felt obligated to say something, and this was a situation that could have exceeded the limits of their thinking. We assured ourselves that as soon as they had pulled themselves together, we would no longer hear this word spoken again.

Very quickly, though, we had to face the facts: "re-foundation" had become the leaders' most favored concept.

"Once the emergency is over, we must think about reconstruction. Nay, about the re-founding of Haiti," President René Préval explained on February 9, 2010, to his colleagues of the Union of South American Nations. He continued along these lines: February 15, 2010, during a visit to Haiti from Canada's prime minister, Préval to the *Toronto Star:* "What are we to do in Haiti? It is especially important to take this opportunity not to rebuild but to rethink, to restructure Haiti." The next day, February 16, he said to French President Nicolas Sarkozy: "The country is not to be rebuilt. It is to be built. It is to be reestablished."

Recast, rethink, restructure, change, and even simply construct: There is no lack of words that signify the authorities' resolution to not repeat the past. And the international community was not to be outdone by the national authorities. The Francophone University Agency (AUF) talks about the re-foundation of higher education in Haiti. The Dominican president, Special Envoy Bill Clinton, and the UN secretary-general speak of the desire for the "re-foundation" or "rebuilding" of Haiti. The UNDP website that was created to support the rebuilding of Haiti has the address "www.refondation .ht." Among donors the new fad is to discuss the re-foundation of the state, re-foundation of justice, re-foundation of education, re-foundation of social ties, and so on.

Such determination on the part of the leaders not to rebuild as before should be reassuring. Could it be that the extent of the damage of January 12 has provoked a consciousness such that they are actually taking stock of the enormous task at hand?

Are we on the path of a true re-foundation?

The Long March of the Haitian People Toward Re-Foundation

The Haitian people did not wait for January 12 to think about the problem of re-founding the nation. The fall of the Duvalier regime witnessed across the country the flourishing of many democratic and popular organizations (farmers' associations; trade unions; student, professional, political, civic, and women's organizations; neighborhood committees). They were driven by a very simple but very promising motto, "Change the state." *Tèt an-sanm, tèt anplas* (A united stance means a firm stance), we said. "Change the state to bring it closer to its citizens, so that it serves the nation."[10]

During this post-dictatorship period, seminars, conferences, work-shops, congresses, as well as street demonstrations and radio shows pointed the finger at the country we no longer wanted and produced a series of debates and reflections about the country to be built, the country to be "re-founded." This would mean a true re-re-founding of the country, a thorough overhaul of the state and nation, one that addressed the country's structural problems and that proposed solutions in the interest of the entire nation and its citizens.

The 1987 Constitution: A Will to "Change the State"

Even more significant, the essence of this vision is captured in the 1987 Constitution. The latter prescribes reforms to be enacted on the ground in all areas with the goal of concretizing this vision for a new country and a new state.

While emphasizing independence and sovereignty, the Constitution delineates how to democratize the exercise of power, bring the state closer to its citizens, and promote "citizen participation in major decisions affect-ing national life" (Preamble of the Constitution, no. 7). In this vision, in addition to the three traditional pillars of power, the executive, legislative, and judiciary branches, two other "pillars" are introduced: independence and decentralization within and among state institutions.[11] The Constitu-tion places special importance on decentralization as a constitutive process: new autonomous regions are created, each with its respective representa-tives, each of whom are assigned roles that condition the operation of the executive and legislative branches and operate within the establishment of key state agencies.

In its economic plan, the Constitution "guarantees economic freedom in so far as it does not work counter to social interests" (Article 245).[12] Private business is protected by the state if it contributes to "the growth of national wealth" and "the participation of the greatest number that may benefit from that wealth." To realize this prospect, the Constitution cre-ated the National Institute of Agrarian Reform (INARA), "responsible for organizing the overhauling of the basic structure of the agrarian system and

for implementing land reform for the benefit of those who actually culti-
vate the land" (Article 248). Agriculture, our domestic industry, our source
of domestic capital accumulation, national production directed first and
foremost to meet the needs of domestic consumption, cohesion among
the various components of the domestic economy and a means to protect
the domestic market—these goals were all clearly outlined. Such an orientation defeats that "concurrent" project parented by international donors
and maligned in its popular dubbing, "The American Plan for Haiti."

Regarding the social sphere, education, specifically the education of
the masses, is "the first task of the state and local authorities" (Article 32.2)
who "must make schooling free for everyone" (Article 32.1). The Constitution orders within the same article that a literacy campaign be undertaken (Article 32.9). It promotes higher education and emphasizes the
importance of the State University of Haiti (Articles 208–211). The family
and the child, defined in the broadest sense, are protected. It does not
discriminate between legitimate and illegitimate children. "All children are
children." It guarantees social rights, including the right to housing, work,
education, and social welfare for all citizens.

For the first time, the Creole language was declared an official language
on the same level as French (Article 5). A Haitian Academy was to be created to establish and develop the Creole language. Freedom of thought and
of religion are guaranteed. From then on, all legislation that discriminates
against the Vodou religion should be retracted. And there are provisions
to protect and promote the national cultural heritage, including material
culture and intangible cultural heritage. These provisions that stem from
the popular movement of protest in 1986 and made into law in the 1987
Constitution should have initiated a real break with the status quo. All
of these constitute major innovations perfectly compatible with a nation
re-founded to become more inclusive while expanding the body politic.[13]

As for decentralization fundamental to the establishment of a new
state, we no longer keep count of the maneuvers, each cruder than the
next, taken to prevent its implementation. The most recent example is
the rescheduling of the indirect elections of 2007, which were to put in
place the municipal and departmental assemblies as well as the department
councils and the Interdepartmental Council. The establishment of these
bodies would have met the essential conditions for the creation of the permanent Electoral Council and the Reconciliation Commission as well as
for standardizing the status of important officers of the judiciary. A cabal
emerged against the Electoral Council, which had organized the elections.

When the members of that Electoral Council were replaced, the new council was given quite different tasks. And that's it. Therefore, the institutional structure established by this Founding Charter remains partial, incomplete, flawed, illegitimate. We can similarly speak of the executive's hesitancy to share power with the town halls and the CASEC[14] regarding education, health, environment, culture, and taxation as well as of the limited resources allocated to local authorities. All this demonstrates the clear resolve of various executives from 1987 onward to block the dawning of a new state.

Representatives of the media, intellectuals, and in some instances reformists outside of the purview of the state have made the few visible advances in recognizing Creole as a national and official language. Rare are the initiatives by the state itself to register in its acts the new status of our national language. The National Academy of the Creole Language has never been established. We could find many other examples that attest to the lack of political will to implement what the Constitution stipulates: education for all, the literacy campaign, funding for the State University of Haiti, and so on.

Ultimately, it is the same authorities who suddenly and in its entirety let go of the Founding Charter with the argument that the charter itself is not a stable, consistent enough basis of governance. Thus, all those who have succeeded to power from 1987 to the present day have made it a point of honor to systematically refuse to "change the state," to re-found the nation. Are these not the same people who today speak of rebuilding?

We are at liberty and in a rightful position to ask the following questions: How can we explain that the most popular and legitimate project that could boast the support of a national consensus and clear origins within popular social movements, that constitutes a demand of the Founding Charter—this project otherwise known as the "National Project"[15]—has been thrown into oblivion, suppressed, scorned? And how did that other project, "the American plan for Haiti," or the strategy of international donors—roundly and openly fought against and identified as that which we were not supposed to do—become the one that has prevailed from this period onward? How do we explain that what is essentially the rejection of the notion of re-foundation returns to us in a form that is recognized as the true re-foundation?

The actors behind these measures found themselves allied with forces that have no interest in re-foundation: the traditional oligarchy, allied with the army, and enjoying the support of a segment of the international community which refuses any real change, any genuine re-foundation.

Are these not the same forces that we find at the heart of the re-foundation in 2010?

- The international community, deeply enmeshed with its millions, its MINUSTAH, its NGOs and its funding agencies.
- The Haitian government, the same authority that for the last 20 years has taken on the task of avoiding the real re-foundation, is now attacking the re-foundation's most striking tool, the Constitution.
- And finally, members of the local oligarchy, the beneficiaries of all the proposed subcontracting and trade liberalization, the heirs of incomes passed down for over a hundred years, and the visible partner of PARDN.

Some Paths and Means Toward a True Re-Foundation of the State and Nation

The extraordinary damage attributed to the January 12 earthquake in human, physical, economic, and social terms has laid bare the deep structural weaknesses of our society: it struck the heart of our capital, a republic all its own,[16] and it struck the republic's most important symbolic monuments.

We must rebuild but on new foundations. We must (now) re-found, say the authorities. But 25 years ago, the Haitian people already agreed on the urgent need for profound structural changes in all areas of national life: economic, political, social, and cultural. Change the state, they demanded.

We must re-found the nation. Better to lay down its foundations. Broaden its citizen-base. Create the conditions necessary to make it safer, friendlier, more sovereign, to its core based on a citizenry that meets on common ground, in a common homeland, with common objectives. We must see an end to the following:

- The model of accumulation that blocks productive development by allowing 0.05% of the population to corner 40% of the national income and by allocating less than $2 US in wages per day to 80% of its workers.
- The spatial distribution of power and resources that concentrates 65% of economic activities in the metropolitan area[17] and prevents the country from actualizing its potential, its abilities, and its production capacity.
- The multiple dichotomies of rich/poor, black/mulatto, Creole/French, Christian/Vodouist, and urban/rural that keep us from developing a

genuine community where our members find themselves united by common interests and where our differences, instead of marking superiority or inferiority, may enrich our collective.

- The massive and intense obstacles blocking the way to national sovereignty and manifested in the long foreign military presence and food, economic, and banking dependency, which feed on each other and grow each day, and in so doing, further prevent the nation from taking charge of itself.

It is important, it is even urgent that we re-found the nation. But what kind of re-foundation? What strategy?

The Constitution? Developed within a highly participatory framework, voted in by over 90% of the Haitian people, the subject of what Marcel Gilbert calls the historical unity of the people, it is an excellent warhorse and must be equipped, nourished, and cared for in order to achieve the real re-foundation.

The Constitution is still in effect. We must fight for its implementation. Despite the time that has passed, our country in its marrow is still ready:

- For a real decentralization of power and resources
- For a genuine agrarian reform
- For universal education, and the literacy campaign
- For the realization of the status of the Creole language as official and the promotion of national culture
- For a "strong and stable state, capable of protecting the values, traditions, sovereignty, independence and national vision"[18]
- For "a Haitian nation that is socially just, economically free and politically independent"[19]

Notes

1. Originally published in the *NACLA Report on the Americas* 143, no. 4 (July–August 2010), 37–41, 43.

2. See Gina Athena Ulysse, "Dehumanization & Fracture: Trauma at Home & Abroad," socialtextjournal.org, January 25, 2010.

3. David Brooks, "The Underlying Tragedy," *The New York Times,* January 14, 2010.

4. Michel-Rolph Trouillot, *Silencing the Past: Power and the Production of History* (Boston: Beacon Press, 1995), 72.

5. Anténor Firmin, *The Equality of the Human Races* (1885; Urbana: University of Illinois, 2002), 398.

6. Mimi Sheller, *Democracy After Slavery: Black Publics and Peasant Radicalism in Haiti and Jamaica* (Gainesville, FL: University Press of Florida, 2000).

7. J. Michael Dash, "The Disappearing Island: Haiti, History and the Hemisphere," the Fifth Jagan Lecture and the Third Michael Baptista Lecture, York University, March 20, 2004.

8. Michel-Rolph Trouillot, "The Odd and the Ordinary: Haiti, the Caribbean, and the World," *Cimarrón: New Perspectives on the Caribbean* 2, no. 3 (1990): 3–12.

9. This piece is an adapted selection from *Et si la Constitution de 1987 était porteuse de Refondation?* (Port-au-Prince: Éditions Cahiers Universitaires, 2011). Translated from the French by Lynn Selby and Valerie Kaussen. *Translators' note:* There is no precise English equivalent of *refondation*. The word "rebuilding" does not connote quite strongly enough the sense of a complete overhaul, remaking the foundations of society. In other senses it is used to denote "restructuring." To keep clarity and to focus on the linguistic power of the word, in this essay we use the word "re-foundation."

10. Fritz Deshommes, *Décentralisation et collectivités territoriales en Haïti* (Port-au-Prince: Editions Cahiers Universitaires, 2004), 15.

11. Bureau du Premier Ministre/PNUD, "Bilan Commun de Pays," Port-au-Prince, 2000.

12. Unless noted otherwise, all cited legal articles in parentheses are those from the 1987 Constitution.

13. Note that the Constitution was approved by a large margin by the Haitian people at the March 29, 2007, election [during which amendments were proposed]. Of 1,496,210 voters, 99% voted in its support.

14. *Translators' note:* Conseil d'Administration de la Section Communale, most often translated as the Communal Section Board.

15. For more details, see Fritz Deshommes, *Haiti: La Nation Ecartelée/Entre Plan Américain et Projet National* (Port-au-Prince: Editions Cahiers Universitaires, 2006).

16. Often referred to as the "Republic of Port-au-Prince" by critics of centralization.

17. PARDN (Action Plan for National Recovery and Development), March 2010, 5, www.haiticonference.org/Haiti_Action_Plan_ENG.pdf.

18. Constitution of 1987, Preamble, no. 2.

19. Ibid, no. 3.

Contributors

Batay Ouvriye is an organization that regroups factory unions and committees, workers' associations and militants, all struggling in Haiti to construct an independent, combative, and democratic union movement, and to organize wage workers, self-employed workers, and the unemployed to defend their rights.

Rachel Beauvoir-Dominique was trained as a sociocultural anthropologist at Tufts University and Oxford University. She has headed the University of Haiti's Department of Anthropology and currently teaches at the School of Ethnology and the School of Social Sciences. An initiator and active member of two foundations dedicated to the preservation of Haitian cultural traditions, she is also a founding member of the Centre de Recherches Urbaines–Travaux (Urban Research Center–Works). Beauvoir-Dominique is the author, with Didier Dominique, of *Savalou E* (Montreal, 2003; Casa de las Americas Prize, 1989) and the author of *L'Ancienne Cathédrale de Port-au-Prince, Perspectives d'un Vestige de Carrefours,* ed. Deschamps (Port-au-Prince, 1991), as well as various other articles and publications concerning Haitian anthropology, archaeology, history, and culture.

Roland Bélizaire is a professor of economics in UEH, the State University of Haiti. He completed a master's in politics and economic reform for development in the Catholic University of Santo Domingo in 2003. Belizaire also has training and work experience in international relations.

Beverly Bell is the founder of Other Worlds and associate fellow at the Institute for Policy Studies. Bell has worked for more than three decades as an advocate, organizer, and writer in collaboration with justice movements in Latin America, the Caribbean, southern Africa, and the United States. In addition to dozens of articles and book chapters, Bell has written *Walking on Fire: Haitian Women's Stories of Survival and Resistance* (2001) and the forthcoming *Fault Lines: Views Across Haiti's New Divide* (2012).

Jean-Yves Blot is a political anthropologist and vice dean for research at the Faculté d'Ethnologie, Université d'État d'Haïti, where he has taught for two decades. He is a specialist in political anthropology and was director of the Bureau National d'Ethnologie from 1998 to 2007. In this post, Blot has conducted research related to preserving and analyzing Haiti's cultural heritage.

Brennan Bollman has worked in Haiti since 2008, primarily with a neglected tropical disease program led by the University of Notre Dame. Following the earthquake, she took a leave from Harvard Medical School in order to return to Léogâne and help coordinate a field hospital there for several months. She is now continuing her medical studies.

Bri Kouri Nouvèl Gaye is a Creole-language journal in the popular sector aiming to democratize information in Haiti and help spread information where it had never reached. In a country where more than 90% of the press is privately owned, the journal's editors decided to create a grassroots source of information.

Bureau des Avocats Internationaux (BAI) in Port-au-Prince helps prosecute human rights cases and trains Haitian lawyers. Founded in 1995, BAI has pioneered a "victim-centered approach" that combines traditional legal strategies with empowerment of victims' organizations and political advocacy.

The Center for Human Rights and Global Justice (CHRGJ) brings together and expands the rich array of teaching, research, clinical, internship, and publishing activities undertaken within New York University (NYU) School of Law on international human rights issues. The Global Justice Clinic (GJC) at NYU School of Law—a project of the Center—provides human rights lawyering services to individual clients and non-governmental and inter-governmental human rights organizations, partnering with groups based in the United States and abroad.

Myriam J.A. Chancy is Professor of English at the University of Cincinnati. She is the author of several books, including *Framing Silence: Revolutionary*

Novels by Haitian Women (1997), *Searching for Safe Spaces: Afro-Caribbean Women Writers in Exile* (1997), and *From Sugar to Revolution: Women's Visions of Haiti, Cuba and the Dominican Republic* (forthcoming 2012). Her third novel, *The Loneliness of Angels,* was recently awarded the Guyana Prize for Literature Caribbean Award 2010, Best Fiction. She was past editor-in-chief of *Meridians: feminism, race, transnationalism.* She currently sits on the editorial advisory board of *PMLA,* the journal of the Modern Language Association, as well as on the advisory council in the Humanities of the Fetzer Institute.

Manolia Charlotin is the editor and business manager of the *Boston Haitian Reporter.* Charlotin is a social entrepreneur, advocate, and community organizer who has worked in community development, immigrant civic engagement, political campaigns, youth organizing, and cultural awareness for the last 10 years. She is the cofounder of Haiti 2015, a grassroots campaign to advance access to opportunities in Haiti, whose launch in January 2011 connected community-based organizations all across Haiti.

Lisa Davis is human rights advocacy director for MADRE and an adjunct professor of law for the International Women's Human Rights Clinic at CUNY School of Law. For the last 10 years she has worked in the women's human rights field both as a consultant for Treaty Body members and an advocate, working on successful petitions to international human rights treaty bodies as well as amicus briefs and expert testimony for the Inter-American Court. Davis has testified before various UN human rights bodies and has written extensively on international women's human rights issues, including on gender-based violence and torture.

Lise-Marie Dejean, a Haitian physician and the Executive Director of the organization Solidarite Fanm Ayisyen (SOFA, Solidarity with Haitian Women), is a well-known activist for women's rights. She was Haiti's first Minister of Women's Condition. She was recently elected to Latin America and the Caribbean Women's Health Network's Board of Directors.

Eramithe Delva is the executive director of KOFAVIV, the Commission of Women Victims for Victims, herself a victim of rape in 1992. Delva has represented rape victims, members of KOFAVIV, since she cofounded the organization in 2004. Since the earthquake, Delva has testified before numerous international agencies, including the UN, the US State Department, the Senate Foreign Relations Committee, and the Inter-American Tribunal on Human Rights.

Fritz Deshommes is a founding member of the Haitian Association of Economists and teaches economics at the Université d'État d'Haïti, where he is vice rector in charge of research. He is considered one of the pioneers of contemporary economic journalism in Haiti, and he is the author of eight books. Recent titles include *Salaire Minimum et Sous-Traitance en Haïti* (Minimum Wage and Subcontracting Industry in Haiti, 2010) and *Vie Chère et Politique Économique en Haïti* (*The High Cost of Living and Political Economy in Haiti,* 2nd ed., published in 2008).

Disaster Accountability Project was founded in 2007, following the experience of Katrina survivors and volunteers, led by the efforts of law student Ben Smilowitz. Its mission is to improve disaster management systems through public accountability, citizen oversight and engagement, and policy research and advocacy. Since its creation in 2007, the Disaster Accountability Project has benefited from the support of over 500 volunteers and interns.

Isabeau Doucet is a journalist based in Port-au-Prince. She has been writing about the conditions in camps and the reconstruction process for *Haïti Liberté* and the *Christian Science Monitor,* and has produced for Al-Jazeera. She is a graduate student in anthropology at Goldsmiths, University of London.

Etant Dupain is the director of *Bri Kouri Nouvèl Gaye,* Noise Travels News Spreads, the grassroots partner of TransAfrica's Let Haiti Live Project. Dupain is trained as a journalist and community organizer. He has lived in Venezuela and the Dominican Republic and underwent an intensive six month training in Brazil with the MST, Landless Peasants' Movement.

Alex Dupuy is the Class of 1958 Distinguished Professor of Sociology and Chair of African American Studies at Wesleyan University. He has published broadly on social, economic, and political developments in Haiti and the Caribbean. He is the author of *Haiti in the World Economy: Class, Race, and Underdevelopment since 1700* (1989), *Haiti in the New World Order: The Limits of the Democratic Revolution* (1997), *The Prophet and Power: Jean-Bertrand Aristide, the International Community, and Haiti* (2007), and more than three dozen articles in professional journals and anthologies.

Kevin Edmonds is an independent journalist and graduate student at the University of Toronto. His research interests include the political economy of the Caribbean, military and economic destabilization in Latin America and the Caribbean, and free trade's impact on agriculture in the developing world. He is an active member of the Canada Haiti Action Network and a former research associate for the North American Congress on Latin America.

Yolette Etienne has decades of experience working on development in Haiti, including being the country director for Oxfam GB for over fifteen years. Since the earthquake Étienne has worked with the Agriculture Cluster, and is currently the Haiti program director for Oxfam America.

Carine Exantus is a student at the Faculté des Sciences Humaines and the author of a blog on Haiti's IDP camps, "Diary of a Survivor in Haiti," published on the Conversations for a Better World website.

Marshall Fleurant is a general medicine research fellow at Harvard Medical School. He received his medical degree at Albert Einstein College of Medicine and trained in internal medicine at Thomas Jefferson University Hospital in Philadelphia. Dr. Fleurant is an active participant of Unity Ayiti and Physicians for Haiti in Boston. He has completed his master's at the Harvard School of Public Health and researches health information technology and its effect on primary care and health disparities.

Patrice Florvilus is a human rights attorney working in Haiti, specializing in housing rights, squatters' rights, and other rights of Haiti's IDPs. Florvilus offered free legal services to over a dozen IDP camps facing the risk of forced eviction. He is the founder of Defenseurs des Oprimées/Oprimés (DOP), a group of human rights attorneys accompanying the grass roots.

The Force for Reflection and Action on Housing (FRAKKA) is a coalition of 40 grassroots groups founded in March 2010 to unite grassroots groups and residents of internally displaced people's camps to win their human right to housing.

Haiti Grassroots Watch (*Ayiti Kale Je* in Creole) is a collaboration of two well-known Haitian grassroots media organizations, Groupe Medialternatif/Alterpresse and the Society for the Animation of Social Communication (SAKS), along with students from the State University of Haiti's Faculty of Human Sciences (FASCH), and members of the network of women community radio broadcasters (REFRAKA) and the radio stations in the Association of Haitian Community Media (AMEKA).

Ansel Herz is an independent multimedia journalist. A survivor of the January 2010 earthquake, he has reported from Haiti since 2009 for Inter-Press Service, Reuters Alertnet, and Free Speech Radio News and has been a commentator on Haiti for the Canadian Broadcasting Corporation and *Democracy Now!*

Institute for Justice and Democracy in Haiti (IJDH) was founded in 2004 as an offshoot of BAI to work with the people of Haiti in their non-violent struggle for the consolidation of constitutional democracy, justice, and human rights. It distributes information on human rights conditions in Haiti and pursues legal cases, cooperating with human rights and solidarity groups in Haiti and abroad.

Louise C. Ivers is chief of mission for Partners in Health (PIH) in Haiti, an international nonprofit organization that provides direct health care and social services to poor communities around the world, supported by research and advocacy. She is an assistant professor of medicine at Harvard Medical School and an associate physician in the Division of Global Health Equity at Brigham and Women's Hospital (BWH).

Kim Ives is an editor of *Haïti Liberté* newsweekly, the host of a weekly Haiti show on WBAI-FM, and a filmmaker who has helped produce several documentaries about Haiti. Ives is also a regular columnist for the UK-based *Guardian*.

Chenet Jean-Baptiste has a PhD in political science from Université Paris 3–Sorbonne Nouvelle and is a professor at the Université d'État d'Haïti at several schools, including Sciences Humaines. Jean-Baptiste has decades of experience working in the rural sector with peasants' associations, including serving as the director of ITECA (the Institute of Technology and Animation) for the past eight years. Before this he was the program director for the National Commission for Justice and Peace and the secretary general of POHDH (Platform of Haitian Human Rights Organizations).

Mario Joseph is managing attorney of BAI. He has co-managed or managed the BAI since 1996, and has practiced human rights and criminal law since 1993. The *New York Times* called him Haiti's "most respected human rights lawyer." He spearheaded the prosecution of the Raboteau massacre trial in 2000 and has represented dozens of jailed political prisoners, in Haitian courts and in complaints before the IACHR.

Valerie Kaussen is an associate professor of French at the University of Missouri–Columbia, where she teaches Francophone Caribbean literature, film studies, and cultural studies. She is the author of *Migrant Revolutions: Haitian Literature, Globalization, and US Imperialism* (Lexington Books, 2008). Her articles have appeared in *Research in African Literatures, Small Axe,* and *Monthly Review,* as well as in a number of volumes devoted to Francophone Caribbean and Haitian studies.

Janil Lwijis was a professor and activist, teaching at the Faculté des Sciences Humaines and author of three books about NGOs in Haiti. His doctorate was in social work at the Universidade Federale de Pernambuco, in Recife, Brazil. Lwijis founded the Asosyasyon Solidarite Invèsite/Invèsitèz Desalinyen. He passed away minutes before the earthquake struck.

Isabel Macdonald is a journalist and a PhD student in communication at Concordia University in Montreal. Her master's thesis at York University, Toronto, examined international media coverage of the 2004 coup d'état in Haiti.

MADRE is an international women's human rights organization that works in partnership with community-based women's organizations worldwide to address issues of health and reproductive rights, economic development, education, and other human rights. It provides resources and training to enable its sister organizations to meet these goals by addressing immediate needs in their communities and developing long-term solutions to the crises they face.

Hervé Jean Michel is a freelance writer and political activist in Haiti. Jean Michel has been a staff writer, author of weekly columns for *Haïti Progrès* and *Haïti Liberté.*

Melinda Miles has worked for over 10 years with Haiti's popular movement and community leaders on issues ranging from democratic participation to increasing national production while protecting the environment. After the earthquake on January 12, Miles cofounded the Haiti Response Coalition, a unique collaboration of international and Haitian nongovernmental organizations. Miles is the director of Let Haiti Live, a multidimensional advocacy and solidarity project at TransAfrica Forum that brings together alternative media, community mobilization, coordination of international advocacy, and grassroots-based efforts for reforestation and family-level food security.

Pablo Morales was the editor of the NACLA Report on the Americas (nacla .org), a bimonthly magazine covering Latin American politics and U.S. policy toward the region, and currently works at Time Magazine.

Anthony Oliver-Smith is an anthropologist who since the 1970s has written about disasters and involuntary resettlement in Peru, Honduras, India, Brazil, Jamaica, Mexico, Japan, and the United States. He has served on the executive boards of the National Association of Practicing Anthropologists (NAPA) and the Society for Applied Anthropology (SfAA) and on the Social Sciences Committee of the Earthquake Engineering Research Institute. He is a member of the editorial boards of *Environmental Disasters* and *Desastres y Sociedad.* His work focuses on post-disaster social organization, including class/race/ethnicity/gender-based patterns of differential aid distribution, social consensus and conflict, grief and mourning issues, and social mobilization of community-based reconstruction efforts.

Veerle Opgenhaffen is the executive director of the Center for Human Rights and Global Justice at NYU School of Law. She was the co-investigator of the center's project researching the links between food insecurity and gender-based violence in Haiti's IDP camps, and also worked on the center's previous two research reports on economic, social, and cultural rights in Haiti, *Wòch Nan Solèy* and *Sak Vid Pa Kanpe* (both copublished with the RFK Memorial Center for Human Rights and Partners in Health/Zanmi Lasante).

Deepa Panchang works with the organization Other Worlds. She became involved in Haiti after the 2010 earthquake, working in Port-au-Prince on issues of forced eviction and human rights for earthquake survivors, and cofounded Unity Ayiti, a Boston-based Haiti solidarity group. She completed her master's degree at the Harvard School of Public Health, where she researched the right to water in Haiti, and holds a BA in economics and environmental science.

Nicole Phillips is a former union lawyer who after the earthquake left her career in 2010 to join the IJDH, where she is now a staff attorney. She is also an adjunct professor and assistant director for Haiti programs at University of San Francisco's Center for Law and Global Justice. Phillips has served since 2000 as a member of the board of directors of Human Rights Advocates, an NGO based in California with consultative status to the United Nations and has appeared before the UN Human Rights Committee, Committee on the Elimination of All Forms of Discrimination and Commission on the Status of Women on various human rights issues.

Renaud Piarroux is a specialist in infectious diseases and parasitology at Université de la Méditerranée. He began studying cholera in various African countries in 1994, when he first experienced a cholera outbreak in a refugee camp in Goma, Democratic Republic of the Congo.

Rishi Rattan is a resident in the Department of Surgery at Tufts Medical Center. Since 2007 he has worked in Haiti's Central Plateau with Zanmi Lasante. He is a founding member of Physicians for Haiti, a not-for-profit organization developing sustainable medical education and leadership opportunities for Haitian physicians. Over the last decade, he has lectured, trained activists, and organized successful national and international campaigns on issues including the right to health, access to essential medicines, health-care worker shortages in the developing world, reproductive health, and gender-based violence.

Jane Regan is a multimedia journalist and scholar who has worked in and on Haiti for almost three decades. She is currently teaching journalism in Haiti, as well as collaborating with a multimedia, multilanguage reconstruction watch partnership of Haitian alternative media institutions Groupe Medialternatif/AlterPresse and the Society for the Animation of Social Communication (SAKS) along with students from the State University of Haiti's Faculty of Human Sciences (FASCH), and journalists from the network of women community radio broadcasters (REFRAKA) and community radio stations.

Margaret Satterthwaite is a professor of clinical law at New York University and faculty director of NYU's Center for Human Rights and Global Justice and the Root-Tilden-Kern Program. She is the author of numerous articles, book chapters, and reports on human rights. She is the director of an interdisciplinary team researching the link between food insecurity and gender-based violence in Haiti's IDP camps, following two research reports, *Wòch Nan Solèy* and *Sak Vid Pa Kanpe,* both copublished with the RFK Memorial Center for Human Rights and Partners in Health/Zanmi Lasante.

Lindsay Schubiner became involved with Haiti solidarity work after the earthquake, building on her background in social justice organizing. She helped found Unity Ayiti, a Boston-based group that supports liberation and self-determination for the majority of Haitians. She received a master's degree from the Harvard School of Public Health.

Mark Schuller is an assistant professor at York College (CUNY) and the Faculté d'Ethnologie, (UEH). Supported by the National Science Foundation and others, Schuller's research has been published in over twenty book chapters and peer-reviewed articles as well as public media, including a Huffington Post column. He wrote forthcoming Killing with Kindness: Haiti, International aid, and NGOs and co-edited four volumes. He co-directed/co-produced documentary Poto Mitan: Haitian Women, Pillars of the Global Economy. Schuller chairs the Society for Applied Anthropology's Human Rights and Social Justice Committee and is active in solidarity efforts.

Jeena Shah is a fellow at the Lawyers' Earthquake Response Network (LERN) of the BAI. She focuses on securing the rights of IDPs who are facing forced eviction. Shah represented pro bono clients in immigration, family, labor, and environment cases, and was a Clinton Fellow at Navsarjan, a grassroots NGO in Gujarat, India, where she authored a report on the failure of the state government to enforce legislation on caste discrimination.

Mark Snyder is a founding member of the US-based human-rights civil-society group International Action Ties. Working as a community mobilizer he has lived and worked in rural and urban India, Peru, and the United States. As an active partner in a anti–forced eviction initiative developed with Haitian civil society groups and organizations, IDP groups, and international NGO partners, Mark has spent the majority of the past year working alongside the IDPs of Port-au-Prince, Haiti.

Patrick Sylvain is a Haitian language and culture instructor at Brown and Harvard Universities. He is also a lecturer in anthropology at the University of Massachusetts, Boston. He is a writer, social critic, and photographer. He has published in numerous anthologies and journals, including *Agni,*

The Butterfly's Way, Callaloo, Caribbean Writers, Haiti Noir, Human Architecture: A Sociology Journal, Poets for Haiti, Fixing Haiti and Beyond, and *The Oxford Book of Caribbean Verse.* Recently featured in *PBS NewsHour,* NPR's *Here and Now* and *The Story,* he is a contributing editor to the *Boston Haitian Reporter.*

Evelyne Trouillot is the director of pre-Texte, an organization that sponsors reading and writing workshops and elaboration of pedagogical materials, and is a professor at the Faculté des Sciences Humaines, Université d'État d'Haïti. Along with her two children's books, Trouillot is the author of an essay on children's and human rights in Haiti, *Restituer l'enfance,* two collections of poetry, *Sans parapluie de retour* and *Plidetwal;* books of stories, *La chambre interdite, Islande,* and *Parlez-moi d'amour;* and four novels, among which the first, *Rosalie l'infâme,* was awarded Le Prix Soroptomist de la Romancière, and the last one, *L'oeuil totem,* was awarded Le Prix Carbet de la Caraïbe et du Tout-Monde in November 2010.

Gina Athena Ulysse is associate professor of anthropology, African-American studies, and feminist, gender, and sexuality studies at Wesleyan University. She is the author of *Downtown Ladies: Informal Commercial Importers, A Haitian Anthropologist and Self-Making in Jamaica* (2008) as well as numerous articles and essays on research methods, feminism, Haitian diasporic tensions, and Vodou. A performance artist, she has presented her signature piece, *Because When God Is Too Busy: Haiti, Me, & THE WORLD* throughout the United States. She blogs for *Huffington Post* and *Ms. Magazine.*

Malya Villard-Apollon is associate director of KOFAVIV. Her work has taken her to the courtroom, IDP camps, police officers, the UN base, and around the world. Villard has testified before the UN Commission on Human Rights, the U.S. State Department, and the IAHRC. Her analysis has been featured in several media stories and the documentary video *Poto Mitan.*

Charles Vorbe is professor of political science and law at the Université d'Etat d'Haïti (State University of Haiti), chairing the Center for Studies in Population and Development (CEPODE). He has published, among others, *L'Etat de droit en procès: contribution à une critique théorique* (The State of Law in Process: Contribution to a Critical Theory), 1998; Le FMI instrument de l'hégémonie économique des Etats-Unis (The IMF, Instrument of the United States' Economic Hegemony), *Alternatives Sud 6*

(1999): 2. Vorbe co-edited two volumes from *CEPODE* and wrote two articles: Mondialisation néolibérale, droit et sous-développement en Haïti (Neoliberal Globalization, Rights, and Underdevelopment in Haiti), *Cahiers du CEPODE* no. 1 (September 2009), and Séisme, humanitarisme et interventionnisme en Haïti (Earthquake, Humanitarianism, and Interventionism in Haiti), *Cahiers du CEPODE* no. 2 (May 2011).

David A. Walton received his MD and MPH from Harvard. Walton now serves as instructor of medicine at Harvard Medical School and associate physician at the Brigham and Women's Hospital, both in Boston, Massachusetts. Based on his work with Partners In Health in Haiti over the last 13 years, Dr. Walton has emerged as a leading expert in the community-based care of HIV/AIDS, tuberculosis, and non-communicable diseases in resource poor settings. Most recently Dr. Walton has been involved in the cholera response throughout Haiti.

Mark Weisbrot is codirector of CEPR in Washington. He has written numerous research papers on economic policy, especially on Latin America and international economic policy. He is also coauthor, with Dean Baker, of *Social Security: The Phony Crisis* (2000). He writes a weekly column for *The Guardian Unlimited* (UK), and is a regular contributor for McClatchy-Tribune Information Services. He is also president of Just Foreign Policy.

Joris Willems has been a media activist and a freelance reporter with Radio France International and Dutch public Radio VPRO; is correspondent for Belgium's Radio Centraal and the London-based Haïti Support Group; and has published in the Belgian written press. Willems has been in Haiti since 2008, working with groups such as Broederlijk Delen, PAPDA, and Other Worlds. He conducted a major study of the Haiti Interim Reconstruction Commission and is a Ph.D. student in International Development at the Ghent University (Belgium).

Index

Also available from Kumarian Press

Dual Disasters: Humanitarian Aid After the 2004 Tsunami
By Jennifer Hyndman

"Hyndman skillfully draws together an array of fascinating and disturbing material to reveal the double-edged character of dual disasters—which bring both misery and opportunity. This wide-ranging volume interrogates the now-common aid refrain 'building back better' to ask the crucial question 'build what back better?'"

—Nicholas Van Hear, Centre on Migration,
Policy and Society, University of Oxford

**Building Back Better:
Delivering People-Centered Housing Reconstruction at Scale**
By Michal Lyons and Theo Schilderman

The devastating impact of disasters on the world's population is on the increase, influenced by climate change, urbanization, and persistent high levels of poverty, among other factors. There is a growing demand for reconstruction at scale. This book asks whether large-scale reconstruction can be participatory and developmental; can rebuilding be truly people-centered, contributing to breaking the cycle of poverty and dependence? Can reconstruction reduce people's vulnerability to disasters and other shocks?

Building Back Better examines the context for reconstruction, and shows how developments in the fields of housing, participation and livelihoods have changed and enriched approaches to reconstruction. It goes on to explore the practice of implementing large-scale reconstruction through in-depth case studies of recent programs in Sri Lanka, Pakistan, Indonesia and India. Finally, an analysis of selected projects in six additional countries over a longer period of time adds other relevant issues to people-centered reconstruction at scale.

The book intends to inform policy, program design, practice and evaluation.

It will be of interest to agencies regularly involved in reconstruction, to consultants and specialists involved, to aid agencies, to the authorities in countries regularly faced with disasters, as well as to students, academics and researchers.

Visit Kumarian Press at **www.kpbooks.com** or call **toll-free** 800.232.0223 for a complete catalog.

Kumarian Press, located in Sterling, Virginia, is a forward-looking, scholarly press that promotes active international engagement and an awareness of global connectedness.